Daniel March

Morning Light in many Lands

Daniel March

Morning Light in many Lands

ISBN/EAN: 9783337253776

Printed in Europe, USA, Canada, Australia, Japan

Cover: Foto ©Suzi / pixelio.de

More available books at **www.hansebooks.com**

Morning Light

In Many Lands

BY

DANIEL MARCH

BOSTON AND CHICAGO

Congregational Sunday-School and Publishing Society

PREFACE.

AFTER the long night of ages, the morning light is breaking on all the lands of the old East. It is a new creation of hope in the hearts and joy in the homes of millions. I have only tried to point out some of the high places, where the light is beginning to shine, and some of the low valleys, where the clouds look darker, just because the morning is on the hills. The book would have been much larger, and I hope much better, if a messenger of the prince of darkness had not come in the night and stolen away all that I had written, with painstaking care, of mission work seen on the journey from Prague in Bohemia to Shanghai in China. The plunder did naught to enrich the thief and it left me poor indeed. If he had been half as ready to bring back the spoil as I was to forgive the theft and reward the return, my readers would have had a better book and I should have been spared the one great loss in a long journey.   D. M.

CONTENTS.

	PAGE
CHAPTER I.	
A Short Chapter on a Long Journey.	7
CHAPTER II.	
Modes of Travel in Many Lands	17
CHAPTER III.	
Extremes and Contrasts.	29
CHAPTER IV.	
The Southern Cross	42
CHAPTER V.	
Holy Mountains and Sacred Rivers in the East	49
CHAPTER VI.	
How to See Mission Work in the East.	59
CHAPTER VII.	
Grand Experiments and Great Success	70
CHAPTER VIII.	
The Motory Power of Mission Work.	81
CHAPTER IX.	
What Can We Teach China?	95
CHAPTER X.	
John Chinaman	106
CHAPTER XI.	
What Can China Teach Us?	120
CHAPTER XII.	
The Common People of the East	145
CHAPTER XIII.	
Faith and Hope in Heathen Lands	163

CHAPTER XIV.
Having Eyes and Seeing Not 182

CHAPTER XV.
Light in the East 196

CHAPTER XVI.
Views from Car Windows in India 236

CHAPTER XVII.
The Power of the Gospel 264

CHAPTER XVIII.
Work Already Done 281

CHAPTER XIX.
Forward 295

CHAPTER XX.
One Law of Duty for All 318

CHAPTER XXI.
The Consecration of Wealth 330

CHAPTER XXII.
The Higher Education 339

CHAPTER XXIII.
The Christian Press 349

CHAPTER XXIV.
The Last Crusade 361

CHAPTER XXV.
Recruiting Offices 369

CHAPTER XXVI.
Cooperation in the Field 385

CHAPTER XXVII.
Recruiting on the Field 397

CHAPTER XXVIII.
Faith in Success 409

Morning Light in Many Lands.

I.

A SHORT CHAPTER ON A LONG JOURNEY.

How far is it round the big ball of our earth? If you take a line and stretch it eastward from Boston and keep going straight forward till you come back to Boston again from the west, how long would the line be? Every schoolboy can answer from the geography. But suppose you put the answer in terms of travel, what would it be? Just about as far as a camel would go, if he should move at the common pace of the desert and keep going straight on, six days in the week, without stopping for four years. Just about as far as you would have to travel in going from Boston to Chicago twenty-five times. My neighbor, the captain, tells me that he has been round the world seven times, and his voyages, the way he went, would just about reach from the earth to the moon. My friend, the conductor, the first man to shake hands with me when I came back, has run on the railway far enough to encompass the earth thirty-two times. And the captain and the conductor are still good sound men, much younger than I am, and likely to have many more miles of travel before they start on the last journey. The captain never lost a spar, and the conductor never smashed a train. And that looks as if traveling on long journeys had come to be quite safe and easy in our day.

But is the journey round the world pleasant and easy all the way? That depends upon who goes and what he goes for. Some go, like the sea birds that follow the ship all the way across the ocean, never seeming to rest and never getting tired. Some go, as the camel goes in the desert, groaning and complaining when the Arabs place the burden on his back in the morning, and complaining and groaning just as much when they take it off at night. Some travelers come home from the long journey and say they found the best of everything all the way, the best ship on the sea, and the best train, carriage, donkey, and bandy on the land, the best fare at hotels, the best company on the road and the best sights to see; they never lost the way, never had an accident and never saw one; if they were ever cheated or misled or lied to, they did not know it, and so they had nothing to complain of. Other travelers come back and say they started at the wrong time, took the worst route, and experienced all manner of hindrance, accident, and delay, from beginning to the end of the journey. They were sick on the sea and tired on the land, and anxious and troubled everywhere. When they tell the story of their travels, it is a tale of accident and annoyance and discomfort, from heat and cold, rain and drought, vermin and filth, from beginning to end. Such people will do best to stay at home, sit by their own fireside, read books of travel, long to go, but never start. The other class of travelers can go anywhere, at any time of the year, by whatever route they please, and they will be sure to find friends and sunshine all the way, and when they come home and tell their story they make it so bright and cheery that everybody who hears wants to go too.

How long does it take and how much does it cost to go round the world? You can make the journey in three months, and you can spend thirty and wish you had more. If you cannot spend a year, you had better not go at all. It is not worth the cost in time and money and labor to go and come back and read books of travel to find out what you ought to have seen but did not. That is about all that some do. They take the best ships on the sea and the fastest trains on the land. They run across the country in India from Bombay to Calcutta, they stop a day or two at Singapore and Hongkong and Yokohama. They look up to the distant mountains and across the broad plains and down upon the muddy water of the sacred rivers. They visit a few temples and tombs and monuments. They talk with steamboat officers and hotel keepers and guides. They bring home photographs and curios and cunning work in brass and ivory and stone. They take a ride in the jinriksha through the streets of Tōkyō and the English settlement in Shanghai. They try a sedan chair for an hour in Canton, and an ox-bandy for a night in India. They gather up the commonplace talk which is retailed to all travelers without money and without price in hotels and on shipboard; they while away a weary hour in reading guidebooks when waiting for trains or steamers. And then they come home and say they have seen the "gorgeous East" with all its splendors and all its misery, all its legends of mystical lore, and all its traditions of ancient glory.

And yet they have seen very little of the actual condition and character of the swarming millions of human beings that make up the living population of town and country in the great East of to-day. If one cannot make more than that out of the journey round the world, he had better stay at home and read books written by men who have spent a lifetime of laborious study and observation in the endeavor to find out the mysteries of the eastern mind and the marvels of its ancient story. An industrious and scholarly man told me that he had lived in China thirty-four years and he had been studying the Chinese mind all the time, and still to him it was a great deep which he could not understand. That being true, a traveler who does not know a word of the language, and who steps ashore for a few hours at Shanghai and Hongkong, is not likely to come home with full right to say that he has seen the Central Flowery Kingdom with his own eyes and that he knows all about it. If he cannot afford a year in making the circuit of the globe, he will be wiser to stay at home and read the books of men who have been studying the eastern mind for a whole generation and are still very far from boasting of their attainments in eastern lore.

As to the cost of the journey, seven hundred dollars will pay the first-class fare of one who goes by the shortest and quickest route, and only wishes to say he has been round and come back safe. The fare will include board on the sea, and three dollars a day will be enough for board on land. But to make the journey with profit and satisfaction, fifteen thousand miles must be added to the twenty-five thousand miles round in a direct course. If one gets back to the place of starting with less than forty thousand miles and sixteen months of time in travel behind him, he must have missed much that he went to see, and he will have many regrets that he did not go farther and stay longer.

The facilities for travel in our time have taken away a large part of the terrors of the deep and the hardships of the land. We have made roads for everything on the earth and the water, and we are only waiting for inventors to finish work already begun and we shall trample the winds and traverse the fields of air. Mighty kings in ancient time could not fly as fast or as far on fiery steeds as the peasant and the plowman travel in our day. The chariots of heroes and conquerors, whose names are great in eastern story, were ugly carts compared with the flying palace of our time. The highways, which subject nations made for kings when Solomon reigned in all his glory and Xerxes scourged the sea for breaking his ships, were only mule tracks among the mountains or cow paths on the prairie compared with roads which now climb the steep with easy grade and cross continents with unbroken chain. We have tunneled the mountains and bridged the rivers and filled up the valleys and made the rough places smooth with arches of stone and rails of steel. It needs no prophet's vision to say that there is sure to be a road sooner or later wherever multitudes wish to go, and means of transportation will be supplied for all the goods they wish to carry. The old and the young, the sick and the well, the rich and the poor, all travel. Every nation has its representatives in every other, and many private families have members on all the continents of the earth.

I have traveled as far as I could possibly get from home, and yet I have heard my name called as a familiar sound on the other side of the globe by men who had been my school-fellows in boyhood, and I have met my next-door neighbor in the Land of the Midnight Sun. I have heard men who never saw a snowflake express an eager desire to visit our colder clime, and I have heard the praise of American arts and industry from the lips of men who could not pronounce the name of our country correctly. We give to every land, and we get back more than we give. Our houses are garnished with the manufactures of all nations, our tables are loaded with the luxuries of all climes, because we have made highways over all seas and continents of the earth, and whatever is made or grown in one land is sure to be brought within the reach of every other. The products of the shop and the field are as sure to be carried wherever they are wanted as the springs among the hills are sure to find their way to the sea.

At such a time it seems a small matter for one to say that he has passed around the whole compass of the globe and returned safe to his home without accident or delay. He has only dropped into the currents of travel that are always flowing, and he has floated on to the end of his journey without touching a hand to the oar to pull against the stream, without once holding the reins of the fiery steed that has drawn his palace car swift as the wind. And yet to one who has completed the full round of circumterranean travel, the journey is something more than a holiday excursion. In the review of the route he must needs remember many rude jolts on the land and worse tossing on the sea, many hard lodgings which no enthusiasm for travel could call easy, and many irritations which the sweetest temper would scarcely meet with a smile. The winds do not always blow softly from sunny isles, nor are the senses oft regaled with

"Sabæan odors from spicy climes".

in the streets and lanes of eastern towns. He must see many sights which are not fit for the sun to look upon, and he must hear tales of misery and degradation which a becoming regard for the decencies of speech will forbid him to repeat. Nevertheless, when he gets well home, he finds the hardships of the way the pleasantest things to talk about next to the hospitalities of friends that made him add a hundred homes to the one which he had left behind. He thinks it worth the while to make so long a journey just to learn by his own experience that the bands of human kindness and sympathy already encompass the globe, and that the time is coming when the names stranger and foreigner will give place to friend and brother.

Which is the better way to go at the start, east or west? I should say decisively east. Then you seem to be tracing the stream of emigration and empire up to the source from which it has been flowing down to us from the far distant ages. First after Young America comes Old Europe, and then by slow and imperceptible changes the lands of the morning and the most ancient East. Every day brings you nearer to the sunrising, and as you press on you half fancy that by-and-by you will find the king of day girding himself in his secret chambers and coming forth with all his glories for his journey through the heavens. The light grows more intense and the sunbeams smite with a severer stroke as you round out from the Red Sea into the Indian Ocean, and the land breeze which comes out to meet you from Ceylon seems as if it were laden with the suffocating fumes of ancient altars, or the deadening exhalations of forests and rice fields that never felt the healing touch of frost. You traverse the whole great land of India from its southern cape to the wall of the snow mountains made without hands on the north, and you see everywhere gross darkness resting on the people, and yet also everywhere light breaking through the cloud and giving promise of approaching day. You pass on to Burmah and Siam, and there sits Buddha enthroned in everlasting sleep and his worshipers round him seeming as if their god had poured upon them the spirit of deep slumber and had closed their eyes that they might not see the light of the new day dawning on all the great eastern world. Then comes the climax of all that is ancient and unchangeable, all that is mysterious and incomprehensible to western minds, in China. You have got as near to the origin of things as you can go. Everything is old. Ask how long a temple or a wall or a bridge has been built, and you will be answered, as a priest answered me at Ningpo, "Tens of thousands of ages." You pass on to Japan and you breathe more freely when you find forty millions of people waking from the sleep of ages and breaking forth into a wild and wondering life which mingles the dreams and delusions of the past with the practical science and the rational faith of

Christian nations. A month or two of time in the Island Empire of the Mikado breaks the suddenness of the transition from the deadening lethargy of the old East to the intense and fervid life of the New World. In the long and quiet passage of the Pacific you have time to think over all you have seen and balance the account of thought and theory about the Old and the New, the East and the West. You find that a year's travel towards the sunrising has put you ahead one day in the reckoning of time, and you are obliged to drop the extra day into the deep in order to make your Sundays agree with those which you find the people keeping when you get home. The first Wednesday out from Yokohama on the homeward voyage, you go back and count the day over again so as to be ready to keep step in the march of time with the fast and furious life about you, when first you set foot on the shore of the New World of the West.

Forty thousand miles are about equal to one fourth the length of all the railways in the United States if they were stretched in one continuous line. It is surely something to be thankful for that one has passed over all that distance at a speed varying from sixty miles an hour to the slowest walk, and has trusted to all kinds of conveyances and to all sorts of people and yet has never experienced or witnessed an accident or disaster of any kind on the way. It seemed to me when I reached home that the hard trot of the Syrian horse and the measured swing of the Arabian camel and the heavy jolt of the Chinese cart and the pleasant whir of the Japanese riksha and the restless tossing of the sea were all shaken out of me, and I stood on my feet as firmly as if I had not walked on the other side of the globe with men whose midnight marks our noon. My journey led me hundreds of miles through great and strange cities, where the crowded streets were as intricate as the meshes of the spider's web; and then again I passed through solitudes and waste places of the earth where there was no inhabitant and no sign that human foot had been there before. I was dependent upon others for information, and they spoke fifty different languages, all equally unknown to me. But I never missed a desired connection, never failed to get conveyance when I wanted it, I never was misled, I never lost the way when there was any way to lose; if I ever were cheated or lied to, I did not know it and so it did not hurt me; the houses of strangers were opened to me with hospitality, the courtesies of princes and the service of coolies were offered with equal kindness, the public conveyance and the private carriage were always at command, all questions of wonder and curiosity were answered with equal frankness in the government office, the heathen temple, and the mission school. I came home with the feeling that the promised time of universal brotherhood among men of all nations is nearer at hand than we are apt to think. And I thought too that every traveler who goes round the globe with a considerate mind and kindly heart must do something to strengthen the bonds which are bringing all nations into one united family.

II.

MODES OF TRAVEL IN MANY LANDS.

IN making the circuit of the globe the traveler must needs trust to a great variety of conveyances and a great number of unknown guides, and he will be surprised to find with what ease and safety they all bear him on his way. For days and nights and weeks in long succession his home must be upon the great iron steamer, whose vast hulk is bound and barred with ribs and rods of steel, whose mighty engines toil without rest under the fiery torture of the furnace heated sevenfold, whose keel plows the waves ten times deeper than the subsoil plow the prairie, and yet leaves no furrow behind. No returned voyager can tell the next what experience awaits him on the sea or on the land. One takes one route, another another; one finds fair weather all the way round, and another is burnt by the sun and beaten by the tempest and tossed by the typhoon. I can tell my experience; let the next man tell his. If the two are unlike, let none say that both cannot be true. I passed through the whole length of the British Channel and over the German Ocean, which has been the terror of mariners for ages, and both were as calm as a summer lake among the hills when the winds are hushed in noontide repose. I was many days and nights on the Mediterranean, where ships have been caught by mighty tempests ever since the voyage of Jonah and Æneas, but the winds were asleep in their secret chambers and I slept soundly on the sea. I passed through the Red Sea, where men die of heat every year, and my cabin was so cool that I sometimes closed my window to shut out the west wind that came in from Nubia and Abyssinia fresh as the morning breeze in our October days. I passed over the Bay of Bengal and the China Seas, where many a gallant ship has gone down under the stroke of the terrible typhoon, and where our captain said the best and bravest of seamen had found a burial place in the bottom of the deep. But the typhoon was busy at its wild play out on the Pacific Ocean and it let us pass in peace. Once we anchored two nights and a day under the shelter of hills above Hongkong, waiting for the cruel scourge of the Eastern Seas to blow its breath away before we ventured out upon our northward voyage. But the implacable Nemesis of the deep howled about us all the time with a voice which seemed to say, "You laugh at my power while hugging the safe shelter of the hills; but let me catch you out on the China Sea, and you will never laugh again."

On the Bosporus, the Hoogly, and the Meinam, and in the Bay of Jaffna, I took passage on the miniature steam launch which was run by an engine little bigger than a bushel basket, and it bore me as safely as the mighty hulk which could hang a score of such launches along its bulwarks and carry a thousand men inside. On the coast of India I trusted myself to surfboats that went through the breakers like the stormy petrel rejoicing in the tempest. The white spray covered us like a cloud, but we escaped safe to shore with only a little wetting and a feeling of great relief that the sea had its bounds that it could not break over and that we had passed beyond its wild domain. Many times for short distances I trusted to craft so small that I was told to sit down and sit in the middle of the boat and not lean to one side or the other, lest the little cockleshell should go over and empty its living cargo into the deep. On the rivers and canals of Siam and China and on the Pei-Ho, the main water way to the great capital of the Middle Kingdom, I lived for weeks in a house boat which was propelled by poles and oars and sails or drawn by men who made a towpath of the bank and who sometimes waded waist deep in mud and water while pulling the rope. The boat moved so slow at times against wind and current that four men had hard work to gain a mile in an hour, and it took them six full days to complete a journey of a hundred miles, though they worked with quiet and uncomplaining constancy from before sunrise in the morning till after sunset at evening. The roof of the house in which we lodged and dined and wrote was so low that a tall man must stoop to stand, and the boatmen lived so near to a state of nature that the captain had a small wire ring on his left ankle and that was all the clothing that the four men wore.

My conveyances on the land were not less diverse and interesting than those on the water. In all the East the donkey is always and everywhere at home. There, as everywhere else, he is kicked and cuffed and starved. He pays back as many kicks as he can, and he is always lively enough to make the night hideous with his terrific squeal and his awful bray. And he is always ready to be the meek and much suffering servant of any traveler who can accept lowly conditions without complaint, and who will not object to an occasional blast of music without words on the way. He is small but spunky — so small that a tall man mounted may sometimes doubt whether it is his own feet or the donkey's that are doing the walking. It was a constant wonder to me how the poor abused animal could live and find enjoyment in making mischief for his tormentors, although every show of temper on his part was sure to bring more blows, and every good service was repaid with heavier burdens and harder fare. Some kept for travelers in Cairo are sleek and well fed. Some that trudge up and down the stony paths of Palestine feed on thorns and thistles by the wayside. Some stand with purple housings and gilded bridles at the rich man's door. But the donkey is a donkey the world round, meek and lowly in manner, obstinate and vicious in spirit, like the camel, intolerable in temper, and indispensable in use.

From Jeypoor to Amber and back I rode on an elephant so large that it seemed as if we had mounted a black bowlder of the hills and it was rolling along the highway without knowing or caring that two pigmies were perched on its back and wondering what made it go at the word of command. For an evening excursion of eight miles an elephant was thankfully accepted both as an honor and a pleasure. But for a longer journey I should have thanked the Maharajah of Jeypoor, who sent the elephant as a princely courtesy, and I should have felt obliged to say that a due regard for the comfort of body and brain required me to prefer a horse or a camel or even a donkey. I would not speak disrespectfully of the service of the elephant. I wondered as much at his intelligence and docility as I did at the cunning and the pretended stupidity of the donkey. I saw the great black beast piling heavy teak logs in the shipyards of Rangoon. He would lift an enormous beam to its place in the pile, then step one side to sight across the end to see if it were even with the rest of the logs. If it projected two or three inches, he would make a battering-ram of his head and bunt it back to an even face with all the other logs in the pile. When I saw the great beast do that, I wished that some human laborers had as good an eye for order and harmony as the elephant.

In Bulgaria I made long journeys in a phaeton drawn by four horses harnessed abreast and driven by a turbaned and bearded Turk at a speed that would satisfy the fast and furious life of young America which bowls along the macadam roads in the suburbs of our great cities. Then again in the same Bulgaria I crossed the Shipka Pass of the Balkan Mountains drawn by four oxen at a pace so slow that a moderate walk would leave it far behind. The galloping horses on the dusty plain and the laboring oxen on the rugged mountain made no greater contrast than the palace of the prince in the city and the hovel of the peasant in the villages of the same country. Still again in Tinnevelly and Travancore, in Southern India, I rode all night in an ox-bandy, lying on my back in a bed of straw. The oxen were driven at a trot by a coolie, who twisted the tails of his team instead of applying the lash to quicken their pace. The long-horned trotters were changed every hour, and the relays were so well arranged that I found myself fifty miles away in the morning from the place where I crept into my bed of straw the evening before.

I made an excursion from Calcutta to Darjeeling to see the three highest mountains in the world, Kunchin-Junga, Dhawalaghiri, and Mount Everest. The distance there and back is seven hundred and forty-six miles. I slept on the hard boards of a second and third class car and found it comfortable. I paid less than five dollars for the whole distance and thought it cheap. Our first run to the river Ganges was at the rate of forty-two miles an hour over a broad-gauge road. Our third and last run was over a two-foot gauge, and the train was forbidden by law to run more than seven miles an hour. We dodged into and out of ravines and defiles and gorges so often that the spunky little engine was in sight far above us climbing the steep all the while. It seemed to me as if it were a Bengal tiger or some mighty beast of the cat kind which had been caught and tied by the tail to our train and it was sputtering and spitting fire with fear and rage as it was trying to escape back to its mountain den and dragging our train by the tail up the steep all the time. Often the driving wheels of the engine on ahead were as high as the roof of the car in which we were riding. If the coupling had broken, we should have had such an experience in tobogganing as a Canadian winter never gives to those who travel far to the north to find it. But the fastenings held firm and we made one fourth the ascent of the highest mountains with the ease and the pleasure of a holiday excursion on the plains.

In Northern Syria and Asia Minor I rode days and weeks on horses whose hard trot made the camel's long, swinging gait seem like lullaby to the weary rider. I passed over plains and ridges of rocky mountains which reminded me of the time when I rode thirty days on the living ship of the desert in the wilds of Arabia. The day before reaching Carchemish, the ruins of the ancient Hittite town on the river Euphrates, I lost my riding-stick, and I then traveled on two days under the burning sun before I found tree or shrub or bush big enough to supply me with another. Sometimes we went five and six hours without seeing a sign of water, and when we came to what was called a well it would often be nothing but a pool, turbid and muddy, trodden into mire by the coming and going of camels and cattle.

In Hongkong and Shanghai and Tientsin and all over Japan I was whirled along over smooth roads in the snug little man-cart called the jinriksha. I felt unwilling at first to be drawn as babies are drawn in our streets, and to see the strong-muscled coolie sweating and puffing between the shafts just to relieve me of a little effort and to earn a few cash for himself. It looked to me as if it were making a beast of the man to make him draw in the shafts like a horse, and I was afraid it might have a worse effect on me to ride while human muscles were tugging and pulling to put me over the road. But such is the effect of use that I came to like it well in the end. And when I reached home I did not notice any sensible letting down of my manhood, and I had a higher respect for the coolie who had drawn my majesty in the streets of Tōkyō and Tientsin. The man who rides with an umbrella to shelter his head from the sun and the man who pulls with head and feet bare are not so far apart as they look to be, so long as each fulfills his duty well.

In the Jaffna district of Ceylon I rode in an American rockaway wagon which was propelled at a rapid pace by five coolies, two before to pull and three behind to push, and each party responding to the other with shout and cheer as they flew before the wind. The smooth road went winding in graceful curves among lofty palms and spreading banyans, slender bamboos and sacred bo-trees. The thatched cottages of the natives nestled under the shadows of lofty forests, seemed like cool retreats from the burning heat at noon, and they lined the way with cheery lights by night. Occasionally the coolies gave a spring and a scream when they came upon a deadly cobra creeping across the path. But the cobra was very glad to get out of the way when he heard the sound of the coming carriage, and the coolies were still more glad not to provoke the fatal fang of the serpent with their feet.

In Peking, the capital seat of a government which rules over more millions of people than any other government on the face of the earth, I rode through broad streets a hundred and twenty feet wide. My carriage was a springless cart, the common conveyance of passengers in the great imperial city of the Central Flowery Kingdom. The body of the cart was bolted to a wooden axle, the wheels were loaded all over spokes and felloes with iron spikes having solid heads as large as a silver dollar. The cover or body of the carriage was shaped like a dog kennel with a rounded roof not high enough to stand up in and with no seat to sit down upon. The only endurable place for the passenger was on the shaft at the tail of the horse. In the wet season you are covered with mud, in the dry season with dust; but bad as is the riding it is better than walking in the streets as you find them in wet or dry. The roadway was a bank of mingled mud and dust in the middle of the street and four or five feet above the level where the sidewalk ought to be. The ridge was made from the accumulated offal and filth of ages. On the sides of the central causeway which constituted the only road was a stygian abyss of mire and all manner of foul and abominable sewage so deep that in the rainy season, I was told by long-time residents, it was no uncommon thing for a driver to lose his way on the central ridge of mud, pitch down the bank, and man and horse and passenger all be drowned together in the deep mire that makes the broad street. And all that under the very eye and hand of the imperial government which has camped down in that abyss, that reeking quagmire of filth, as if it were ambitious to show its magnificence by surpassing all the slums and sewers of all the cities of the empire.

I was carried through the streets of Canton and over the millet fields from the Western Hills thirteen miles to Peking and thirteen more over an imperial stone road from Peking to Tungchow and across rice fields from Fuchau to the Fushan Mountain in a chair borne on the shoulders of men. I never seemed to myself so heavy as I did when I sat in the chair and saw the hard bamboo carrying poles resting upon the bare shoulders of the men, and I heard them panting up the steep places to save me the weariness of walking. I found that mode of riding a little more trying to my feeling of independence and self-respect than conveyance in a man-drawn riksha.

And yet, last of all, and most astonishing of all to myself

as I remember it now, I must confess that I was carried up a mountain five hundred feet high to visit an old Buddhist monastery near Suchau in a sedan chair, and the bamboo poles which bore my masculine weight rested upon the shoulders of women. I was slow to consent to what seemed to me an indignity both to myself and the women, although they were coolies and were accustomed to many kinds of work much less suited to their sex than carrying sedan chairs. I consented at last when told that the women would be greatly disappointed if they did not have the opportunity to earn a few cash by the service. I was willing to give the money and go up the mountain on foot. But I was told that that would demoralize the people and make much trouble for them and for other travelers that might come afterwards. So I took my seat in the chair and the women lifted the weight to their shoulders and moved on. They sung and shouted at their work, but I shadowed my face with my umbrella for very shame to see myself carried in such fashion. Finally I made signs to the women to put me down and I would pay them full fare for their work and take my own time to climb the steep in my own unaided strength. The mercury was in the nineties and there was no punka to take the place of a breeze on the hills. But the height was gained in good time, and the poor, stolid women wondered at the strange sight of a man willing to walk when he had the best opportunity to ride — an unusual thing to see in China or anywhere else in the East.

The women of America, the most highly privileged and blessed of all the women of the earth, sometimes complain that they are shut out from occupations which are open to men. Let them go to the far East and they will find some of those restrictions removed. In India and China and Japan they will find full and free permission to carry coal in baskets for the supply of steamboats lying in the harbors; they can carry baggage and heavy loads of merchandise on their heads and so cultivate an erect and easy gait in walking; they can gather offal and remove sewage in the open streets of great cities and nobody will forbid them, nobody will think they are doing anything unsuited to their sex or inconsistent with the usages of good society. They can creep on hands and knees in mud and water six inches deep, pulling up weeds between rows of rice in the paddy fields, and breathing the odors of sewage with which the grain is watered from the town. They can even carry strong men in chairs supported by bamboo poles resting upon their tender shoulders. They can climb, panting for breath under such burdens, up the steep sides of mountains and receive a small string of copper cash for the hard service. They can be permitted to do many other things which a due regard for the decencies of the printed page forbid us to mention. The women of China and India may well teach the women of America to guard well and sacredly the great honor and privilege enjoyed by them now, and not lightly throw away or neglect the keeping of what they have, for other supposed privileges and official responsibilities of doubtful worth and dangerous tendency. Of all lands on earth, America is the paradise of women, and it becomes them to preserve that paradise in pure and holy keeping, lest rash and restless spirits, under the name of reform, should make it a pandemonium of contending passions or a trampled arena of political strife. What is gained by contention and controversy may be little compensation for what is lost in delicacy in feeling, modesty in deportment, peace and purity in all the relations of home and domestic life. The people of the East have harems and hovels, zenanas and cloisters in abundance, and there is little to choose between the selfishness and profligacy of the princes and the ignorance and degradation of the people. Both have yet to learn that the new life, the glorious and immortal hope which gives strength and progress to western nations must come to them from the Christian home. And it is the great and divine mission of Christian women to teach that lesson to the millions of Asia that know it not. In that service American women will find greater honor and more abundant reward than in passionate struggles for responsibilities which they are not fitted to bear or in the feverish and wasteful rivalries of fashionable life.

III.

EXTREMES AND CONTRASTS.

IN making the circuit of the globe and turning aside from the direct course to see whatever is best worth seeing on the way, the traveler lights upon every variety of scene which the earth presents and every variety of animal and vegetable life which the earth produces. Once I went northward to sit with the Lap in his turf-covered cabin and to watch the reindeer on the moss-covered hills about the North Cape in the gentle light of the Midnight Sun. The birch and spruce and pine did not venture so far into the kingdom of eternal cold. But the summer's day took in the whole night, and there was neither morning nor evening in the whole twenty-four hours. I seemed to stand on the top of the world, and the king of day went round and round in a coronet of light just above my head. And then again in this last journey I went southward till I saw the north star go down to the horizon and the southern cross come up with the dazzling retinue of the many-throned powers of the heavenly host that surround the starry symbol of the world's redemption.

Many times in the long journey I gazed with wonder and awe upon the ranges of mighty mountains, Alps and Apennines, Rhodope and the Balkan, Olympus and Parnassus, Taurus and Lebanon, Sinai in Arabia and Adam's Peak in

Ceylon, Fusiyama in Japan and Hindu Kush in Afghanistan, and the mighty wall of the Himmaleh, the highest on the face of the earth, the ridge of the world which human foot has never climbed, the abode of snows which the sun has never melted, the source of rivers that bear the food of millions in their waters, and that traverse a thousand leagues of land on their way to the sea. Then again many a time I looked around the whole circle of the horizon in vain to find a hill high enough to break the dead level of grain and grass and cultivated field. The thatched roofs of villages and the yellow heads of sorghum and millet and rice and corn looked so much alike that it was a relief to the eye to see the antlers of the deer sometimes rising above the grain and the black wings of the rook and the raven casting a shadow upon the glittering ocean of sunlight. The plain of the land was like the plain of the sea, "boundless, endless, and sublime." Then again I passed over a treeless and burning waste, where for miles and hours of travel I found no well or fountain of water to wet my parched lips or slake my thirst. The birds overhead flew in flocks and all one way, as if fleeing from a land that famine had made a desert.

From such scenes, in Northern Syria and on the banks of the ancient river Euphrates, I turned southward on the long voyage by Suez and the Red Sea to Ceylon. When I first landed at Columbo, on that beautiful island, my first experience was a feeling of inexpressible delight and surprise at the wild luxuriance and endless variety of vegetation. The wide-branching banyan and the sacred bo-tree, the feathery palm and the graceful bamboo, mangosteens and mangoes, dorions and bheels, and nameless trees ablaze with blossoms, camphor and cinnamon, climbing vines and ferns a hundred feet high, bananas and plantains and palmyras, the lofty eucalyptus, the medicinal cinchona, the hillsides covered with the garden-like culture of tea and coffee, the lowlands waving, like our wheat fields, with rice, and the higher grounds with the heavier growth of maize and millet and sorghum — all seemed like a new creation when compared with the naked hills of the Euphrates and the sunburnt plains of Bulgaria, which I was traversing in the early days of autumn. To be transferred at once from the barren sea and the more barren mountains of the North to such a scene of life and luxuriant vegetation made it seem to me as if some omnific word had gone forth upon the waste and bidden it blossom like the rose and bring forth fruit in perfection, like the garden of Paradise under the culture of a divine hand.

On that fertile and steamy island of the great sea a seed need only be dropped by a bird of the air or a breeze from the mountains and something useful to man will grow — some blooming flower will breathe its perfume on the air, some climbing vine will wreathe a bower to shade the weary from the noontide heat, some fruit-bearing tree will load its branches with food for the hungry and invite them to eat. The native people, with rice enough for daily want and fruit in abundance to be had for picking, do not mind it much if they have nothing to wear. They seem to grow out of the earth like the palm and the banyan; their complexion is like the brown soil which they lazily till and tread upon, and when they go back to the earth like the leaves and the blossoms there are so many of them left to fill their place that nobody is missed and few tears are shed for those that are gone. It is one of the saddest developments of heathenism in the old lands of the populous East that a man's life is worth so little to himself or to anybody else. If he live long, there is little chance that he will make the world any better by his life; if he die early, there is just as little chance that the world will lose anything by his death. There were more people in the world than were wanted when he came into it; the crowd and the competition for food and subsistence will be just as great when he has gone out of it. To him and to all, the human family is like the crew of a sinking ship thrown out upon the deep and all struggling and contending with each other for the possession of a plank or a piece of furniture on which to float for a while, in hope of rescue or of reaching the shore. The strongest survive and the feeble go down and none can say which is better, to drown at once or to endure the torture of thirst and weariness and cold a little longer in hope of rescue.

In the course of the long journey I passed through all extremes of climate, from heat to cold and from rain and hail to drought and sunshine. At Newara Eliya on the mountains of Ceylon, within seven degrees of the equator, I crouched for an hour over an open fire at evening to get warm enough to go to bed. I slept under a thick pile of blankets and forgot that I was in the torrid zone. In Northern Syria and Turkey I slept on the roof of the guardhouse, where soldiers kept watch to be within call of travelers who might fall among thieves or get lost in the waste places of the wilderness. I waked many times and found it convenient to look up to the stars instead of the clock face to see how far on the hours of the night had passed and when the herald of the dawn would appear. It was pleasant to think that my timekeeper hanging high over head beyond my reach had been wound up and set a-going from of old by a divine hand and that it had not lost a minute in thousands of years. In all my wanderings I was glad to look up to that great dial-plate of the heavens and feel assured that the standard of time for all ages and nations is kept by One whose ways are everlasting and with whom there is no variableness nor shadow of turning.

At Madras I was hospitably entertained by one of the Council of Five, who made and executed law for thirty millions of people. My bedroom at his house was forty feet long, thirty feet wide, and twenty feet high. On the steamer Yokohama Maru my room was just long enough for me to stretch my length from end to end, and just wide enough to let me extend my two arms the other way. And I slept equally well under the high ceiling of the honorable Councilor's chamber, and under the higher canopy of the stars and in the narrow crib of the rocking and rolling ship. My thank offering in the morning was as sincere in the one case as in the other. One of the lessons which I went around the world to learn was, how to sleep peacefully wherever night overtakes the traveler, and how to rise up with gratitude and praise wherever morning breaks and brings the new day. Sleep, in any case, seems like the twin brother of death, and waking is as nearly related to the resurrection from the dead, and both come evening and morning to teach us gently, silently, the blessedness of the sleep which

God will give to his beloved when their day of life is done, and the glory of waking into a life which shall have no end. To him who learns that lesson well, it matters little whether he lies down for his last slumber alone in the waste places of the earth, or he finds his last resting-place in the bosom of the great deep. The angel messengers, who come to bear his emancipated spirit home, will find him as easily in one place as another.

At Naina Tal, on a spur of the Himalaya Mountains, a hailstorm burst in my window at midnight, and hailstones lay in banks like drifted snow about the house in the morning. I rode down the mountain through a jungle, where a tiger had been seen the week before leaping over the high grass and brushwood in the wild freedom of his native home. I slept the following night at Bareilly in a room so hot that when I laid my hand upon the marble table it felt to me as if it had been heated over the fire. I was thankful for the hailstorm of the mountains, not less so for the bed in the hot room on the plain, and I only wished that I had seen the tiger at a safe distance in the jungle to complete the climax in a day of wonder and varied delight. The main objection to the climate in most countries of the East is its uniformity. Six months of cloud and rain, and then six months of sunshine; wind blowing from one direction all the time for half a year, and then wind blowing just as long from the opposite quarter; temperature at ninety and a hundred from May to November, and then temperature at sixty-five and seventy to May again; and so runs on the even tenor of dull life for millions in the populous lands of the East. And the same uniformity is in food and fashions of dress and modes of living. Rice in the morning, rice at noon, and rice at night; a few rags of clothing in winter, a few less in summer, and a house of mud and reeds all the time. How to awaken any degree of mental activity or moral aspiration among millions of such people is the great question which confronts all Christian missionaries in the East. People who complain of frequent changes in weather and fashions in dress and modes of living in our cold and hot New England climate forget that they are indebted to such changes for a large part of their energy, vivacity, invention, and enjoyment of life. The people in the tropics must look to the temperate zone for the stimulus which will rouse them from the sleep of ages and inspire them with faith and energy to join the grand march of the Christian nations toward a greater and truer life than has ever yet been lived on the face of all the earth.

In the course of five thousand miles of travel in India, and as many more in the farther East, I saw all extremes of poverty and riches, princely magnificence and pariah degradation. The wealth displayed in the construction of palaces and temples and tombs was the spoil accumulated by ages of cruelty and oppression. The poverty was the inevitable consequence of ignorance and superstition and it had been for centuries the uniform condition of an oppressed and plundered people. I sat on the "Peacock Throne" of the mightiest of the great moguls. The golden plumes and the flashing gems that canopied the head of the great emperor were gone, but the marble seat and the gilded ceiling were still there as in the days of Aurungzebe and Akbar. It was the highest representative of royal state as it once appeared adorned with pearl and gold in eastern story. Travelers and ambassadors from the West, who were favored with an audience by the grim despots of Delhi and Agra, brought home tales of the dazzling splendors and the exhaustless wealth of the "gorgeous East." And yet they had only to look out from beneath the gilded arches of the audience chamber upon the surrounding country and they could see the landscape covered with the mud cabins of the poor, whose forced toil had built the palaces and supplied the riches and splendors in which despots reveled and which poets celebrated in lofty rhyme. At Delhi and Agra and Muttra and Jeypoor and Amber and Ahmenabad and Aurungabad I walked through the halls of princes that were adorned with marbles cut with every device of art and emblazoned with gold-covered ceilings and arches and columns and glittering with precious stones that it cost a kingdom or a great battle to buy. They had been all built out of the guilty spoils of war or the cruel oppressions of the poor. It made my nerves tingle to hear the tales of crime and profligacy which had held high carnival within those gilded walls and chambers which men travel thousands of miles to see and which poets adorn with all the fascinations of royal magnificence and romantic love. They seemed to me cheerless and cold and tomblike, and little better fitted to be the homes of peace and purity than the mud hovels of the poor whose unpaid labor had hewn and polished the marble and burnished the gold and set the precious stones that emblazoned the walls.

I sat on the platform with rajahs and princes of India in the great Hall of Calcutta, on the occasion of presenting a testimonial to the retiring viceroy, Lord Dufferin. The chairman was a maharajah with many titles of great renown, a descendant, I was led to suppose, of some mighty mogul or magnificent shah of the olden time. He wore a coronet of gold, and an aigrette of diamonds, set in the crown like plumes of the peacock, was tossing and flashing with light at every movement of his head. I fancied he might be a representative, in a small way, of Akbar or Aurungzebe or Jehan, as they sat in royal state on the Peacock Throne in the golden audience chamber at Delhi. I had seen him, as he came down on the train from Benares, stepping out upon the platform of the railway station at Patna, with a retinue of servants about him. When he called, they approached him half-bent to the earth and with hands clasped as if in the act of worship. They seemed to think it the highest honor to walk in his train or to lift his pipe to his mouth, or to pick up and replace his golden slipper, if it should chance to fall from his foot. But to me the grand maharajah looked coarse and lazy, vulgar and sensual and beastly, in the presence of the whirling wheels and the hissing steam of the nineteenth century. And I thought that possibly the great moguls themselves would not look much better to us if seen in the clearer light which shines on princes and people in our day. In that same great Hall of Calcutta, where maharajahs were clothed in purple and flashing with diamonds, I saw the poor pariah, the carrier of burdens, the scavenger of the streets, with only a loin-cloth to cover his nakedness, and with nothing better than the bare earth or the stone pavement for a bed when night came. And I doubted which found most to live for, the proud rajah with a harem of sensuality for a home and a retinue of servants to save him the trouble of lifting his hand, or the poor pariah who earned his rice by toil and slept soundly wherever the night might find him.

I saw the marble tombs and the mighty mausoleums of the great moguls, Aurungzebe and Jehangir and Shah Jehan of Agra and Delhi and Aurungabad. I saw by daylight and by moonlight, the Taj, the wondrous tomb that cost twenty millions of money and twenty thousand lives of laborers and twenty years of toil. I saw the scarcely less costly resting places of the great daimiōs and shōguns and mikados of Japan. I stood in ignorant wonder as I tried in vain to read the long inscriptions upon the marble columns that stood upon the back of enormous marble tortoises at Nanking and Peking and along the imperial road leading to the capital city, and telling the greatness of whole dynasties of princes and emperors whose ashes lay beneath the stone. I sat and cooled myself from the hot sun in the shadow of the great domes of Golconda in Hyderabad where the great Mohammedan princes sleep in glory each in his own bed. Kingdoms had been impoverished to build those monumental tombs. They were emblazoned with gold and marble and precious stones, and they were adorned with every device of exquisite art. Weary thousands of unpaid laborers had toiled for years in building up lofty platforms of stone and raising graceful minarets and columns and arches. They were not consecrated with shrines and altars and incense and images and idols as the heathen dedicate their tombs. But they were accounted so holy that in some cases I was required to put off my shoes from my feet before I could enter. As I walked through miles of arched corridors and shady retreats, where the dim light fell on tessellated floors and walls set with precious stones, it seemed to me as if the fleeting centuries of the past had come back and spread their cloudy wings around me, and the pagan and Moslem princes of other times were frowning upon me from their gilded thrones because I had intruded upon their repose with the tread of unhallowed feet. The echo of the slightest word that came back redoubled from the vaulted ceiling seemed like the whisper of pitying angels that had come there to lament the vanity of all human greatness and to bewail the transitory state of man on the earth.

But then I looked out upon broad fields where the naked pariah dragged his rude plow over the ashes of millions of the dead who died with no pitying eye to weep their fall and no friendly hand to set up a memorial stone to mark the spot where they were buried. And I thought the ashes of the pariah slept as peacefully in the open paddy field or on the sunny hillside without a shrine or a monument, as did the ashes of moguls and daimiōs and shōguns under roofs of fretted gold and in mausoleums of sculptured marble. The mere earthly elements of the story of birth and death, the coming and the going of a human life, are very much the same in either case. In the palace or the hovel there is a little flutter of excitement, a faint cry of mingled pleasure and pain over the coming of a new claimant for all the honors and joys that earth can give, or a new subject to all the burdens and sorrows that earth can impose. It may be that the kingdom has already too many competitors for its crown and the newcomer is not wanted. It may be that the hovel is already more than full and it gives little joy that there is one more hungry mouth to swell the daily cry for bread. But the years pass swiftly on and the struggle for life is as sharp for the prince as for the pariah. There is toil and weariness, brief success and bitter defeat, in either case. To the prince, the crown is not worth the purchase of rivalry and battle and blood. To the pariah, a life of toil and hunger and pain is not worth living if that is all there is of man. At length, after a time that always seems short, however long it may have been, there is a sudden going out of a life which had just begun, just as a puff of air coming in at the window at evening blows out the flame of a candle. Then the great world goes on just as before. A slight ripple has risen upon the great sea of existence and then sunk back again into the deep, and no mark on the surface shows where the little wave went down. That is the story and the whole story of a human life, whether of prince or peasant, if earth be our only home and death ends all for man. It is only the great hope of the endless life to come that gives greatness to man here, whether he be the monarch on the throne or the pariah in the rice field, whether he lie at last enshrined in marble and canopied with gold, or his dust mingle with the common soil which "the rude swain turns with his share and treads upon." But the other life, which lies beyond this, is so great and mighty that all distinctions of earthly rank or riches or power sink into insignificance when compared with the infinite destiny of immortality. If this life be all, there is not much to choose between the greatest of the moguls of Delhi and Agra and the meanest pariah, who finds an unknown grave in the mud of the Ganges or on the mountains of the north from which the sacred river flows on its way to the sea. Palaces and temples and tombs, crowns and scepters and royal robes, are but trifles, playthings of an hour, to him who shall wear the crown of immortality and shine like the stars in the firmament forever and ever.

IV.

THE SOUTHERN CROSS.

A JOURNEY round the globe gives one a grand opportunity to see the great and marvelous works of the Lord Almighty in many lands and on the boundless sea. In passing from land to land and from ocean to ocean it is an unspeakable satisfaction to feel that you can never go beyond the reach of the upholding hand and guiding eye of Him who made the heavens and the earth and filled them with riches and glories for his children to enjoy. The earth flies in its orbit a thousand times faster than the swiftest railway train, and yet the mountains stand firm upon their base, the sea is not shaken out of its bed, the feathery palm and the delicate bamboo are not swayed by the swiftness of the motion, and you feel that the everlasting arms are about you in every clime, and all the powers in the heavens and the earth are harmonized by an everlasting covenant well-ordered and sure. You traverse plains and climb mountains and cross seas; you observe every variety of tree and plant and fruit and flower; you find all living creatures making their congenial home on the earth, in the waters and the air; you study the aspects of the earth and the heavens at all seasons and under all changes, — and you come home from the long journey with a deeper feeling than you ever had before that one Mind created and one Will controls all forms and forces, all life and being, on the face of the earth. You settle down more content to live in the great house which your Father has made for his children, and more thankful for the varied and exhaustless riches with which the earth is filled for all creatures to enjoy.

As I sailed southward toward the equator I saw the north star go down to the rim of the horizon and at the same time I saw the sacred constellation of the southern cross come slowly up night after night to look in pity on the darkened millions, who were just beginning, one by one, to look up and rejoice in the brightness of its rising. I remember well a pleasant night in June when we were plowing through the broad, dark-blue China Sea, where the monsoon blows with its strong and long-continued blast, and the more terrible typhoon exhausts its short-lived rage in a few hours and yet in that time strews the bottom of the deep with wreck and fills many homes with wailing and sorrow. The only movement in the air was made by the motion of the ship, and the sea was as calm as a crystal lake in a summer's noon. The stars shone out with dazzling brilliancy and the reflection on the smooth face of the water made a heaven below as bright and beautiful as the heaven above. The pole star was low down towards the horizon, but the pointers in the Great Bear high up in the heavens showed the place where the North forever holds its throne. The sons of Arcturus and the princes of the heavenly host were circling round the pole with faces turned in homage towards their king. Wonderful, infinitely wonderful, seemed the starry heavens, and their mystery of depth and magnitude seemed so high and deep that no mortal mind could attain unto it.

And there still my attention was called to the brilliant cluster of the Cross more than to all the rest. It is composed of four stars, clear shining and well set, to represent the sacred symbol of divine suffering and human redemption. No wonder that mariners look to its rising as a sign of peace and goodwill to their homes on the land and to themselves on the sea. About it is gathered a larger constellation of brilliant stars than can be seen in the same space anywhere in the northern heavens. I looked out to see it every night from the deck of the ship on the sea, and I even thought I could sleep more calmly if I went out upon the house-top or threw open the window to look at the sacred sign before I retired to rest at night on land. In countries where the Cross is little known it seemed an especially fitting symbol to hang out in the sky every night to induce the darkened millions of the East to look up and hope and rejoice that the day of their redemption draweth nigh.

To me it was a peculiarly suggestive thought that the brightest of the starry host were gathered about the symbol of the world's redemption. The thrones, dominions, principalities and powers in the heavenly places were set in glorious array, like the twenty-four elders of the Apocalypse, about the starry figure which calls to mind the most astonishing and satisfying revelation of the divine love to man. The highest and mightiest of the princes of heaven stand gazing in rapt and voiceless contemplation of the great mystery of the divine incarnation, as if it gave them such a manifestation of the mind and heart of God as they had never seen before in the ages of their existence. It is set high and resplendent in the southern heavens as if to say that the work of redemption by the cross of Christ is for all nations, and that the isles of the utmost seas may know him who was lifted up from the earth that he might draw all men unto him. That sacred and glorious constellation shines forth with equal brilliancy upon the sea and the shore through all the changes of opinion and all the conflicts of nations. To the discouraged and the wandering and the darkened, it brings the best hope and it shows the way to the port of peace. It shone there clear and serene for ages before Christ came to give some foregleam of the brightness of his coming. It will shine on till all things in heaven and in earth are made one in Christ, and the ransomed nations join in crowning him Lord of all.

To me, that sacred constellation of the southern heavens suggested the other great thought that in the infinite ages to come and in the infinite worlds of immensity, the story of the Cross may be told and millions of immortal spirits, that have never fallen from their high estate in glory, will wonder and adore as they hear how their one supreme and eternal King once was crowned with thorns and crucified that man might regain his lost estate of life and immortality. We are told in the sacred story that the crucified One of Calvary now wears the crown of heaven and that the stars are at his feet. And in that state of supreme exaltation he still displays on his forehead and in his hands the signs of the sacrificial suffering borne by him for man's redemption. And if so, then the hosts of the blessed in all worlds must forever look upon the mystery of the divine incarnation as a revelation of God worthy to be made the science and the song of unwearied students and worshiping hosts, in all worlds, throughout all ages, world without end. I would not dare say that the sign of the Cross was set to shine among the eternal stars on purpose to teach that lesson. But to us who are saved by the Cross, it may be permitted to look up and rejoice when we see that sign in the most ancient heavens and we associate its significance with the deepest mysteries of God's universal and everlasting kingdom.

When once we believe and confess the first great fact in the gospel story, the divine incarnation, when we look by faith to the dying Sufferer of Calvary and we say with devout heart and thoughtful mind, "This was the Son of God," then it will be impossible for us to overestimate the meaning, the greatness, the far-reaching consequences of the sacrifice made by Christ for our redemption. We cannot conceive of any mode or means by which the infinite God could convince us more fully that he is mindful of our need and that he is visiting us every moment in kindness and tender mercy. So great a revelation of the love of God cannot be for us alone, but it must be made known to all worlds and it must be the theme of wonder and joy to all ages. Believing in that revelation we just begin to see how great a thing it is to be a man, made a little lower than the angels, a little less than divine, and crowned even now with glory and honor. Taking the gospel of Christ for the ground of our faith and the guide of our life, we have the highest incentives to walk worthy of our immortal citizenship in the redeemed earth and the eternal heavens. In the full blaze of science and art and culture, in the forefront of all advance in knowledge and riches and power, we may still count it the highest attainment in knowledge to know Christ, and the highest attainment in culture to be made like him higher than the heavens after the power of an endless life. Having learned the first and simplest lesson of faith on earth, we shall be ready, at his call, to enter into that other home where we shall see him as he is in the glory which he had with the Father before the world was.

By invitation from the official Astronomer of India, I climbed up into the lofty chamber of the observatory at Madras. There I saw the electric finger of the clock whose delicate touch fired the noonday gun at the same instant at Madras and Bombay and Calcutta, and so regulated time for public use all over India from Cape Comorin to the Himalaya Mountains. I looked through the great space-piercing tube of the telescope at the planet Saturn. I saw the double ring and the great white globe poised in the center of the two without touching either. I could not but ask myself silently the question, "Whose hand held that mighty orb in its place without any visible fastening or support? Who kept the surrounding ringed worlds from falling upon the globe and covering it with confusion and desolation?" And the blazing constellations, rising rank on rank, throne above throne, in numbers without number, seemed to answer back with a voice which the soul could hear, "God." The glittering cross, with its attending princes of light, and all the infinite expanse of the eastern heavens, responded with the glad refrain, "God." And the very silence of the immensities of space, the everlasting order and beauty with which the starry host kept on with even march and unbroken ranks across the fields of light, repeated back the ceaseless proclamation which the soul can hear in its silent depths, "God!" God measures the heavens and sets the stars for beacon lights on the infinite deep, and he calleth them all by name, and he marshals them forth upon the plains of immensity night by night, as the shepherd leads his flock on the hills of the morning.

V.

HOLY MOUNTAINS AND SACRED RIVERS IN THE EAST.

IN going round the globe one can easily take within the compass of the journey the great mountains, the highest and mightiest on the earth, the holy mountains where God came down in thick darkness and mighty thunderings in ancient time, the calm and blessed mountains where men heard voices from heaven and saw the human form transfigured in the brightness of the divine glory. Lebanon and Hermon, Tabor and Carmel, Olivet and Sinai — I saw and ascended them all in the glow of the morning and in the gentle light of the setting day, and I was glad to find that the scenes of sacred story are so much like hills and valleys and high places which have been consecrated by Christian faith in my own land, and that the people of the Western World need not cross the sea to find holy ground on which to worship the Father in spirit and in truth. On the more familiar ground of Europe and in the far East, I saw the snow-crowned summits of the great mountains reddening in the rising and setting sun, seeming like altar-flames lifted up in continual prayer and worship from earth to heaven. And I too bowed in worship as in the presence of the Infinite, when I thought of the power which had lifted up those mighty masses far higher than man's intrusive foot has ever climbed, and made them fountains of perpetual streams that fertilize the plains and fill the hearts and homes of millions with food and gladness. The mountains are barren and cold, but they are sources of life to all that live. Without them the fertile plains would be a desert and every living thing would die. The rice plains and the palm groves of the Ganges are kept alive by the annual tribute brought from the icebergs and the snows of the far-off mountains. The clouds that bring the rain, when the whole continent of India is grievously tormented by the flame of the sunbeam, are gathered and sent forth upon the air by the snow mountains a thousand miles away from the parching fields. No wonder that the mystical mythology of the East should make the mountains the habitations of gods that utter forth their voices in the thunder and send their best gifts to man in the flood of the fertilizing streams! No wonder that the extravagant superstitions of the East, in glorifying the mountains, should make their height a thousand times greater than the whole diameter of the earth and their foundations as far beneath the level of the sea! No wonder that the worshipers of the powers of nature should build their altars on the high places of the hills, and the saints and the sages, who spend their lives in meditation, should seek the solitude of the mountains and make the clouds of the morning and the stars of night their companions! Of all holy places which men have consecrated by offerings of devotion and pilgrimages of faith, the mountains are most worthy of the name. And the intelligent Christian traveler is always glad to bring them within the range of his journey.

I traveled three hundred and seventy miles north from

Calcutta to Darjeeling, to see the great white wall of the snow mountains, the highest of the Himalaya range and the highest in the world, Kunchin-Junga, Dhawalaghiri, and Everest. We rushed away at the rate of forty-two miles an hour till we came to the Ganges. We crossed the sacred river on a ferryboat and then went on half as fast upon the meter gauge road. Finally we came to the foot of the mountains and began the ascent upon a railroad of two feet gauge, darting in and out of the narrow ravines at what seemed a rapid rate but which really was only at the slow pace of seven miles an hour. The road company was forbidden by law to run at a greater speed. When we had reached the utmost height that the panting locomotive could climb, the mountains, the great mountains, rose twenty thousand feet higher still. But they were hidden away behind a thin, silvery veil of mist or haze, so that we could not see them on the evening of our arrival. The next morning we rose early and went out to see the great sight of the earth reaching to heaven and leaving man far below. But the veil was still there. We could not see the white face of the great mountain wall, which no human foot has yet been able to climb. The next morning came, and it was our last chance. We looked out early and anxiously for the great sight; we almost thought we could see it. Our friend, who lived there and whose eye was familiar with all the changing aspects of the earth and sky in his wild home, thought he could pierce through the veil and see the awful face of the three great hierarchs throned among the hills. But then the white mist was so like the white snow that he confessed himself deceived and gave it up at last.

Our search and our disappointment reminded me of the efforts which I had been making for many months to sound the depths and scale the heights of Indian wisdom. I had been told many times that the Indian philosophy was deep and high, such as no western mind could attain unto. But I humbly thought I could approach the brink and look down into its great, unsounded deep, or I could stand reverently afar off and gaze at the awful and inaccessible heights. But in all my reading of the sacred books ascribed to the saints, in all my study of the philosophy taught by the sages of the East, I had found nothing but a blind and baffling mist, a bewildering haze, which left me only to conjecture what might lie beyond. I had read many books which gave great promise of things hidden from common eyes, too subtle and ethereal for common minds to grasp. It had been promised that glorious, transporting revelations would be made to those who persevered in the study and followed in the steps of the sages. I had done so before I visited the East. I did so again on the ground where the sacred books were written and the philosophy sprang into being. But I seemed to myself to have been floundering through bogs and fens, sinking deeper in the mire the farther I went on, or to have been climbing up steep places to get a broader and brighter view, and all the while I was getting into thicker clouds and deeper darkness. If there be any wisdom hidden away in the mass of contradiction and nonsense which makes up the contents of the sacred books of the East, it must be hard to find and not worth the search.

I do not reject the boasted wisdom of the East because

it is mysterious and incomprehensible, but because its claim to mystery is false and affected. Its greatest mystery is that it has nothing to conceal. It cannot be made to carry any intelligible meaning except by putting a far-fetched and figurative interpretation upon language which was intended to be taken literally and which, when so taken, is absurd and ridiculous. Any truly great and divine revelation must have mysteries past finding out. Nevertheless they are realities, and the more we come to understand them the more rational and significant they are seen to be. We can believe in the reality of things which we have not seen because we have the testimony of competent witnesses and the confirmatory evidence of revelations which we can understand.

We came back to the hot and sultry plains of the Ganges and the Hoogly without seeing the snow-crowned summits of the highest peaks in the world. But we believed that the mountains were there as firmly as we should if we had seen them with our own eyes. We should have been thought fools or madmen if we had insisted that there were no such heights as Dhawalaghiri in the world because we had traveled so far and had tried so hard to see them and we did not see them at all. So I believe in the reality of things that I have not seen with my own eyes just as firmly as I believe in things that I have seen. Others have seen, if I have not. Millions have acted upon the truth and reality of things they have not seen, and they have found it safe and rational so to do. It is wise and prudent, it enlarges the mind and uplifts the soul, to believe in the reality of things that we have not seen and in the infinite importance of revelations which we cannot fully understand.

It is darkening and debasing to insist that we will be governed only by our senses, that we will believe only in a world that we can see and measure and comprehend, that we will go no farther in faith and duty than we can be led by the feeble lamp of our own experience or by the touch of a hand that is material and muscular like our own. We should not blame the Hindu for believing in things above and beyond the range of present experience and observation, but for believing in things absurd and contradictory. The faith which rests upon a firm foundation must agree with the soundest reason and it must answer the deepest necessities of the soul. The mystical philosophy and the monstrous faith of the Hindu never did either.

I saw the storied rivers which millions worship in the East. I saw the sacred waters to which devotees from distant lands came by hundreds and by thousands every year in the hope to wash away their sins. I saw them plunging into the turbid current and coming out more defiled than they went in. But they thought the water holy, and thenceforth they wore the rude garment, which had been dipped in the stream, as a robe of righteousness to which the gates of heaven would surely open. The devotees of the Holy Orthodox Church of Russia traveled a thousand miles for the opportunity to plunge into the muddy Jordan at the supposed place of the baptism of Christ. They carefully rolled up the wet garment in which they had taken the bath and carried it devoutly home that they might wear it as a shroud in the coffin and be wrapped in its folds in the grave. I saw women dressed in the finest silks that eastern looms can weave, glittering with gems and gold as they went down the stone steps to wash their hands and faces in the water of a tank that looked and smelt as if it were the drainage of all the sewers of the city. Two hundred and fifty thousand pilgrims gathered in Allahabad, at the junction of the Ganges and the Jumna, that they might wash away their sins in the doubly holy water of the united streams. Many died on the journey; some were drowned in the river; all suffered greatly from want and weariness and hardship of every kind. One day four hundred of them laid aside every particle of clothing, covered their bodies with the vilest filth they could find, and then marched in procession with an English official riding on an elephant and leading the line down to the sacred waters. Their hideous and disgusting appearance, their wild cries and their fierce excitement, made it seem as if all the madhouses of the world had turned loose their inmates upon the flat of ground at the junction of the rivers. Some were there to tell the infatuated worshipers of the waters of a Fountain which God himself has opened for sin and uncleanness. But the blinded pilgrims of the Ganges and the Jumna looked upon the herald of glad tidings as one that mocked, and they drowned his voice with their continual cry unto gods of silver and of gold, of iron and of stone.

At different times in the course of my long journey my movable home was by the far rolling Danube, the strong current of the Bosporus, the classic scenes of the Hellespont and the Isles of Greece, the turbid stream of the Irrawaddy and the Meinam, the Yang-tse-Kiang and the Pei-Ho. On a previous journey I had bathed in the Red Sea, the Dead Sea, and the Sea of Galilee. I lapped water with

Gideon's three hundred at the Spring of Harod under Gilboa, and I sat by while the women came to fill their pitchers at the fountain of Nazareth. I had crossed the ancient Kishon and camped by the fountains of the Jordan at Cæsarea Philippi. And now again I was glad to enlarge my sacred geography as I rode beside the Cydnus in whose cool waters young Alexander of Macedon endangered his life, and upon whose banks Paul, a greater conqueror, mingled in the sports of childhood. The morning star shone so brightly that I could see the shadow of myself and horse as I crossed the Orontes and rode away from Antioch, where Paul and Silas preached the gospel in love and parted in anger. I paused a moment and slipped down upon my feet to drink of the spring which is called by the great Apostle's name, and which was holier to me than the muddy tanks of Benares or the gushing fountains of Daphne, where apostate Julian revived the rites of a worship which his father Constantine had abolished. I camped beside the ancient Euphrates, where the Hittite kings dwelt in Carchemish when the terror of their name was enough to raise the siege of Samaria, in the days of Elisha, and put to flight the armies of Syria. I crossed and recrossed the Ganges, the Jumna, the Indus, the Chenab, the Sutlej, the Djhelum, and the Godavery. I rode in a boat over the tops of the full-grown millet and sorghum on the banks of the Pei-Ho, and I saw the pure water of the Po-Yang Lake come down into the muddy Yang-tse-Kiang and push the turbid stream for a while out of its own channel and then at last lose itself in the mighty flood of the great river. Everywhere the rivers, turbid or clear, swift and roaring like the Jordan, or silent and slow like the Nile and the Hoogly, bore the life of millions in their waters. If they should dry up or cease to flow, millions would die. And the traveler must be very thoughtless if he does not think with wonder and awe of the one almighty Hand which brings the waters of the ocean from afar across the pathless fields of air to fill their fountains full. If for one year the ocean should withhold its tribute and the clouds refuse to form, all languages would be loaded with cries of woe and the earth would become one universal grave. To save the nations from such death, the great rivers of God go forth from the sanctuary of the mountains and carry life and growth to all the fruits and fields of earth. So every man's life is held in the grasp of a power as completely beyond his control as the gathering of the clouds and the fall of the rain.

As one meditates upon these great and marvelous works of the Lord Almighty in many lands, it does not seem strange to him that blinded and brutal men should worship the stars, the mountains, the rivers, and the seas, when once they have forgotten Him who commands the stars to shine and the rivers to flow and the ocean to enrich all lands with the abundance of its treasures. The great powers of nature are so utterly beyond all human control that the ignorant and the superstitious are awed into worship and sacrifice, and the scientific and cultivated talk of nature as if it were a power in itself independent of one supreme, all-ruling Mind. And yet the ignorant and the debased are lifted up to a new life when they look upon all material forces as the putting forth of one infinite Will, and the truest and most advanced science agrees with divine revelation in bringing man everywhere into the presence of the Infinite. Both agree in showing the wisdom and the power and the love of the one Almighty Father equally in the life of the smallest creature that lives and in the infinitude of worlds that emblazon the midnight heavens with their glory. And one does not need to go into the uttermost parts of the earth or to compass the globe in long travel to learn that lesson. Every blade of grass that grows in the field, every flower that blooms in the meadow or the garden, every snowflake that flies through the wintry air, is a witness to the presence and power of the one Almighty Father; every whisper of conscience is the voice of God in the secret place of the soul.

The people of the East have yet to learn the first great truth taught in the first verse of the Bible, and all the way through to the end: "In the beginning God created the heaven and the earth." Some of them say that neither the heavens nor the earth were ever made. All things that exist have always been and always will be. Others say that all things that exist are God; they themselves are a part of the divine nature and cannot but do God's will. Independent of all theories and philosophies of the universe, the common people of the East make to themselves millions of gods and they endow them with all the exaggerated imperfections of their own character. So neither the philosophers nor the common people have any proper idea of worship or trust in the one Almighty Father, maker of heaven and earth. When they receive that first great truth of divine revelation, they will be new men, and the whole meaning of life in the world will be new to them.

VI.

HOW TO SEE MISSION WORK IN THE EAST.

SOME travelers go all the way round the globe and never meet a missionary in all the journey. They come home and say they have little confidence in reports of conversions among the heathen, for they saw no Christian natives and no signs that the people of the East are forsaking the religion of their fathers. Nevertheless the journey gives grand opportunity to those who will use it to study the advance of the nations of the East in light and truth, and the signs of the coming righteousness and peace in every land. It was for that especial purpose that I made the circuit of the globe and directed my course all the way round just where I was most likely to find what I went to see and hear. I was indeed interested in the historic memorials and the great works of art which testify the greatness of former generations in the East. But I would not have gone so far and given so much time and toil and money just to say that I had seen the relics of the bygone ages and had satisfied my curiosity with the journey. My main reason for studying the men and the monuments of the past was to see what hope there can be that the populous East will produce greater and better men and mightier works in the future. Some travelers seem to take satisfaction in sending home messages that missions among the heathen are a failure and the best hopes of the world are doomed to disappointment. It certainly would be a sad journey if one must bring home the message of despair.

I went, however, on the long journey, resolved to look on the dark and discouraging side of mission work, if such a side there be. I did not go as an agent or committee or secretary of any society or organization whatever. I had no commission save from Him from whom all can receive the highest and the best. I was not bound to report what I saw or tell what I heard unless I chose so to do. I went just where I pleased, stayed as long as I pleased, paid my own expenses, and came home when the Lord's good providence brought me back in safety and in peace. My most esteemed and excellent companion in travel was as free as myself in his choice of times and routes and modes of investigation. There was no necessity upon us to agree in the impressions we received, the opinions we formed, or the conclusions to which we came. Now that both are safe home again, neither is bound by what the other may say as to the results of our observations. I say thus much of personal matters in order that it may be understood fully that I speak only as an independent witness and that I have quite as much right to my opinions and impressions of the work of missionaries in the East as the self-styled liberal travelers who send home letters about the failure of missions in China and India, and who say they know all about it, when really they have never visited a single mission station, never talked an hour with a missionary or a heathen convert. To justify myself in what I say in this book, I must give a little in detail my method of gathering information.

I traveled more than forty thousand miles, and I kept my eyes and ears open and all of my faculties for observation in full exercise all the way. I asked questions everywhere and of everybody who could give information. I saw personally more than seven hundred missionaries who had made it the sacred service of their lives to find out the thought, the feeling, the faith, the hope and the fears of the heathen people in order to lead them forth into the great light and liberty of truth and salvation. I did not seek opportunities to make public addresses, because I went on the journey to learn rather than to teach. And yet many times the opportunity came in such form that I could not in common courtesy decline. So in one hundred and sixty-eight instances I gave such address, sermon, or lecture, as I could in answer to kindly request. Sometimes I spoke to students who were preparing for the ministry in colleges and theological seminaries; sometimes to schools of boys and girls preparing for the common duties of life; sometimes to companies of missionaries who had come together especially to hear what we had seen of Christian work in other lands. I spoke with equal freedom to heathen and Christian, in the church, the schoolhouse, the public street, and the jungle. By the help of interpreters I made use of twelve languages besides my own. I tried in them all to tell the people by public address and afterward in personal conversation what wonderful things the gospel of Christ had done for our own land and what it would do for theirs if they would receive it to the heart and make it the guide of their life. I made special effort to find out whether my words were understood, and also whether I rightly understood what they said to me in reply.

I was received and hospitably entertained by missionaries and people of every denomination, Congregational, Presbyterian, Methodist, Baptist, London Mission, Church of England Mission, Scotch Assembly, Reformed Dutch, China Inland Mission, Canadian Mission, Southern Methodist, Southern Presbyterian, Wesleyan, United Presbyterian, Independent. I received information and hospitality from all these and also from merchants, judges of English courts, officers in the army, presidents of colleges, consuls, foreign ministers, members of council, civilians, and business men of every kind. I visited the native Christians and heathen in their houses, the native pastors in their fields of labor. I visited and examined all grades of schools, sacred and secular, heathen and Christian. I asked all manner of questions about studies, discipline, behavior, proficiency, character, and results of instruction. I visited hospitals and I asked physicians to tell me faithfully what their profession and practice had taught them concerning the social life and moral character of the people as they were under heathenism and as they are under the influence of Christian instruction and the personal presence of missionaries among them. I wished especially to know how the converts to Christianity are regarded by their own countrymen — whether they are generally thought to be more virtuous, reliable, trustworthy, than they were before they renounced heathenism. I talked with men in hotels and railway trains, on steamships, in shops and offices and streets, and I asked employers, both native and foreign, whether they preferred Christian converts or heathen for servants, workmen, clerks, messengers, and marketmen. I sat with the judge on the bench, with the professor before his class, with the physician at his dispensary, with the priest in his temple, the monk in his monastery. I saw the Buddhist preacher in his pulpit; the story-teller with his audience about him listening in the street; the fortune teller making grimaces and mumbling incantations in the market place; the diviner shaking rods from his bamboo box before an idol to find a lucky number; the astrologer drawing diagrams and making horoscopes for the newborn child; the gambler plying his trade in the sacred apartments of the temple; the opium smoker lying stupefied and oblivious in his reeking den, — and I was told the meaning of what I saw and heard by men who knew the language and the people well.

I listened to men who ridiculed, or criticized, or condemned all methods of missionary labor and who thought it sharp and severe to say that all missionaries had better go home and convert the heathen in their own country before they seek to make converts in foreign lands. I heard the talk of men who say that the many denominations of Christians had better agree among themselves what are essential articles of faith before they undertake to teach the heathen what to believe. I heard the stories that have been told these twenty years on the decks of oriental steamers and the verandas of eastern hotels about the luxurious living and the lazy lives of missionaries, and I traveled more than ten thousand miles among the heathen in search of missionaries so living, but I did not find them. I found hundreds of missionaries wearied with work, yet rejoicing in it; meeting great difficulties, yet overcoming them; subjected to long delays and hindrances, and yet succeeding at last; suffering unutterable things from the filthy manners of the heathen about them, yet never complaining. But idle, inefficient, luxurious, self-indulgent missionaries I did not find, though I went in search of them through the length and breadth of India, through large portions of Burmah and Siam, and China and Japan. I saw many zenana women, Bible readers, native catechists and their teachers, and I asked them to tell me what kind of homes they found in their visits, and what they thought of social life among the Mohammedans, Hindus, and Chinese, and whether the homes of the heathen converts looked brighter and happier than those of the people who poured water and oil upon idols or burnt joss sticks before the tablets of ancestors in their houses every day. I saw great numbers of heathen converts. I attended their churches and Sunday-schools; I heard them preach and sing and pray. I could not understand what they said, but I tried to read their faces, their behavior, their manifestations of emotion, which are the same to people of all languages and nations. I saw them often when they were under no restraint or impulse from the presence of the missionary, and they had every opportunity and inducement to act themselves out freely. I visited a great many heathen temples, shrines, sanctuaries, holy places, where often the devout were gathered in great numbers, having come on long and painful pilgrimages and having made costly sacrifices to answer the demands of their faith. I saw them at their devotions, witnessed their gifts and prostrations and sacrifices. I inquired of those who could understand them what they said and what was the meaning and intent of all their worship. I made myself a learner everywhere with no theories of my own to advocate, no preconceived opinions or prejudices to confirm as the result of my inquiries. And I must have been a very dull scholar indeed if I did not learn something reliable, trustworthy, about the present condition of the great eastern nations and about the probability that they will ever rise from darkness and degradation into a truer and greater life in the future.

As the result of all my inquiries and observations, I came home with the decisive conviction that there are signs of a great awakening in all the East and that the time is drawing near when a new day shall dawn upon those who sit in darkness and in the region of the shadow of death. The great missionary enterprise is of God and it can no more fail than the promises of God can fail of fulfillment. Already in all heathen and Mohammedan countries the thrones of darkness are shaken and the strongholds of superstition are besieged by forces that no power on earth can resist. The walls of defense are strong and they will stand a great deal of shaking, and they will not go down in a day. But go down they must before the silent shafts of the Prince of light. They have been built for ages, but they are things of the past and they cannot live in the light of to-day. The great monuments, the gorgeous temples, the magnificent tombs of heathen and Mohammedan art all tell of an age which has gone never to return. There is no sign that such great works will ever be repeated to witness the power of a false faith. I counted two hundred Buddhist pagodas in a small town far up the Irrawaddy River, and saw thousands besides in Burmah and Siam, but I did not see one in the process of building, not one of the many crumbled and decaying which men were engaged in repairing or rebuilding. All over China I saw temples, pagodas, monasteries, Buddhist, Taoist, and Confucian, but I never saw one which was new, not one that was being built. I asked the age of a temple in Ningpo, and, as already said, the priest replied, "Tens of thousands of ages." That was his way of saying that the building was very old. I asked the same question and received the same answer in reference to a famous bridge at Fuchau. I saw one of the finest of pagodas eight li from the walls of Peking. When asked, the people of the village were modest enough to say at first that it was only six hundred years old, but the next moment they took back the estimate and put the age at twelve hundred years. I asked an old resident, who had lived in the country more than thirty years, which number was nearer right. He said it was safest in China to take the larger number. I asked him if, during the whole time of his residence in the country, he had seen a Buddhist temple or pagoda built or a city surrounded with walls or any great monument reared, and he said, No. I saw one temple to Confucius at Nanking which they said had been built within twenty-five years. But the open courts and corridors were overgrown with weeds and briars and bushes like a jungle. I found a pleasant resting-place for three weeks at a Buddhist monastery, or rather temple, it was called, on the slope of the western hills fifteen miles from the walls of Peking. There were eight similar temples on the face of the same hills. All but one of them were rented for summer residences to foreigners who belonged to the embassies and missions in Peking. The most sacred and consecrated part of the temple where I rested, the holy house which contained the images of Gautama, was used by servants as a wash and ironing room, and that with the full knowledge and consent of the priest who had charge of the whole structure. It was named the "Temple of Everlasting Rest." It looked to me as if it were a fit place where Buddhism might be buried in its chosen and everlasting sleep, a Nirvana from which it will never wake again.

I visited the rock temples of Elora in India. Two miles length of a mountain-side facing the north had been cut at intervals into the most elaborate cave sanctuaries for heathen worship. One of them is more than three times as large as the largest Protestant church in America, and it is all cut out of one solid stone. There were altars and shrines and sacred retreats for priests and pilgrims, images of monkeys and serpents and gods. And they were all of one piece, cut out of one ledge of solid rock. That one temple must have cost enough to endow a dozen colleges, to build a hundred churches, to educate a thousand men in all the arts and sciences of the world. And yet it was utterly deserted, and so were all the rest that the workmen of some far distant age had sunk into the face of the mountain. The altars and shrines and idols were without worshipers, save when some strolling company of howling and crazy pilgrims came from afar to make the caverns echo for an hour with their wild cries. Nobody is cutting out such temples from the rock in India or anywhere else at this day. There is no probability that such mighty monuments of superstition will ever be raised there or anywhere else in the world again. The broad kingdoms and fertile provinces, which once supplied their most skillful workmen and their richest revenues to build vast temples and carve colossal images and celebrate great feasts in support of heathen superstition, are now devoted to the support of the human family and the increase of human good.

All over India and Burmah and Siam and China and Japan I saw monumental evidences of a power which was great and mighty in former ages, but which has now no part in the great moving forces of the world. It dazzled with its magnificence and it deceived with its falsity in a past age, but it cannot live in the light which is coming in from Christian nations and which is overspreading all the East silently as the morning breaks on the mountains, progressively as the dawn advances to the full day. The great mass of the people of the East are still sitting in darkness and in the region of the shadow of death, but they are losing faith in their old superstitions, they are beginning to see that the new religion from the West comes to them with a message of truth and of power, of life and liberty. It will take more than one generation to break the long bondage of ages and set the imprisoned millions free, but the day of redemption draweth nigh. The dawn brightens in all the eastern heavens, and it is as sure to move on to the high and glorious noon as God's covenant of the day and of the night is sure not to be broken. We are not to lose faith or slacken effort for the redemption of the East because the promised day comes slowly on and sometimes the night comes with the morning. It took a thousand years to bring forth the best life we have in America. And we must not faint or be discouraged in Christian work and giving if it takes a tenth part as long to bring the multiplying millions of the East into the glorious light and liberty of the children of God.

VII.

GRAND EXPERIMENTS AND GREAT SUCCESS.

THERE was a time within the memory of some now living when Foreign Missions were looked upon as a mere experiment. Some were sanguine of success, some were open in opposition, some wished well but doubted whereunto the thing would grow. The conversion of the heathen was a thing to be desired and prayed for, but few thought it likely ever to come to pass in the ordinary course of Christian toil and faith. The onlookers and the laborers were equally divided in sentiment and in opinion, and the outside world ridiculed or, with patronizing pity, said it was a religious craze which must have its day and would soon come to an end. Reviewers and newspaper writers played off their small wit upon the folly of sending warm blankets to the sweltering islanders of the tropics and shedding tears of pity over cannibals in the ends of the earth while the home heathen are dying at the door. The great and the honorable East India Company, a business corporation, the richest and the mightiest that England made, after due examination and long debate, solemnly declared the sending of missionaries to heathen lands to be "the maddest, the most extravagant, the most expensive, the most unwarrantable project that was ever proposed by a lunatic enthusiast." That time has now long gone by. That same company gave seventy-five thousand dollars to print a dictionary which one of those lunatic missionaries made while hiding himself from arrest by the agents of the company who had been ordered to seize and send him home. That great and mighty board of directors, who ruled over more millions than the Cæsars in the height of their glory, and who, in their pride of place and power, resolved to rule the kingdom of God out of their dominions, has been dead and buried more than thirty years. In the last generation it could stand against the world; now there are none to do it reverence. But the missionary enterprise, which the directors stigmatized as a waste and a madness, and which the wits and the worldlings tried to overwhelm with ridicule and contempt, was never so full of life and power as it is to-day. It never was advancing so rapidly, never had so fair a prospect of making a full conquest of the whole heathen world.

Never in all time has there been put before men so great an enterprise as that which is enjoined upon the followers of Christ in the divine charge to go forth and disciple all nations. The possibility of fulfilling that command is only just beginning to be seen and felt in our day. Many who take no part in the work are already talking as if they thought the thing would be done. Success has convinced the doubting, experience has taught the believing, hard work and heavy burdens have chastened the zeal of the sanguine, the growing prospect of final triumph has fired the hearts of the cold and calculating into fervor of feeling and assurance of faith. Continual progress has been made in the face of difficulty so great, in circumstances so varied, after delays so long continued, that nobody now thinks that there may be greater trials and severer tests of faith and strength in the future. Nobody now thinks that any hindrance can arise in the progress of the work which has not been already met in some form and overcome in the past. The gospel has been brought into contact with all grades of human society, all depths of ignorance and degradation, all extremes of savagery and superstition, and it has proved to be the power of God and the wisdom of God unto salvation among them all.

The proud Brahmin boasts of his divine descent. He exacts worship of the despised pariah at his feet. He denies all brotherhood between him and the low-class coolie who toils in the rice fields and takes poverty and contempt as the portion of himself and his children forever. When asked if he worships the gods, the Brahmin proudly replies, "The gods worship me." It used to be the law and the custom in Travancore for the pariah to go seventy paces to the right or the left of the public path for the Brahmin to pass, lest the holy man should be polluted by a nearer approach to his brother man. His food is prepared for him in secret, lest it should be defiled by the glance of human eyes. He eats alone and in silence as if it were an act of worship and he himself were the god to whom offerings and libations should be presented. For ages he has lived his life of self-adoration and walked the earth as if it were not worthy to sustain the pressure of his foot. And yet that most conceited and self-assured creature, under the teaching of the gospel, has been constrained to own himself a man; he has learned to sit at the same table and drink from the same cup with the coolie, whose touch he once thought was pollution; he has heard the story of One who humbled himself and made himself of no reputation for the good of all, and the proud Brahmin himself has been humbled in the dust by penitence and exalted by faith to the divine rank of sonship in the kingdom of God.

The idle Buddhist withholds his hands from all manner of useful work. He walks dreamily up and down the courts and corridors of his temple as if in sleep. He goes out into the street in the morning with servants to carry his begging bowl and screens of palm leaf to shelter his head from the sun. He counts his silent presence at the door of a house a divine visitation to the people inside, and it is an act of great condescension in him to accept the gifts for which he will not deign to ask. He does nothing for the public welfare; he denies all bonds of kindred and brotherhood of humanity; he shows no pity for the poor, no sympathy for the suffering; he has no intellectual aspirations for his own improvement, no plan or purpose for the relief of the misery about him. He considers it a merit to repress all desire and affection, all thought and feeling, all interest in the well-being of his fellowmen or the advance of the world in knowledge and virtue and truth. He considers God's precious gift of life an affliction, and his whole study and effort is to make his life as little as possible like what God intended it to be. He stifles his intellect, starves his heart, degrades and dishonors the mysterious and wonderful work of God in the whole constitution of his being. In the solitude of his temple he drones out endless repetitions in prayer, and yet he has no God to pray to. As he moves about his monastery he seems like one walking in his sleep and waiting to be caught up into a paradise of dreamless and everlasting slumber where Buddha himself sleeps beyond all waking. Education, art, philosophy, can do nothing to inspire him to effort in seeking the grand purpose of his being, for to him life has no meaning, no purpose; there is nothing worth laboring for. Ask him to do something for the people about him on whose charity he lives; he will tell you that they can have nothing to do better than to serve him, and they are doomed to endless transmigrations of misery in the world to come. Endeavor to enlist his sympathy in behalf of the suffering, and you will find that he considers it a merit deserving the highest commendation to have no pity, no sympathy, no affection for anybody. Now the gospel of Christ comes into contact with that dark, selfish, idle, conceited man, and he wakes from slumber as the soldier rouses from sleep at dead of night when he hears the drum beating the long roll of battle. He is no longer a dreamer walking in his sleep and not knowing the darkness from the day. He is a living man, full of the fire and activity of the time, animated by high purposes and immortal hopes. He is no longer a drone, an idle, selfish beggar living upon the labor of others and never thanking them for their gifts. His heart is touched with sympathy for all that suffer, he is ready to deny himself for the good of others, and he finds a new and strange joy in effort to scatter the cloud of ignorance and superstition from the minds of his fellowmen. The gospel of Christ has done all that for many a blinded Buddhist in our day, and it can do it for millions more.

Of all the peoples of the East the bigoted and fanatical Moslem is commonly thought to be least susceptible to the spirit and the power of the gospel. In the day of his pride and conquest he had but two articles of faith in his creed, the Koran and the scimetar. The nations must accept one or submit to the other. And the spirit of the followers of Mohammed is the same now that it was when they flung out the crescent in fierce defiance of all the world. Theirs is a religion of pride and passion, of conquest and cruelty, of submission to fate and subjection by the sword. There is nothing merciful or humane in its spirit, nothing fatherly or forgiving in its God, although every chapter but one of its sacred book is given in the name of the Most Merciful. It is cold, hard, cruel; it degrades individual character, it crushes out the life of nations, it defiles the sanctuary of home, it stimulates the basest appetites and passions, and it makes the countries where it rules a wilderness of uncultivated fields and decaying towns inhabited by a hopeless, false, and licentious people. The devout Moslem has the name of God ever upon his lips while cursing and profanity are in his heart. He sends the parting guest on his journey with words of blessing and peace while meditating on the means of robbing him before he is out of reach. His religion is hard, cold, cruel. It has no element of life and growth, no capacity to adapt itself to the changing and advancing life of the world. I asked old residents in Northern India many times whether they had ever known a person to be converted to Mohammedanism by faith in its truth and divine character, and they all said, No. And yet even there seven elevenths of all the native preachers of Christianity in the service of the Church Missionary Society are converts from Mohammedanism. Followers of the false prophet of Mecca have learned that the cross of Jesus is mightier than the sword, and coming to Jesus they have found in him the rest which Mohammed never can give. In a church of more than five hundred members I found that two hundred and twenty-five were converts from Islam. The spiritual weapons used by our missionaries in preaching the gospel have already proved mighty enough to pull down all the strongholds of Mohammedan faith. The prophecies of the ancient time and the indications of our day agree in giving us the hope that the cold, cruel, and crushing sway of Islam is soon to end and that in all the East the war-loving crescent will give place to the peaceful cross.

In the ancient city of Damascus, on the street once called Straight, I looked for some memorial of the house in which Saul of Tarsus received his sight after three days of blindness, and where a new and more glorious light than that of the sun shone in upon his soul. I desired, if possible, to stand at the starting place of that great career on which the new Apostle went forth to consecrate the cold intellect and chasten the wild fancy and enlighten the dark hearts of the heathen world. I would stand on the spot where the holy light of the ancient East began its westward course which still keeps pace with the journeys of the sun and which grows brighter with the increase of years. After eighteen centuries of change and conflict there was no trace left of the crumbling walls, and there was no sign by which the site of the house could be known; but on either side of the street there were broken columns between which the Roman legions marched and the conquering eagles flew. Down deep beneath the rubbish of a thousand ruins was the pavement over which the chariots of Ben-hadad and Naaman rolled. In the windows and doorways and arches were stones which had trembled at the tramp of the hosts of Cambyses and Sennacherib and Nebuchadnezzar. The dust of the footways had been trodden by Abraham and Elisha.

I turned aside into a crowded bazaar where sandal-makers and silversmiths made the roof and walls resound with the clank of their tools and the clamor of their tongues. The precious things of the "gorgeous East" lay all around. Diamonds and emeralds and rubies shone like stars in the red light of furnaces. Dark-browed men braided and twisted and linked and spun and wove the ductile gold.

I ascended a stone staircase and went out upon the housetop. I then passed on from roof to roof till I came to an open space between one house and the next as wide as many of the narrow streets of an eastern city. With a short run and a long leap I cleared the chasm and went on till I came to a broad, high wall on which was carved in a curved line and in letters larger than two handbreadths this inscription in the ancient Greek language: "THY KINGDOM, O CHRIST, IS THE KINGDOM OF ALL AGES, AND THY DOMINION IS FROM GENERATION TO GENERATION."

The stones which bear that inscription form the main wall of a vast Mohammedan mosque. The letters are cut on the curve of an arch which once covered a lofty gateway and beneath which countless Christian worshipers had passed in and out in the long succession of ages. High above rises the slender minaret, which the muezzin climbs five times a day, and from the lofty portal of which he comes forth upon the narrow balcony, thrusts his thumbs into his ears to shut out every other sound save his own voice, and sends over the city the wild, wailing call to Mohammedan prayer, which, once heard by the Christian traveler in a Turkish town, can never be forgotten, "God alone is God, Mohammed is the prophet of God." Thus for twelve hundred years the false prophet of Mecca has been proclaimed five times a day from a hundred minarets in Damascus, while the dumb stones of its oldest and grandest mosque bear the testimony and are ready to break out with the cry, "Thy kingdom, O Christ, is the kingdom of all ages, and thy dominion is from generation to generation."

The explanation of this singular fact is easily found. That ancient structure was built before the age of Mohammed, and it was occupied for centuries as a Christian church. That sacred inscription was then fittingly engraven deep upon the walls both as a promise and a prophecy to help the faith of all that entered the open door. Through the ignorance, the indifference, or the contempt of the Moslems, the text was permitted to remain on the outer wall when the Koran had supplanted the Bible in the pulpit and the crescent had supplanted the cross on the tower and millions of scimetars were ready to flash out in defiance of the old prophecy and in defense of the new and false faith.

The streets of Damascus have many times been stained with the blood of the martyrs of Jesus. The fanatical followers of Mohammed have many times sworn upon the Koran and upon their swords to blot out the name of the Nazarene from the city where the apostle to the Gentiles received his divine commission to bear that name before kings and peoples of the earth. But still those words stand there, in the oldest city in the world, graven on the walls of its oldest and grandest temple, to proclaim to the nations and the ages, like the threefold inscription on the cross, that Christ is King, and that his dominion shall endure throughout all generations. The day is fast coming when that prophecy shall cry out from the dumb stones of the mosque and shall speak with living voices through all the streets and in all the temples of Damascus, and Lebanon shall take up the cry through all its mountain homes and the wandering Arab shall make the wilds of the desert resound with the song, "Thy kingdom, O Christ, is an everlasting kingdom, and thy dominion endureth throughout all generations."

There are more Mohammedans in India subject to the Christian government of England than in all the Turkish Empire. At Delhi and Agra and many other cities of India they see the signs of the greatness of an empire which was once theirs, but which has long since passed away. They have no expectation that they will ever again recover the supremacy which they once held in the East. Neither have they any faith that the Koran will supplant the Bible or that the crescent will ever take the place of the cross. In the Punjaub multitudes of young men are breaking away from the cold, hard, repressive spirit of Islam and are preparing to take their part in the onward march of the nations under the leadership of Him who trains his followers in truth and conquers by love. Even in Constantinople the Bible House stands face to face with the Sublime Porte; the Christian college overtops the towers in which the Turks first entrenched themselves in Europe, and wise men foresee the day when St. Sophia shall be rededicated as a Christian church and the name of Jesus shall take the place of Mohammed in the daily call to prayer.

VIII.

THE MOTORY POWER OF MISSION WORK.

THE Chinese coolie works all day in the rice field, half knee-deep in mud and water; or he trundles his heavy-laden wheelbarrow from sunrise to sunset along the narrow ridges of earth that take the place of roads; or he tugs at the boatline and the oar against the current of the river, naked and hungry, until the evening star tells him it is time to tie up for the night; or he bends his shoulders to the bamboo pole, carrying burdens that task his utmost strength, and then he seeks the solace of opium to relieve the gnawing in his empty stomach and the pain in his weary muscles and to give him a few hours of forgetfulness in sleep. He goes on using the stupefying drug till it becomes his merciless master and he is ready to sacrifice everything he has in the world to buy a few hours' release from his misery. He gambles away his last cash to get more opium; he cuts off the fingers of his hand for something to stake in the dreadful game; he sells his wife and child and himself also into perpetual slavery for one chance more at the dice to win an hour or two of seductive oblivion with the certainty that it will soon be gone and he will wake up in deeper misery than he was before. The poor wretch knows no other life. He is insensible to argument or rebuke or entreaty. No threats or scourges or tortures will induce him to surrender the treacherous opiate which gives him all the relief he has and then leaves him in a lower deep of wretchedness and despair. His self-mastery is all gone; his will is as weak as water; he is bound and held captive by a tyrant that is as greedy as death and as pitiless as the grave.

The divine power which goes forth with the missionary of the gospel to the ends of the earth touches the heart of that poor coolie. He starts with a strange surprise and joy as if a voice from heaven had bidden him rise up and walk. New light breaks into his dark mind, new strength is imparted to his enslaved will, hope dawns upon his world of darkness and despair. He is a man again; a stronger and better man than he was before or ever thought he could be when he was at his best. He shakes off the chains of his tormentor and he goes forth to proclaim to others the liberty which has come to himself. That mighty change, that complete spiritual transformation of the whole man, has been accomplished many times in China; it can be accomplished millions of times more. And there is only one power on this earth that has ever been able to do such mighty works in behalf of the lowest of the children of men. And that power is engaged by the covenant of the immutable God to go forth and work its wonders of new creation with the preaching of the gospel unto all nations.

Many stories of actual conversion might be told confirming the truth of the general statement made above. Take one as given by an eyewitness whom I met in the mission field, the largest and hardest in the world. In one of the poorest counties in all China, not far from the city of Amoy, there is a village beautifully situated at the foot of a mountain so high as to command a view of the whole surrounding country. The little low-roofed mud cabins are built on the banks of a bright stream, which bursts out of the base of the hills and goes forth gladdening the plain with music and life through all the year. The streets of the little town are narrow and filthy, the people are ignorant and poor, the children go unwashed and naked. The ducks and the dogs, the pigs and the puppies, the geese and the swine claim equal rights with their human companions, in the mud of winter and in the dust of summer and all the year round.

On the banks of the stream, a little way from the village, a small farmer cultivated a few acres of ground which had descended to him from his ancestors of many generations. He had less energy and endurance than the average of his countrymen, and he had hard work to keep himself and his family from starving. He was a restless, shrinking, diffident creature, with not enough force of character to look his fellowmen in the face, or to go about his business with mind and will enough to do it well. It was very easy for him to fall into the seductive and ruinous habit of opium smoking. As the appetite grew upon him it became impossible for him to get enough out of his little farm to support his family and supply himself with the deleterious drug. So he began to sell off a few rods at a time until at last he had so little left that he began to balance the question of selling his wife and children to satisfy his craving. Before adopting that last desperate expedient he resolved to go down to Amoy and try to start anew in some kind of work or trade. He had no faith in God, in himself, or his fellowmen. He had no conscience or principle or manliness or sense of right to inspire him to effort. He had no hope of ever being anything else than a miserable, disheartened, utterly abandoned creature till death should take him out of the world.

In that state of body and mind he came within hearing of a street or chapel preacher who was setting forth the simplest elements of gospel truth. From mere idle curiosity he listened and caught the meaning of the words spoken. It was the first message of hope to wretched men like him that he had heard in all his life. He took it so well to heart that he sought out the preaching place again and again. He believed the word of Jesus, and with that act of faith a new and divine power came upon him like an inspiration from the Almighty and it made him a new man. He mastered the appetite which was dragging him down to ruin. At once he became eager to tell his fellow-villagers at home what a wonderful blessing he had found, what a free and joyous life he had started upon with the gladness of immortal youth. He hastened back to the place of his birth and the lost inheritance of his fathers. In spite of all his personal disadvantages and all the discredit which was attached to his name as a weak and worthless man, he taught the truth which he had learned so effectually that his friends and neighbors also believed his message and other villages were eager to hear him tell what great things the religion of Jesus had done for him. At the time when the missionary told the story, eleven churches had been organized and seven mission stations had been taken and occupied as the result of that one man's labor in preaching the gospel. The churches so formed chose their own pastors, paid them well for their services, and maintained the ordinances of the Lord's house with order and propriety. The power which made that poor, ignorant, half-demented slave of opium a leader of men and a competent teacher of the highest truth is the power which is enlisted for the conversion of all the heathen. And it will not fail or be exhausted till it has set righteousness in all the earth and brought light and liberty to all people.

Every traveler, in passing through the streets of Chinese cities, falls frequently upon groups of men, six, ten, twenty in number seated upon the ground, listening to one who stands and talks to them with great freedom and animation by the hour. He is a story-teller. He recites romances of his own invention, or he takes up traditions that have been afloat among the people for ages; he dresses them up with additions and exaggerations of his own, and he hopes to interest his hearers so much that they will contribute a cash, a tenth part of a cent, apiece as a compensation for the entertainment, and so he shall get his living. He makes many gestures, throws himself into various and expressive attitudes, stands erect, sits down, flourishes his fan, distorts his face, clutches at his queue and his rag of a garment, often displays much skill and invention in devising illustrations, choosing the best language and working up the stolid minds of his hearers, who listen as if they did not hear and look as if they saw nothing to look at.

Now the fact of the story-teller's profession and his power over his rude audience arrested the attention of an ingenious and observant missionary. He had been in the country for a long time, laboring hard to find out the best way of bringing the spiritual truths of the gospel into the unsusceptible minds of the Chinese. Their feelings were so stolid, their consciences so inactive, their modes of thinking on all subjects so different from his own, that he seemed for years to be baffled and defeated in all his attempts. His own ideas of reason, truth, duty, religion, God, heaven, endless life, had grown up with him from childhood. They seemed to him all perfectly plain, reasonable, easy to comprehend. But with all his zeal, culture, ingenuity, he could not make the conservative and conceited Chinamen see things at all as he did. He had gained a rare mastery of the language, he had studied the traditions and customs of the people, he had mingled with them freely everywhere, in order to get at their innermost thoughts and feelings. And yet he felt all the while that there was a great deep between his mind and mode of thinking and theirs. In whatever words he tried to convey his meaning, his hearers were quite sure to give them a different interpretation from the one in his own mind.

For example, he would speak of God, using the best word he could find in their language for the divine name, and they would think he meant the material heavens, the forces that rule in the material world of nature, the stars, the thunder, the sea, the storm. They would say, "Oh, yes, we believe all that! We have seen God many times. That is all right; we think just as you do." He would go on to explain that he meant the one great God who made the heavens and the earth and all things therein and who gives life to all that live. And again they would answer, "Yes, we know him; we have seen him often. He is the middle one of the three that sit in the temple. We burn joss sticks and make offerings to him every day." Again the missionary would speak of the soul, the spiritual and immortal nature of man, and they would think he meant one of the spirits that escape from the body at death, and that must be propitiated with paper money and material sacrifices lest they come back from the grave and plague the living. Again they would say, "Oh, yes; we know all about the soul; the souls of our ancestors are all about us. We feed them, clothe them, honor them with incense and offerings every year. We could not live safely in our houses, we could not cultivate our rice fields with success, if we did not honor the spirits of our fathers and see their wants in the other world well supplied. We do not allow telegraphs and railroads and mining operations in our country for fear the spirits would be disturbed in their habitations of the earth and the air, and they would blast our fields and kill our cattle and we should all die of famine." Again the missionary speaks of sin, doing aught that is displeasing in the sight of God, and they answer just as readily, "Oh, yes; we know all about that: it is missing the mark, failing in business, losing health or property; it is to incur the displeasure of the spirits and suffer persecution from them. We are always trying to avoid sin. We draw lots and shake the divining rods and consult the augurs and the fortune tellers and the astrologers; we watch for signs and omens for good luck, and we do it all to avoid sin, to find out the way of escaping the consequences of sin."

Still again the missionary speaks of right-doing, rectitude, holiness, need of salvation; and they make answer at once, "We are always trying to do right: we bring offerings to the spirits of the dead; we revere the ancestral tablets every day; we reverence the aged; we keep joss sticks burning in our dwellings from morning to night; we carefully observe all the rules of courtesy and honor and reverence to superiors. We want a saviour to bring us good crops in the field, good trade in the shop, good health in the house, good luck in everything. We would gladly welcome a saviour who can do all that for us and for all China."

So whatever words the missionary might use in their own language in teaching the great spiritual truths of divine revelation, the Chinaman had a meaning for them all; but it was not the meaning that the missionary wished to express. Their language, with all its copiousness, was never made to be the vehicle for conveying the spiritual truths of the gospel. It is cast into rigid, inflexible forms; its characters are tied up with endless and complex qualifications; it is with the utmost difficulty that it can be made to convey anything else than the hard, material, unspiritual ideas which for ages have made up the whole range of Chinese life and thought.

Beset with so many difficulties in the way of getting access to the Chinese mind, the missionary, who was not a man to be easily baffled in anything he might attempt to do, resolved to take a hint from the story-teller whom he saw every day plying his profession in the street. He cast the main facts and teachings in the life of Christ into the form of a connected narrative. He began with the annunciation to Mary at Nazareth and he ended with the resurrection and ascension from Olivet. He adhered strictly to the gospel record, and yet he made the story vivid, full of action, and fitted for popular address. He described persons and places; he introduced question and answer; he filled the whole narrative with life and action from beginning to end. The simple and sublime sayings of Christ; his mighty works done for the good of men; his human kindness; his tenderness and pity for the poor and suffering and afflicted,—all came in to give meaning and grace to the sacred story.

When all was done the missionary selected a Chinese Christian, a man quick-witted, susceptible, and fluent in speech, and to him he told the story with the charge to give close attention and be ready to repeat what he had heard. All the education the poor coolie had ever received had been a training of memory, learning to repeat the names of signs which had no connection and, often to the learner, no meaning. So it was comparatively easy for him to remember a vivid, interesting, and connected narrative. A second and a third time the story was told and the listener required to repeat it as nearly as possible word for word. It was enough: he knew it now as well as his teacher. He was then charged to go home and tell it to his friends and neighbors. He lived some two hundred miles away in the country, and he must make the journey on foot and in company with others as poor as himself all the way. Home he went, traversing the narrow and crooked paths among the rice fields, crossing the great plains and climbing the low hills till he reached his little mud cabin, which made one of a hundred in his native village. He had been conning over the story on the journey, and when he arrived he knew it better than when he started.

He was now to try the effect of the wonderful narrative upon the minds of men who had never seen a missionary and had never heard the name of Jesus. He was like the first disciples who were driven from Jerusalem by persecution and who went everywhere telling what they knew about the crucified One. True to the charge which he had received from the missionary, on the evening of his arrival he called his nearest neighbor into his mud cabin, seated him on the ground, and said, "I heard a good story while I was gone down to the seacoast, and I want to tell it to you. It is about a strange, good man who lived in a land far away and a long time ago, and it will do your heart good to hear about him."

So he begins about the wondrous birth and the Holy Child and the village home among the hills of Galilee. He goes on to the opening of the public ministry of Jesus, and he weaves into the simple story many of the gracious words of the great Teacher. The listener wonders at first, and then he is chained and delighted with the blessing pronounced upon the poor, the hungering, the merciful, the pure in heart, and the peacemakers. He breaks in upon the story, and says, "They are good words which this man spoke. Confucius never spoke like that. None of the sages of China ever said such beautiful and kindly things about the poor and the suffering. The greatest of our philosophers never said, Come unto me, all ye weary, and I will give you rest. The whole land is full of the weary and heavy-laden, and there is no one to give them rest. I wish we had such a man in our country. Oh, if he would only come to us, we would all be so happy to obey him!"

The story goes on, and it tells of the mighty works done by Jesus, opening the eyes of the blind, restoring the palsied arm, giving hearing to the deaf and speech to the dumb, raising the dead to life. Again the wondering listener breaks in upon the speaker, and says, "Oh, that we had such a friend of man in China! Everywhere the blind are wandering about the country in darkness, and there is no one to give them sight. My poor lame neighbor has not walked for a year, and nobody can restore strength to his paralyzed limb. With my loudest call I cannot make my old father hear a word. I had the best doctors I could find for my dear boy when he was sick, but he died, and now I have no son to bury me and maintain the honor of the ancestral name in my family. If this Jesus, of whom you say so much, had been here, perhaps my son had not died."

The wondrous story still goes on through all the teaching and miracle-working days of Jesus' ministry. He is made to stand forth everywhere in the narrative as the helper of the poor, the comforter of the sorrowing, the friend of little children, and yet the ruler of the storm, the master of evil spirits, the conqueror of death. At last he voluntarily, silently, uncomplainingly submits to mockery and scourging and death. The poor Chinaman wonders why he should do that. He was expecting that the story would end by setting him forth as a great and mighty king, the lord of all the nations, the conqueror of all the armies of the earth. And yet he dies, dies the death of a defeated man and a malefactor, dies on the cross as the worst and weakest men die. The grave closes over him and his enemies triumph. The poor coolie wonders at all that. At last the thought steals in upon him that somehow this Jesus suffered and died for him. He begins to think he himself is not what he ought to be. The story about that holy, beautiful, blessed life has made him wish he were a better man, more like the meek, the mighty, and the merciful friend of the poor, comforter of the sorrowing, healer of the blind. No story told by men in the street ever made him have such feelings about himself, ever made him wish he were a better man. He feels saddened over the death of one who lived so long ago, and in a land far away, and somehow it seems to him almost as if it were the death of his own brother, and yet a brother greater far and better than himself. But he is taken by surprise at last when the story ends with the resurrection and the return to heaven. The wondering listener goes home to his own mud cabin to make the bare earth his bed for the night, questioning deeply in his heart what that strange story can mean and why it had such power over him as he listened.

The next evening the man comes back and he brings two or three others with him, and they all want to hear the strange story about the wondrous Friend of the poor, the blind, the lame, and the sorrowing, who appeared on the earth a long time ago, and in a land far away, and who died in love for all mankind. A second time the story is told, and the one who heard it first is more deeply touched to the heart than the rest. Ignorant, stolid, impassive as he is, he drops a tear of pity at the last bitter cry of the cross, and when the resurrection proclaims the triumph over death he shares the gladness of the disciples who rejoiced when they saw the Lord. And so the story of the life and works of Jesus slowly steals into the hearts of the villagers by constant repetition until they build a rude gathering place large enough to receive all who come. They learn to read the gospel from the sacred page; they pray together and sing praise, and they gather for worship every seventh day; they put away lying and licentiousness and all evil communications out of their mouths; they learn to lead lives of gentleness and purity and truth. And when the missionary comes to see the effect of his story upon the minds and lives of these far-off dwellers on the plains and among the hills of China he finds them already far advanced in Christian life and faith and duty. He gathers them into a sacred brotherhood, named from the name of Christ, and he teaches them the way of the Lord more perfectly than they could learn it from the story as it was first told them. In one province of China there are to-day fifty churches, self-supporting, self-taught in the word of life, growing constantly into greater usefulness and more intelligent faith, and all of them came into being from the simple telling of the story of the life of Jesus as it was cast into popular speech and taught to a single Chinaman by the missionary. They have their own preachers; they pay their own expenses; they keep gathering more and more of their heathen neighbors into the household of Christian faith. At stated times the missionary visits and confirms them all in faith and duty, and when he has finished his circuit and returned to his home by the sea he finds that he has baptized fifty, seventy-five, or a hundred in the course of his visitation. All the while he is laboring to supply the growing churches with better educated teachers than those who at first could do nothing but repeat the story of the gospel as it had been specially prepared for them. Two months of the year ten or fifteen men are kept under the eye and daily instruction of the missionary that they may go back to their village homes and teach their own neighbors the word of life and salvation.

By some such simple, inexpensive process the gospel can be preached all over the great Chinese Empire. The converted natives themselves can preach to their own countrymen better than the foreigner. The very limitations of their learning, in many cases, is an advantage to them in their work. Knowing nothing but Jesus Christ and him crucified, they waste no words on theories, speculations, controversies. They just tell the story with the spirit and manner of men who believe what they are saying, and so their hearers are led to believe it too. They can wear Chinese dress, eat Chinese food, go barefoot, live in a mud cabin, and ask no pay but the few cash which the poorest can give. Through such laborers the self-propagating power of the gospel is best made known, and by such ministrations the truth must eventually make its way through all the great heathen nations.

IX.

WHAT CAN WE TEACH CHINA?

IT is often said that the Chinese are the greatest and oldest and wisest of all the ancient nations that have come down to us from the olden time. They invented the art of printing, the composition of gunpowder, and the use of the mariner's compass long before they were known to western nations. They have the most rigid and effective civil service; they set the highest estimate upon education; they have the most profound reverence for age and dignity and parentage; they excel all other people in agriculture, in domestic economy, and in the capacity to make the most out of the smallest means of living. They have kept their language, their laws, and their religion unchanged for thousands of years, while thrones have been cast down, mighty empires have been broken in pieces, and the whole order of society and opinion and custom in other lands has been overthrown.

In all such statements there is a grain of truth and a great amount of chaff. For the most part the Chinese themselves never know the meaning or value of their inventions, or indeed that they were any inventions at all. It has taken western nations to show them the germ of power and expansion which was hidden in their most ingenious arts, and they knew it not. Their political system, which is best in theory, is basest and blindest in application; their learning is the laborious acquisition of things not worth knowing; their reverence is the worship of things baser than themselves; their social order is blind obedience to custom, and their economy springs from the cruel compulsion of poverty. However old and numerous such a people may be, however proud of their history and tenacious of their traditions, we ought to be able to teach them the first principles of a better faith and the beginnings of a new and higher life.

We can teach the Chinese first of all to believe in the one almighty and ever-living God, the Father of infinite mercies, the Giver of every good and perfect gift, who pours out his heart toward his earthly children with the tenderness of parental affection and with the constancy of immutable law. The Chinese believe in the material heavens, in the blind forces of nature, in the caprices of fortune, in the decrees of destiny, in the foreordinations of mysterious and merciless fate. But the conceited and self-assured disciples of Confucius and the devout students in the dreamy dialectics of Buddha know nothing of one infinite, eternal, ever-present God, whose home is with the humble and whose help may be had by all who call upon him in sincerity and in truth.

The Chinaman prays, but it is unto the material heavens that cannot hear; unto the clouds that heed not his cry; unto the seasons of the year that never vary their annual round; unto the great powers and elemental forces of nature that have no soul; unto the winds that blow where they list; unto the storms that rage on sea and land;

unto the sunlight that shines and the rain that falls alike for the evil and the good. Unto such he prays, as if one should stand on the shore and entreat the tides not to rise, or look up to the brazen heavens in time of drought and implore the sun to withhold his heat.

The Chinaman prays to the powers of nature but not to the One who holds the powers of nature in his hand. In the time of trouble, under the affliction of famine or fever or flood or war, he makes offerings; he burns incense; he leads long processions through the streets; he brings out grand and noisy dramatic representations; he bows to the earth and knocks his forehead upon the stone pavement in the presence of grim idols; he makes temples and tombs resound with chants and wailings; he beats drums and blows trumpets and calls aloud upon the spirits of the earth, the water, and the air. And he does all that to propitiate the angry powers that afflict him with fever in the house or murrain in the flock or blight in the field. If the rain comes when he brings offerings to the thunder god in the temple, then he thinks the pitying heavens have heard his prayer. If the fever abates when he has made night hideous with ghostly masks of demons and noisy processions, then he thinks the cruel power that poisons the air has ceased to breathe upon the people. If the famine no longer fills the streets and highways with the starving multitudes, then he says that the spirits that rule the clouds, the hills, and the stars have heard his cry and they no longer dry up the fountains or burn the fields with drought.

So while the Chinaman recognizes the existence of a

power above and beyond his control, his prayers are not to an all-loving Father; his offerings are not an expression of trust and love such as is due to one ever-living and personal God. He feels that the earth, the air, and the heavens about him are filled with mighty and mysterious powers which are envious of his happiness and unwilling to show him sympathy or give him help in his affliction. All his prayers, offerings, and sacrifices are to beings supposed to be angry and unwilling to be propitiated. He spends millions and millions of money every year in sacrifices to powers that have no mind or soul and to beings that have no existence. He needs to learn first of all that the one supreme power of the universe is not a blind force as unfeeling as gravitation, not a law as mindless and merciless as the storm. He needs to know that the conditions of his life in this world are not happenings of chance or decrees of destiny. The ignorant can never be set free from fears and superstitions, the educated can never be established either in faith or in philosophy, until they are brought to recognize the will of one great and good Father in all the conditions and experiences of life. From him come all chastisements and afflictions as well as all riches and prosperity, and he sends both equally in love to draw the hearts of his earthly children in trust and gratitude to himself as the sole, supreme, infinite, and eternal Good. He must be made to see that the one supreme power which guides the sun and the stars in their courses and makes the seasons maintain their annual and beneficent round, is the will of his greatest, best, most generous Friend, and that Friend has given his greatest and best gift to win men back from their evil, wandering, and ungrateful lives and prevail on them to return in love and duty to their Father.

The Chinaman does not know that. It is very hard to make him believe it when he hears it for the first time. When he has heard it for the hundredth time repeated by intelligent and trustworthy teachers, he is apt to think it a dream of a strange, fanatical, foreign people, who do not know what they are talking about when they tell him such things about God. With all his cunning and conceit, with all his pride of ancestry and wide dominion and imperial power, he does not know, or knowing, dares not believe, the one supreme fact which lies at the foundation of all science and which is the source and fountain head of all reasonable faith. To him all people are barbarians in comparison with his own; he thinks no land worth living in, none fit to be buried in, save his own Central Flowery Kingdom. The laws and the literature of his own language are divine; he is unwilling to be drawn out of his narrow self-conceit into the great brotherhood of humanity; it is the greatest confession for him to make when he reads the simple story of the gospel and he feels compelled to say, "A greater than Confucius is here." He is very practical and businesslike in his habits, very strongly set in his own way, however absurd and foolish that way may be. He has great contempt for all people who come from far-off lands to teach him anything, as if he were not already the embodiment of wisdom and the head of the human race. Conflict with the power of Christian nations has done something to take the conceit out of him. But he is a Chinaman still; bound in hard service to the souls of his ancestors; haunted and plagued by the spirits of the power of the air; trying in vain to make peace with the unpitying heavens and the unmotherly earth.

The Chinaman's first step out of bondage, his first lesson in true wisdom, his first act of rational faith, must be belief in the one ever-living and almighty God, faith in the fatherly kindness and personal care of the one Being whose will is the moving force in all the powers of nature, and whose heart is full of tenderness and pity towards all his earthly children. That one first act of faith will be the beginning of an intellectual and spiritual education, which will correct his mistakes about the material world, dismiss his dread of spirits and demons, give him something higher than the forms and phenomena of nature to worship, devise the best employment for all his faculties, and fill his great land with voices of praise and thanksgiving.

The Chinaman's ideas about God are local and material, confused and contradictory. Whatever name is used for the supreme Being, he thinks he knows all about it, and yet he knows nothing as he ought to know. The name only suggests to him some image that he has seen in the Buddhist temple, or some picture of a many-headed and many-handed monster that he has seen carried in a sacred procession, or some fabulous being that he has been told dwelt on a mountain or by the sea in the olden time, or some venerable sage who spoke words of wisdom for many years while he lived on the earth, and then passed away into the heavens, and was worshiped by men who revered wisdom and set up altars to sages. It takes a long time and many explanations and much patience to get the Chinaman to understand and accept the simple idea of God as it is set forth in the Bible and as it is accepted by all followers of Christ. It takes him still longer to comprehend the one supreme fact of the gospel: God loving the world and giving his Son, his greatest and best gift, for the world's redemption. When the Chinaman gets firm hold of that great fact in the Christian revelation, when he accepts it and lives by it as a principle of living faith, it will make him a new man and his nation a new people. It has taken three thousand years of oppression and ignorance and superstition to make the Chinaman what he is to-day. Give him one hundred years of light and liberty, and he will stand with the foremost in the advance of nations. And when he awakes from the sleep of ages, it will be the awaking of a giant who rejoices to run in the race with the swiftest and to contend in strength with the strongest. Let the millions of China receive the gospel and they will fill the earth with missionaries, and in every land they will testify to the quickening and regenerating power of the religion taught in the Bible.

When the traveler from the new world of the West sets his face homeward and leaves the old lands of the East behind, he looks back upon China as more than all the rest the land of mystery and contradiction. The people seem to him to have brought into the nineteenth century after Christ the pride and the power, the ignorance and the superstition of the great nations of the nineteenth century before Christ. He looks upon them as if they had been preserved unchanged through all the ages of Christian history, as Pompeii was buried and embalmed in ashes, on purpose to show us in this advanced age of Christian civilization what were the greatness and the glory, the shame and the degradation of the ancient heathen nations, and how far forward Christianity has carried the people who have received and obeyed its instructions. The Egyptians and the Tyrians and the Babylonians — even the Greeks and the Romans — had the pride and the conceit, the ignorance and the weakness, the falsity and the cruelty of this great Chinese people of to-day. If the ancients as they lived in the time of their glory had been compared with one of our modern cultivated and most Christian nations, they would have seemed in many respects as weak and ridiculous as the Chinese when compared with England or America.

When the traveler turns his back upon the strange old land of China, and the outline of the shore fades from his sight, and he thinks over where he has been and what he has seen, it seems to him like a dream of things that pass before the mind in troubled sleep, but which are never expected to abide the light of the full day. When he steps foot on the shore of his native land, and he wakes up amid the stirring, matter-of-fact life of America, it seems to him as if he had been carried far off by the illusions and fancies of a feverish sleep and he had been walking among scenes that must flee like the shadows of night before the rising sun. But the worst thing about the old China world is that it is not a dream, but a great and sad reality. The millions of ignorant, superstitious, degraded people are all a living reality. They are all human like ourselves. They have the same essential faculties and necessities that we have. That great, mighty, and mysterious people have been living for ages in the pride of ignorance and the self-conceit of seclusion from the rest of the world. The rush and the roar of the nineteenth century have only broken in a little upon the shore, but the uncounted millions of the interior have not seen the motion nor heard the sound. Famine and war and hunger have destroyed millions and millions, but there are millions and millions more still left. A hundred thousand may be taken from the population anywhere and nobody be missed. They toil, they suffer, they die; and all the way through life they are oppressed with fear of things that do not exist, they are inspired with hopes that are never fulfilled, they offer prayers which are never answered, they make sacrifices which are never accepted. The uncounted millions of China are living all their lifetime in bondage to fears of dangers that never come and hopes that are never fulfilled.

How can the Chinese be brought out of the sad state in which they are living? It is the harder to help them, just because they do not think they need any help. In their own estimate they are the wisest, mightiest, most excellent of all the nations of the earth. Their great, filthy, abominable imperial capital they call heaven. The arm of the sea through which ships pass in approaching the capital they call the gates of heaven. The great city at the mouth of the river which flows down from their capital they call the garden of Paradise. Peking, with its pride and filth and mud, is the Chinaman's highest earthly realization of felicity, beauty, beatitude, heaven. How can such a people be lifted up to a higher, purer, better life until some awful calamity, some crushing blow shall show them their weakness and their folly?

It is idle to hope that China is going to be converted

to Christianity and brought into line with enlightened and progressive nations in a day or during the present generation. The ruling policy of the government and of all high officials is utterly opposed to all change. Nobody knows what they think or believe; nobody finds it safe to trust to what they say. Probably they suppose it will be for their own personal interest and for the honor and safety of the great empire that the people shall be held back from the adoption of western arts, sciences, and religion as long as possible. The mass of the people neither know nor care anything about life or interest or duty farther than to keep on in the old course which their ancestors pursued for ages. All their thoughts and efforts and desires are absorbed in the struggle for existence. The old superstitions, oppressions, and poverty into which they were born, surround them like a thick cloud, and they can see no way out of the encompassing gloom. The religious element is not now as active and aggressive as it once was, either in the minds of the people or the policy of the government. It does not now build temples and pagodas and monasteries of vast size and cost, as it once did in days long gone by, but it still holds the people in passive subjection to its cruel and costly sway.

The language, the laws, and the customs of the Chinese must be very greatly changed before they can begin to look at the great facts of life and duty as we do. Their words must be made to take on new meanings to express the truths of the gospel, and then a generation must be raised up to learn those meanings and add them to the old signs and sounds in which their ancestors bound up the whole range of Chinese thought. For a long time multitudes may hear the plainest preaching of the gospel and go away no wiser in mind, no better in heart, than they were before. For a long time the process of teaching, making disciples in China must be very slow. It can be carried on only with tireless patience and unconquerable faith. The simplest lesson must be repeated again and again. One may teach and talk and labor for years, and then find that he has only just begun to find his way into the mysterious depths of the Chinese mind. Faithful men may spend their whole life laboring and longing to see the millions of that great country turning unto the Lord and die without the sight. And yet the time of promise is sure to come. The long, hard, discouraging work of preparation has made great advances in twenty-five years. In many instances the sorest difficulties and hindrances have been overcome. The divine power which goes with the missionary in his work has proved itself equal to the accomplishment of the mighty task which it has undertaken. The great wall of heathenism has been penetrated in many places, and the host of the Lord is gathering in many bands and they stand ready to march up, each straight forward, to the full possession of the whole land. When that day comes there will be a song of gladness which all nations shall sing, a shout of triumph which will be heard around the world.

X.

JOHN CHINAMAN.

JOHN CHINAMAN is the greatest mystery in our common humanity. Judged after western ways of thinking, he is a great contradiction. He is versatile, patient, ingenious, irrepressible, and yet he is the slave of tradition and custom; he gets little advantage from his ingenuity and he plods on in the same beaten track for ages. He transgresses the prime laws of health and longevity, and yet he works hard; he is almost insensible to pain, and he has lived long in the land which the Lord God gave unto his fathers. He sleeps in close rooms; he breathes bad air; he makes a block of wood his pillow and the dusty floor or the damp ground his bed. Yet he is more healthy than many who take the utmost pains to get fresh air and clean lodgings and comfortable pillows for the night. He does the hardest kinds of work; he carries burdens heavy enough to crush ordinary men; yet he grows strong from the overtaxing of his strength and he never complains of the hard tasks put upon him. He eats all manner of crude, unpalatable, indigestible food; yet he thrives on his hard living, and his stomach seldom gives way under the severe pressure put upon it. He works all day in the paddy field up to his knees in mud and water, and the sign in his language which is the symbol of happiness is a mouthful of rice. When he would salute his friend with the blessing of peace in the morning, he expresses the hope that he has eaten his rice to-day.

The Chinaman smokes opium and tobacco; the streets of his great cities are wallowing places for swine; he practices vices that cannot be named in decent speech; yet he has the most vitality of all the peoples of the East. He pulls out his beard with tweezers, shaves the front and back of his head with razors, but lets the hair on his crown grow as long as it will of itself, and then splices it out with false hair to make it longer; and then he is so puffed up with his fine appearance that he would sooner lose his head than his queue. He exposes his bare head and beardless face to the fierce rays of the sun, and yet I never heard of a Chinaman's getting a sunstroke. He works on ships and boats and steamers, runs on errands, draws the jinriksha, drives dog carts and carriages, pushes wheelbarrows and pulls towlines, and employers say that he is just the man for the job when there is hard work to be done.

Sometimes the Chinaman seems so dull that impatient people cannot get along with him, and yet he is so useful that nobody can do without him. He has a great reputation for lying and stealing in his own country, and just as great a reputation for honesty and truth-speaking in Java and Japan. He packs close on the coolie ship for the long voyage to Australia and the islands of the South Seas; he has no exercise on shipboard; he keeps under decks; he eats the coarsest food and he comes out well and cheerful at the end of the voyage. He builds railroads and highways and canals; he works farms and mines and machines until he makes the owners rich, and then he is told that he is not wanted any longer, he must go and give place to men who do less work and demand more pay. He wears his blue cotton in all climates, and he faces all extremes of heat and cold without whiskey to keep him warm in winter and without ice water to keep him cool in summer. He gets rich when others starve; he keeps healthy when others die; he is quiet and cheerful when others are mourning and complaining; he is peaceful when others quarrel; he is industrious when others are idle and lazy; he flies kites and fights crickets like rude boys, and he cools himself with a fan as if he were the most effeminate of all people. Yet he endures more hardship and he suffers more abuse than any other people on the face of the earth, unless the African be an exception. He is kicked and cuffed and snubbed by blustering John Bull and bragging Brother Jonathan; he is ridiculed and laughed at by all western nations, and yet he comes up smiling from every fall and he makes money out of the people who abuse and banish him.

The Chinaman's country is overcrowded with people. He thinks it the fairest and the most favored of all the lands of the earth, the only land worth living in, the only dust fit to be buried in, and yet he emigrates to all quarters of the globe; he appears to be contented wherever he is, and homesickness is a disease of which Chinamen never die. He mounts on the wrong side of his horse, and yet he rides well when he gets into the saddle; he makes the compass point the wrong way, and yet his junk seldom gets lost on the sea. He begins at the wrong end of his book to read, and he reads backwards, and yet he has been printing and reading books in his own language longer than any other people in the world.

According to our theories and ways of judging, the Chinaman is a great contradiction. He lives and thrives and multiplies when he ought to fade and waste away and die. His tools are clumsy; his methods of working are awkward and ill-adapted to what he tries to do; his taste is unrefined and unnatural. Yet, in his line, he makes the best work and he underbids all manufacturers in the market of the world, while securing a good profit to himself. He pays divine honors to his deceased parents; he worships the god of money, and yet he has little pity for the suffering and the needy; he is cruel and brutal in his punishments; he murders his own children to relieve himself of the burden of supporting them. He paints landscapes without perspective, carves images of animals that never existed, incurs vast expense in support of a religion that has no God. He celebrates his father's birthday by presenting him with a coffin, and he burns paper money to pay the expense of his deceased mother in her journey to the country from which none ever return.

The Chinaman, go where he will, contented as he seems to be everywhere, is really never at home save in his own country; he never becomes a citizen or a subject of any other government than his own. He has no sympathy with the great philosophies, inventions, and progressive ideas of our country and our day. He lives on a relic of the past, a moving and breathing mummy of far distant generations, as if to tell the nineteenth century how the great nations of the ancient world would look if seen in "the fierce light which beats upon the thrones" and peoples of the West.

The Chinese stand before the world in this enlightened and progressive age to tell us what would have been the condition of the most cultivated nations to-day had it not been for the birth of the divine Child that was born in Bethlehem eighteen centuries ago. When students in cloistered halls and theorists in schools of philosophy get weary of culture and dissatisfied with Christian civilization and write books to show that life is not worth living in the West, let them go to the far East and see what life they have been lifted out of by the culture of which they are weary and the civilization with which they are not satisfied.

The Chinaman is a great mystery to us and doubtless we western men are as great a mystery to him. We are ever trying to understand and explain the perplexities and contradictions in him. He does not trouble himself about us so long as we let him alone. His satisfaction with himself and his native land is supreme and his self-conceit is sublime. He only wants to keep his great country all to himself with full liberty to overrun all the rest of the earth in search of riches and the means of living which he fails to find at home. If he had some way to keep the unruly river within its channel and compel the clouds to give showers in their season and the sunlight to return after the rain, he would ask no richer blessing of heaven than long life in his native land. In all matters of business and money transactions he is timid and prudent and cautious to the extreme. But he is the most careless and reckless of all men about his own life and the lives of his fellowmen. If the executioner tells him to kneel down and have his head cut off, he will do it as quietly and meekly as the good child kneels to say his prayers at bed-time. When a man of property has been condemned to death, he can easily get some one to suffer the penalty in his place by paying a small sum of money to support the family of the substitute. When thousands and millions are dying of famine, the starving submit to their fate in silence and the living lift up no cry from the depths of the woe which is upon them. Their nerves are not strung to the keen sensibility of Christian nations. Patients in hospitals are seldom willing to take ether to deaden the pain of surgical operations. The great display of mourning at the burial of the dead is a conformity to custom rather than a confession of grief. The coffin is often kept in the house for ornament long after it has received its tenant, and the long procession which follows it to the grave has the appearance of a holiday excursion rather than a display of sorrow.

Thousands of Chinamen live in boats upon the water. They are born and they make their only home and they die upon the water. They will venture out upon the stormiest seas in their clumsy, high-decked junks. They will rush through the wildest breakers in their flat-bottomed sampans. They will row across the bow of a steamer when it is going at full speed, risking their lives to get a sign of good luck. We would suppose that such people would be good seamen and well able to take care of themselves on the water. But the fact is just the contrary. Very few Chinamen can swim. Multitudes are drowned by the upsetting of boats and the careless management of junks every year. They make very little effort to help one who is in the water and in danger of drowning, and the man overboard makes very little effort to help himself. Often he will just throw up his hands, make no cry, no struggle, but sink and drown at once. It is said that the man thrown out of a boat has the superstitious belief that some evil spirit or demon has pitched him over and is pulling him down, and that he has nothing to do but submit and drown. If a few billets of wood are afloat where the boat went over, there will be a great scramble to pick them up, but the drowning people will be left to sink, because there is a great scarcity of wood, but the land has already more people than it knows what to do with.

A few days before I was at Hankow on the Yang-tse-Kiang River, fifteen persons were drowned by the upsetting of one boat and eight by the upsetting of another, and nothing was said about it by the Chinese themselves. They took it all as a matter of course. So at Canton, where a hundred thousand people are said to live in boats on the river, cases of drowning occur every day, and the great floating city never misses those that are gone, never asks how such accidents can be prevented in the future. The average Chinaman takes his lot in life and in death as a decree of destiny against which it is in vain to contend. He will eat his rice and carry his burden without gratitude for the one or complaint against the other. He will laugh and be cheerful while he can and die when he must. All over the East, submission to destiny is the law of life which suppresses all effort and silences all complaint. If a thing is to be, it is in vain to try to make it otherwise, and if it was to be, it is equally vain to mourn because it came to pass.

With all his blind faith in destiny, the Chinaman has an equally blind faith in luck. He has a thousand devices and observances to secure good luck. He will risk his life to get a good sign when the sign itself has nothing to do with getting the thing he wants. I was just starting off from Shanghai upon a steamer bound for Hankow, seven hundred and seventy miles up the Yang-tse-Kiang River. A poor boatman thought he would secure good luck for himself for the day if he should cross the bow of a fast-running steamer just as it was moving off upon so long a voyage. He rowed right across the line of our course when we were already moving at full speed. The steamer whistled an alarm; the officer on the bridge shouted; the engineer reversed the wheels. But the infatuated seeker after good luck kept on rowing till the bow of the steamer struck his little craft, cut it in two, and he found his luck in a watery grave on the bottom of the river. If the Chinaman could learn that obedience to the laws of nature is better than watching for luck, it would make his daily life all new. But unhappily he supposes that nature, the whole surrounding world of earth and air and water, is possessed and controlled by capricious, willful, and revengeful spirits, and that the great study of life for him is to avoid the displeasure of the invisible inhabitants of earth, air, and water, that are ever looking for an opportunity to cross his purposes, disappoint his hopes, defeat his plans, and bring him to disaster and defeat.

If he can only keep on terms of good understanding with the busy and malignant powers that range through all departments of material nature, he will be permitted to fill the measure of his days with prosperity and to die in peace.

The orthodox Chinaman burns incense all day at his shop door to keep the mischief-making spirits from coming in and interrupting his bargains. He throws burning paper into the sea to prevent the spirits of the deep from rousing up storms and sinking his ship in the depths of the ocean. He shakes his counting frame vigorously every morning to drive out the spirits that may have been meddling with the sliding buttons overnight and thus preparing mistakes and miscalculations for him in his business for the day. He builds a heavy stone wall on the other side of the street opposite to his front door to prevent the spirits from finding their way in and smiting the family with disease or disaster of any kind. He makes the lines of his houses on the street irregular and his paths through the fields crooked, so as to deceive and drive away the spirits that are supposed to move only in straight lines. He watches for a lucky day to begin planting his field, starting on a journey, contracting a marriage, building a house, buying a property, or burying the dead. With all his shrewd, practical business talent, he allows himself to be governed by impressions, signs, fears, that have no foundation in fact, that exist only in his own darkened mind and defiled imagination. In this, as well as in many other particulars, the Chinaman seems a contradiction, doing the thing which we would say he would be least likely to do, believing the thing which we would say is most absurd and unreasonable. And yet, after all has been said of the strange weakness and inconsistencies in Chinese character, there is another side to be shown before we make up our judgment of the sons of Han. And this other view will show that western nations may well go to the Chinese to learn some very important lessons in practical life.

But before we pass on to that more satisfactory view we shall do well to glance a little more closely at the Chinaman's faith in the overruling power of spirits in the earth, the waters, and the air. This base and blind superstition haunts him wherever he goes. It controls all his conduct in the main plan of life and in the smallest affairs of every-day work. It is ever uppermost in his thoughts, and it determines all his opinions on subjects of personal interest to himself or of importance to his country and the world. Whenever a change in his manner of life or in the order of things about him is proposed, his first question is whether the spirits will take offense at the movement, or whether it will interrupt them in their goings forth to and fro through all the earth. Every unusual and every common event in the world of nature and in the condition of the people is referred to the caprices and the intermeddling of mysterious beings that dwell in the clouds, sport in the storm, haunt the caves of the mountains, the current of the rivers, or the depths of the sea. If he stays at home or starts on a journey, if he builds a house or buys a field, if he marries the living or buries the dead, he must consult the pleasure of the spirits and subject his plans and his preferences to their approval. There is no field of work, no department of business, no resort for recreation where the Chinaman can escape the presence of the invisible disturbers of his peace and the malignant tormentors of his life. He dare not build the wall of his house two inches higher than the wall of his neighbor for fear it may obstruct the movements of the spirits through the air, and they in anger will throw down his house upon his head. He makes a turn to the right or to the left in the hall of his house for fear the spirits may find their way in and bring sickness or misfortune upon the whole family. When he dies, his friends make a hole in the wall, and push his coffin through it into the open air, lest, if carried through the common door, the spirit of the departed will remember the way, and come back and find entrance to plague the family. The spirit is supposed to have power to inflict plague and fever, and drought and famine, and yet not to know enough to find the door of a house where he has lived in the body for fifty years. At one time the spirits are so intelligent and cunning and mighty that nothing can deceive or oppose them. At another he thinks them so weak and stupid that they cannot find their way if a wall or a hedge be built across their path, or a street is made crooked instead of straight. Whatever loss or trouble or affliction comes upon the Chinaman, he thinks the spirits have done the mischief, and he must burn joss sticks, or paper money, or pictures of clothes or animals or houses or furniture as offerings to appease their anger. His most bitter opposition to railroads and telegraphs and steamships and churches and schools and foreign-built houses arises from the fear that such changes will offend the spirits, and they will bring plague and disaster upon the people.

This is an old superstition with all the Chinese, and with little modification it exists among all the people of the East. It has little to do with their religion, unless it be understood as a religion in itself. It is all the same to them whether they take the name of Buddhist, Taoist, or Confucianist, or all three together. It existed in the country long before either of the three religions or philosophies was known, and it survives under all the teachings and ceremonies of either faith. The Taoist makes it his specialty to teach and observe the doctrine of the spirits as if it were all his own. And yet it was the doctrine and the custom of the people long before Taoism was ever heard of. Buddhism adopts and encourages the same superstition about spirits as if it were a part of the teachings of its great founder, Gautama, because the missionaries of Buddhism, at their first coming into China, found the people already in bondage to the spirits, and they did not think it possible to persuade them to exchange the old yoke for one brought by strangers from a far country. Confucius had no religion at all, either to observe himself or to teach to others. He was simply a secular philosopher who inculcated the lessons of prudence and profit in worldly affairs. He had little faith in the existence of spiritual beings of any kind. He was a social and political economist, who was so busy in teaching men how to live in this world that he had no time or thought for any world beyond this. If any one questioned him about a future life, he only said it was vain and useless to concern ourselves about another life so long as this present life is only imperfectly understood. He was willing to let the people keep up their superstitious customs, provided they would observe his golden mean of temperance, self-interest, and social order.

So under whatever name of religion or philosophy the Chinese may be classed, underneath all external distinctions is the native Chinaman, believing in the overruling power of spirits more than in Buddhism, observing the modes of propitiating the spirits more carefully than the prudential precepts of Confucius. He believes that the spirits for good or ill fortune are in the cards with which he gambles, the bamboo rods with which he divines, the counting frame with which he reckons, and the tools with which he works. He recognizes the voice of the spirits in the wail of the night wind, the hoot of the owl, and the thunder from the clouds. He dreads the anger of the spirits in the overflow of the river that destroys his field, in the excess of the drought which cuts off his hope of harvest, in the cholera and the fever which carry off thousands of the people every year in the cities and villages of the empire.

The Chinaman must be drawn out of that base and blinding superstition before he can be a free, noble, right-minded man. He must cease to live in dread of shadows, dreams, signs, omens; he must learn to revere, trust, and love one infinite, eternal Father, the Father of the spirits of all flesh. Then he will live a new life and rejoice in the liberty wherewith Christ has set him free. He must cease to live in dread of beings that have no existence, and then he will feel himself to be compassed about with everlasting arms of deliverance, and his daily life, even in the lowest depths of toil and poverty, will seem to him to be crowned with lovingkindness and tender mercies. He must no longer seek help in time of need from astrologers and wizards and necromancers and fortune tellers and exorcists, and then he will rejoice in the presence and protection of an almighty Friend in his humble home, and he can walk through the valley of the shadow of death and fear no evil.

XI.

WHAT CAN CHINA TEACH US?

IN studying Chinese character and history it is easy to make out a long catalogue of what seem to us absurdities and contradictions. Nevertheless there are some very practical lessons which the youngest and most progressive of all the nations may well learn from the oldest and most conservative. If, for example, we were to adopt in some modified degree the Chinaman's habit of economy, there would be no such thing as want in all our land. The poorest in America earn and use much more than the laborer in China who has enough to answer all his wants. And his abundance, even in what we would call poverty, comes from saving that which we throw away. He gathers up coarse grass and reeds and the smallest twigs of shrub and tree and bush for burning, and he cooks his dinner and he keeps himself warm with fuel of which we should make no account at all. He saves every particle of refuse from the house and streets to enrich his ground and maintain its fertility for successive centuries of cultivation. He makes an agreeable and nourishing dish for his dinner out of vegetables and remnants which our poorest families would throw to the dogs. He mends and uses broken crockery and furniture which we would think fit only for the ash-heap or the furnace. He stitches and refits old clothes, and wears as a becoming garment rags and tatters which we throw upon the waste-heap or send off to be ground up for paper. He does fine work with the fewest and the simplest tools, when we should want costly machinery and engines and beautifully polished instruments. He makes his home comfortable, according to his low standard of comfort, with furniture the smallest in amount, and made out of the commonest materials, when we would think it necessary to have articles bought at great expense and made by skillful workmen. He travels on long journeys with only a few cash in his pocket to pay his way, when we would spend more than a Chinaman could earn in a year of toil. He keeps costly goods for sale in shops which have no fine showcases or plate glass windows, or fittings up that take all the profits of trade and double the price of the things sold. When he gets rich or well-to-do in the world, he rides on a donkey or in a wheelbarrow or in a sedan chair, and he pays five cents for his conveyance, when an American merchant would pay five dollars.

The poor Chinaman's economy is not indeed all a designed and cultivated virtue, nor does it always tend to an increase of possessions and general prosperity. It is most apt to be a necessity which he cannot escape, or a habit which he does not know how to break up or to improve. In one case he saves because he must needs do it to live. In the other case he saves because he does not know how to spend wisely or profitably for himself and others. He will carefully bargain so as to save a tenth part of a cent in trade, and yet spend ten or a hundred times that amount in offerings and sacrifices to get good luck in business. He eats little because it is all he has. He wears simple clothing because he can get no better. He is content with little furniture in his house because he can get no more. He walks on long journeys because he cannot afford to ride. And he makes the best of a hard lot because it will only make it worse to complain. But if we, in this favored land of America, practiced from choice more of the economy which the Chinaman submits to as a necessity, we could still live in bright homes, wear our silks and broadcloths, travel at whirlwind speed, and secure all our social enjoyments of life without wearisome struggle to-day and without anxiety for the morrow. There is wealth enough in our land to relieve all want, there is work enough to keep all busy, and blessing of every kind enough to make all thankful and happy, if only we use well what we have, and never expend our money before we get it. With us it is waste that brings poverty, self-indulgence which leads to complaint, and grasping for that which will do us no good that makes us lose what we have. Young America may well learn from old China that self-restraint brings liberty and independence, wise economy tends to abundance, and one of the lessons of home education is to learn what unnecessary things to do without in order to get the things that are best worth having.

The Chinaman may be safely quoted as a conspicuous example of industry. He is never known to complain of too much work or too many hours in the day. Chinese servants, when at their best, seem to work all day and watch all night, and they do both for small wages, and they never complain. Laborers are in the field early in the morning at their work, and they make their daily toil keep pace with the journeys of the sun. Riksha men are at their post waiting for a call to run through the streets at a rapid pace an hour before the sun is up in the morning, and they are within call at all hours of the day and the night. Mechanics will work with the poorest tools, and make up in time and attention and minute skill what is wanting in the tools that they have to work with. Carvers in wood and stone and ivory will produce the most minute and delicate lines and cuttings and the most complete and graceful forms, and they will do it all simply by keeping at their work hour after hour, day after day, with slow, hardly perceptible progress, until the task is done. Weavers and embroiderers in silk and pictures upon satin and porcelain have the simplest possible implements for their trade, and yet they produce the most delicate lines and shadings, just by patient attention to details and the most economical use of materials. House carpenters and cabinetmakers will imitate any pattern that is given them so perfectly that the original and the imitation can hardly be distinguished from each other. Writers will produce the strange and complex characters of their language so perfectly that the printed and the written letters seem to be the workmanship of the same hand. I saw four letters or characters inscribed upon the walls of a guild hall in Canton, and I was told that the company paid four hundred dollars, a hundred dollars a letter, to the writer, simply because they were supposed to be such a masterpiece of fine writing. Another company paid a hundred dollars to a man who only dipped the tassel of his girdle in ink and dashed off the letters with a flourish on the wall. But he was supposed to be a genius, and the Chinese have very few such. They make their way by plodding, persevering industry. We hired four men to take us in a house boat from Tientsin to Tung-cho. The distance by the river is a hundred miles. The four men worked hard from daylight in the morning to dark each day for six days to get us through, and we gave them four dollars and a half for their service, and they never complained of the hard work or the small wages.

Let us imitate the minute, patient, painstaking industry of the Chinese in our common, everyday work, and it will put a new stamp of fidelity and completeness upon all our buildings, furniture, manufactures of every sort. We waste more material than the Chinaman uses, by our national habit of hurrying everything, by our unwillingness to take time and pains to do everything well. The Chinaman is blamed and laughed at by us because he is so slow — he spends so much time on work that our mechanics are expected to do offhand, blow after blow. Nevertheless I think our work would be done much better, our furniture, our houses, our shoes, our clothes, our books, our tools, our machines would give us much more satisfaction, if the makers would take a lesson from the Chinaman, and so take time to do their work well; if the mechanic would never let any article go from his hands until he could say that he had done his best.

It is indeed true that the Chinaman's patience and perseverance are often expended upon things of little value. He cuts several hollow globes of ivory, one within the other, and he makes them all free to move in any direction within the outer shell. The work when done is nothing but a freak of skill. It is very difficult to do, and it is worth nothing when done. The time and labor spent upon it would be more than sufficient to build the house that the workman lives in. A Chinaman will carve in marble the figure of an animal that never existed, except in his own grotesque imagination. And the labor and skill given to the absurd representation of a dragon, a griffin, or a unicorn would make a successful architect or a renowned sculptor. The student who is ambitious of literary honors or of a government appointment spends many years, sometimes fifty, or a whole lifetime, in committing to memory the mysterious signs of his classic language. It is indeed called education, and the man who succeeds in mastering the strange, disconnected symbols is called learned. But it is simply a task of memory. It does not furnish the man with knowledge or discipline or acquaintance with the affairs of the real world in which he is to live and act his part. It is simply a task of committing to memory things that have no connection with each other, and often no meaning to the learner. And yet the task itself is certainly a display of patience, industry, perseverance, worthy of a better object. In Peking I saw a man who had come hundreds of miles to offer himself for examination in the Chinese classics. He said he was seventy-four years old, and he had been studying all his life to commit to memory enough of the grotesque characters to pass examination, get his degree, and go home to die in peace and honor. He had given seventy years of toil to get a degree which would be worth nothing to him but a name when he got it at last.

I sometimes think that students in our own country would do well to task themselves in like manner to master things worth knowing and the knowledge of which will prepare them for the demands of practical life. And I would not say even that the child must needs understand everything that he commits to memory, as fast and as far as he advances. We try to make a great show of teaching the child the meaning of everything as fast as he learns it. And yet we have to give up our theory at the very first step in education. The child must learn the alphabet before he learns the meaning or the use of a single letter. The child must learn the multiplication and the division of numbers before he can understand the endless uses and applications of such tables. So there are many great yet simple precepts of duty and faith which the child should learn long before he understands the importance or the reason of such precepts. The child must learn to obey before he knows the source or the extent of parental authority. The child must learn to look up to God in trust and love before he knows anything more about God than just this, that he is great and good and must be loved and obeyed. The best precepts of duty, those which go with us like guardian angels to direct our steps all the way through life, are those we learned before we knew their meaning or understood their importance. The best guide we have within ourselves, conscience, never reasons or explains. It only whispers in the secret place of the soul the sacred and awful command, "Thou shalt"; "Thou shalt not."

The Chinese may be quoted as an example to all nations for their high respect for reputable authority, a becoming reverence for all that is worthy and venerable in the past, a cautious and conservative clinging to old ways, so far as they are good and so far as they will help the present generation to find out better ways for the future. The Chinese do indeed carry their reverence for form and usage to an absurd and unwarranted extreme. Their best reason for doing anything as they do is the simple fact that their fathers did so before them. With them the ancients are always the sages; they had all wisdom; and the idea of improving upon their instructions or usages is profane and demoralizing in the extreme. The people of to-day must wear the long queue, shave the front and back of the head, set up ancestral tablets, worship the spirits of the departed, just because the generation that went before them did so. They build vast temples and offer sacrifices to Confucius because their fathers did so, and it would dishonor the memory of the great departed to deviate from their customs. The one great, standing law of duty to the well-bred Chinaman is to keep to the old ways, observe the old ceremonies, hold himself and the nation to the same undeviating course from age to age. New customs, foreign ways, western science, are to be rejected just because they are new and different from the ways of the fathers.

All this seems very strange and stupid to us, whose great word for inspiration and effort is Progress: improvement, new departure, new philosophy, new theology, a new world. Yet it is barely possible that we might go more safely if we were less eager to go fast. We might be improved in all that is noble and excellent in character by tempering our desire for new things with reverence for whatever is venerable and true in the old. It is not a good indication in children to speak slightingly of their parents, even though the children may have more education, experience, and property than the parents ever had. Neither is it a good indication in any people to speak contemptuously of their ancestors. A great and strong and progressive people must be a reverent and believing people. A people without faith in truth and duty, in God and in themselves, are open to every disorder and tumult and they are on the high road to decay and death.

To be wise and prudent in adopting changes in laws and customs, in opinions and doctrines, we must have a profound respect for the opinions and customs that have come down to us, hallowed by time and by the memory of the great and the good of other days. There are some forms of faith which are venerable just because they are old, just because they have been accepted and relied upon by the noblest and the best of many generations. We need not adopt the Chinaman's reverence for everything said or supposed to be said by Confucius, or by the greatest and wisest of the men of old time. There are no sages in the history of any nation to whom we can safely ascribe the wisdom which the Chinese find in the father of their philosophy and the founder of their faith. But there have been noble men, giants in intellect, saints in character, before our day. If we are better or stronger in any respect than they were, it is because their strength and wisdom have been added to our own. We are farther on in the progress towards a rational faith and a reputable life just because they started us in the right way and they led us on to the end of their journey.

The Chinese may well teach Young America important lessons in respect for age and obedience to parents. In this, as in many other things, the Chinese carry a characteristic virtue to an absurd and an idolatrous extreme. The son is taught to behave himself with the most abject and servile reverence in the presence of his living father, and he must regard the spirit of his dead ancestor with a worship which can be rightly rendered only to the one infinite Father of all spirits and the Giver of every good gift. Then, too, it is often said, to the disparagement of the Chinese son, that the homage which he pays to his deceased ancestors does not spring from real reverence or affection for the departed, but from fear that their spirits, if offended by neglect, will work him evil by blasting his crops, deranging his business, bringing sickness and death upon his household. However that may be, a large part of the stability of the Chinese character and the permanency in Chinese institutions may be traced to the reverence which the young are taught to show to the aged, the obedience which children render to parents, the honor which all classes put upon men venerable in age and wisdom and authority.

We should not think it a mark of high respect and deep affection if a young man in America should celebrate his father's sixtieth or seventieth birthday by presenting him with a very costly and highly ornamented coffin. We should say it was a sign that the son thought it quite time for his aged father to take to the narrow house himself, and leave the homestead and property to his heir and successor. And yet the Chinese son does all that as a token of profound affection and a fitting expression of his desire that his venerable parent may live many years and keep the carved and gilded coffin ever in sight in the best room of his house, to show to his friends as an evidence of the filial gratitude and affection of his son. Whatever may be said of the selfishness and insincerity of the show of affection and reverence which the Chinese make towards their parents, still it is true that they have the fulfillment of the promise to children who honor father and mother. Their days have been long upon the land which the Lord God gave them as their inheritance among all the nations. No people in all history have held the uninterrupted possession of their country so long, none have maintained the same institutions, social customs, and traditions for so many centuries.

So with all people and always and everywhere: the foundation of all national order, permanency, and continued life must be laid in the family, in the honor which children show to their parents, in the habits of filial obedience which begin with the child and grow strong with the man. Disobedience to parents is the beginning and the fruitful source of disobedience to all laws, human and divine. Rudeness, irreverence, lack of courtesy and mutual honor in the household, are sure to train up a people to be rude, reckless, and godless. Their history will be a succession of revolutions and their prosperity will be the forerunner of social disorder and ruin. Peaceful, well-ordered homes are a more effectual defense of a nation than standing armies, cannon-proof forts, and ironclad ships of war. The obedience which the son shows to the law and order of his father's house, the habits of kindliness and courtesy and fidelity which he practices in his early years, in the seclusion of his own home, will make him brave in the time of danger, patient in the time of trial, true and honorable at all times. Let children in our American homes learn the lesson of law and duty as they learn their mother tongue from the lips of their parents, and our nation will outlive the centuries of China and it will be exalted and honorable among all the nations of the earth.

The Chinaman may well teach us the lesson of contentment with our lot, whatever that lot may be. He can give us an example of a disposition to make the best of everything about us, even when our lot is not what we would choose and many things give us annoyance and trouble every day. Happiness, contentment, come not so much from any outward condition as from the use we make of what we have. The mind, trained and disciplined to right habits of thought and right feelings of heart, is its own master and the master of everything which affects its experiences from day to day. We can fret and complain with everything to make us happy; and we can sing and give thanks under the greatest losses and disappointments.

You may say that the contentment and cheerfulness of the Chinaman come from ignorance and self-conceit. But still he may teach us to make as much of our better knowledge and happier lot as he makes of his mistakes and disadvantages. He thinks his country is the central flowery kingdom of all the earth. On his land the sun shines with the most benignant beams, and the rains fall with the greatest abundance of the blessings of heaven. He has rice to eat, and a reed or a mud cabin to live in, and a cotton shirt to wear, and he speaks with pity or contempt of those far-off tribes who, as he supposes, live in holes in the ground, eat roots and creeping things for food, and go without clothing in heat and cold. He thinks his blind, back-handed language the most beautiful, the most sacred and divine speech ever given to the lips of man. He considers all other languages but jargon, the barking of dogs, the shrieks of monkeys, in comparison with his most ancient and sacred speech. He thinks the sages of his land have all wisdom and all knowledge, and that obedience to their precepts will bring the highest happiness and prosperity possible for man. The babel of noise and confusion which is the sign of diligence in his schools, and the endless repetition of unmeaning sounds by which he learns to read, and the lifelong labor which it costs him to master the lifeless literature of his sacred books, he considers the best evidence that he belongs to the most enlightened people of all the earth. The cheerless hovels which he builds to live in, the clumsy tools with which he works, the coarse manufactures in his shops, and the heavy models of his ships, he takes to be the utmost attainment of human skill. The people who live and work in any other way are to him boors and barbarians.

We smile at the Chinaman's self-conceit and we pity the ignorance out of which it grows. And yet we may well envy the bliss which his ignorance brings; and we would be happier if we had more of the contentment which the poor Chinaman draws from his self-conceit. His devotion to a country which he has so little reason to love should put us to shame for complaining of a country in which the highest attainments of culture and civilization are within the reach of every citizen. If the Chinaman can be content with hard work and poverty pressing him every day of his life, if he can be cheerful with no hope of ever improving his hard lot, how much more should we rejoice and sing for gladness of heart that we have ample pay for work done and abundant leisure for the cultivation of mind, and we can know from personal inquiry that ours is the country where the laboring man has the highest privileges and the most abundant reward for his labor. No land on the face of the earth gives all its inhabitants so many things to be thankful for. Continual indulgence makes us hard to please. It is not what we want that makes us complain, but the many things we have and fail to use well. Self-mastery will make us masters of any lot and give us reasons for gratitude in every estate of life.

The Chinaman may teach us a good lesson in maintaining a high respect for education and thorough discipline in preparation for all the duties of public and private life. In this case too we draw our lesson from a mistaken use of a theory which is good and true. It is assumed by the government that a thorough knowledge of the Chinese classics is the best preparation for the duties of public office. But that is a very great mistake. The Chinese classics give no instruction in the practical and business affairs of the world as men now live and as they must live to keep abreast of the time and the progress of the age. They teach no branch of science as it is now taught in the most advanced schools of the western world; they convey no useful knowledge of processes in the arts or principles of government or sources of national prosperity. They are to be mastered by patience and perseverance in barely and blindly committing to memory words and sounds that have little meaning or connection to the learner when he is first chained down to the dull and unmeaning task. The man who is fifty years of age and who has spent his life thus far in committing to memory signs without connection and words without meaning is a very unfit person for the discharge of the duties of public office or the management of any department of business. He is an imbecile, and he often takes especial pains to show that he does nothing and that he does not intend to do anything. He cultivates his finger nails till they become so long that he cannot use his hands in any practical work. And he takes especial pride in showing the bird claws on his fingers, for those horny appendages are conclusive proof that he never does any kind of work. Nevertheless he carries out the Chinese idea of education. He goes through a long, laborious course of training to fit himself for a place of honor and responsibility; but the fitting consists, not in a knowledge of the duties he is to perform, but of the sayings of men that have been dead two thousand years. He is not in a hurry to come out of his schooldays early. If he can only begin his public career at fifty or sixty years of age, he is content. He thinks the time and labor given to preparation well and profitably spent.

As a matter of course such a system of education must prove a failure. Brilliant men break away from its trammels and climb to the seats of wealth and power in defiance of its restrictions. Dull men plod through the whole course of classics only to become the dupes of knaves who live by plunder and perjury. Trustworthy officials, if any such can be found, are incapable, and the talented cannot be trusted. Nevertheless the Chinaman's great mistake in making the mastery of dead forms the basis of education may well teach us the grand lesson that thorough preparation for any work or office is the best economy. The Chinaman works hard and long, but his labor is lost because it is misapplied. Let us imitate his diligence and perseverance in learning things worth knowing, and we shall save both time and toil in the end. Hurry is waste. Let apprentices take time to learn their trade and learn it well before they set up for master workmen. Then fewer ships will sink because they were not well put together, fewer houses will fall because the walls were not set on a firm foundation, fewer people will be hurt or killed on land or sea because engineers and captains and conductors had not been sufficiently trained to their business. Let teachers themselves be taught thoroughly before they undertake to teach others, and then fewer scholars will go through the whole course of our schools without getting a practical education. Let all men be content to take the lifelong training in faith and patience and hope which the divine Teacher institutes, and then they will be prepared for that other and greater life, where mistakes and failures cease to be known.

We shall all do well to take lessons from the Chinaman in practical sagacity and energy in the management of worldly business. He is very far from being a model worthy of imitation in honesty and fair dealing. He is not apt to speak the truth unless he sees very clearly that it is for his present and personal interest to do so. He is very slow to believe or to see that there is anything wrong or dishonorable in lying. All the wisdom which he has ever learned from Confucius and all the sages of his native land has only made him shrewd and keen-sighted in looking out for his own interest. And yet he is a model in taking hold resolutely of the first profitable work which comes to hand, be it ever so low and little rewarded. Unemployed workmen in America would never fall into the disreputable trade of tramps if they would let the Chinaman teach them to do well and at once the first work that offers. He does not sit down and theorize as to the best method of work or the just law of wages or the number of hours that make a day, while the work itself remains undone. He does not waste time in waiting for something better to turn up, while the good opportunity of to-day remains unimproved. He takes hold of things, if need be, by the rough handle, and he keeps hold until the rough handle is worn smooth by use.

The Chinaman goes to Burmah and Siam and Singapore and Java, and gets all forms of profitable business into his hands, while the natives lounge in the sun and laugh at the pig-tailed strangers until the lazy lookers-on wake up some day and find that they are in danger of being turned out of house and home by these busy and aggressive emigrants from the great hive of the north. He goes to California and Australia and the Sandwich Islands, and he plunges into dust and mud, doing all manner of work in field and mine and shop and house and street, until a cry comes from the idle and the lazy that these filthy foreigners are growing rich while others are poor, and they are getting all the work while others have nothing to do.

The Chinaman is ready to go to any part of the world where there is hard work to be done and good wages to be given. While other laborers waste their time in strikes and cry themselves hoarse in the demand for more wages and fewer hours of work in the day, the Chinaman strikes hard blows with spade and hammer and axe, and pockets the money which idlers will not take unless it is more. So the Chinaman gets rich all the time on wages which others say are not enough for beer and tobacco for themselves, to say nothing of food and clothes for wives and children. The Chinaman's theory of work and wages is one which does not need to be written out in books and discussed in newspapers and popular assemblies. His first and last rule is to take the work which first comes to hand and accept the wages offered, and so to adjust the profit and loss of trade as to come out with a margin of gain in the worst times.

I should be very sorry to have our American laborers reduced to the low standard of wages which the Chinaman accepts, or the low standard of honor and honesty which the Chinaman approves. But I do think that they might learn something for their advantage if they would imitate the Chinaman in improving present opportunities while waiting for better. Let them give more attention to profitable work than to empty words of complaint. Let them act with energy and decision in the shop and the field, rather than debate and theorize in the clubhouse or the barroom. There is always work enough for those who are willing to do it, rather than spend time in wrangle and debate. There is always wages enough for those who do their work so well that their employers cannot afford to do without them. The

Chinaman grows rich when others starve; he lives and prospers when others fail and die, simply because he is quick and keen in availing himself of every present opportunity without wasting time in waiting for better times to come. His mind is always bent upon securing material and worldly advantages alone. Perhaps for that reason he is more apt to succeed upon his low standard of success. But others, who are just as worldly and selfish as he, fail because they cannot get at once all they want, or because they give themselves up to theories of work and wages, while in practice they lose both. Let the American laborer imitate the Chinaman in accepting the work and the wages which come first to hand while he is looking for better; let him do his work so well that employers cannot carry on business profitably without him, and then he will soon command such wages as the Chinaman never receives, and he will stand in such honor and independence before the world as none but American citizens and laborers can attain.

We can learn from the Chinaman to carry our religion everywhere and into everything, and never be ashamed to show what we believe or to do what is right. We can learn from him to make our faith in the reality of the unseen and spiritual world and in the binding force of religious duty the one most acknowledged and influential law of our life. The Chinaman's religion is indeed very poor and unsatisfactory at the best. It gives him no courage in danger, no comfort in affliction, no hope in death. When heart and flesh fail and all earthly things are gliding from his grasp, his religion is a trouble and a terror to him rather than a strong consolation and a victorious hope. It is hardly worth being called a religion at all. It gives no revelation of the one infinite and everlasting God, the Father of mercies who pours out his heart in lovingkindness over all his earthly children. It does not make known the origin, the duty, or the destiny of man. It does not tell the doubting what to believe, nor the inquiring what to do, nor the afflicted in what to trust, nor the dying where to rest their hope. It is a strange mixture of Confucianism, which is a philosophy, and of Buddhism, which is a superstition, and of the traditions and customs which prevailed in the land long before Confucius or Buddha were known to the world. But such as it is, the Chinaman takes it to heart and carries it with him everywhere and associates it openly with all the affairs of his daily life.

In accordance with the instructions and the usages of his religion, the Chinaman sets up a tablet to his dead father in his house, and he thinks the spirit of the departed one is ever hovering near the sacred symbol, observing all the conduct and hearing all the words of the family. He sets up another tablet at the grave, and there he thinks the spirits of the dead gather to receive the offerings which he brings them to show them honor, and to give them rest in their mysterious habitation of darkness. The whole visible world to him is full of unseen powers, spirits, intelligences, that are ever observing his conduct and ruling his destiny. Spirits in the sun and moon and stars, spirits in the clouds and winds and rain and thunder, spirits in the earthquakes and eclipses and storms, spirits in the mountains and hills and rivers and seas, spirits in the months and seasons of the year, and in all the productions of the earth. He recognizes their presence and pays them homage everywhere. All the operations and phenomena of nature are the evidences to him of the presence and efficiency of spiritual powers which he must revere and propitiate if he would escape disaster and death. When on the seas, he casts offerings into the deep and hangs out flags inscribed with prayers as streamers in the wind, to appease the spirits of the storm and to bring fair weather. On land, the fields and walks and highways and gardens, the trees and wells and fountains, are all set with symbols of the Chinaman's faith in the reality and power of the unseen world by which he is always surrounded and under the shadow of which he is always walking.

He builds temples on the high places of the hills that they may be seen afar as signals of the continual worship which he offers to heaven. He carves out caves in the rocks of the mountains that the spirits which dwell in the deep places of the earth may hear his voice in worship and smell the odor of the incense which he burns. He keeps the smoke of sacrifice ascending all day from the door of the shop where he trades, from the border of the field where he plows and sows and gathers the harvest. And the same sign of his faith is in the schoolroom where his boys are learning to read, on the bench where his apprentices are learning to work, by the chair of state where the judge sits to administer justice. The joss stick must be kept burning on the river craft of the boatman, on the junk and sampan of the fisherman off the coast, in the stifling den of the opium-smoker, and on the pictured stage of the theater in the city and among the divining rods of the gambler in the street. The purchase of a house, the start on a journey, the visit of the physician, the marriage of a son, the burial of a father must all be accompanied with religious rites and acts of worship.

To us the rites seem ignorant, unfitting, and absurd; but to the Chinaman they are recognitions of the reality and the power of the unseen world; they are confessions that man was made to be religious, made to believe in spiritual powers above him, and to be always acting as in the presence of things unseen by the bodily eye, and yet more real and lasting and mighty than the earth on which we tread and the possessions for which we toil. The Chinaman is not ashamed to say all that, to do all that, in his poor, blind way. He would sooner be ashamed of anything else than of his religion. He has never heard of such a thing as an infidel, an unbeliever, an agnostic, an atheist. He does not suppose it possible for a man to live without religion. Even the great Chinese philosopher, Confucius, who cared very little for anything beyond this present world, could not tear from the minds and hearts of his countrymen the faith they had then and have still in the reality of the unseen world and the destiny that awaits all men beyond this life. He had to let them alone in that faith in order to get their attention to his maxims of prudence and worldly wisdom.

Confucius has been dead nearly twenty-five hundred years. His whole teaching was to show men how to preserve order in human society and secure prosperity in this world, and yet, contrary to his instructions, the Chinese to-day worship him as a god simply because they must have something to worship. Stolid and indifferent and reckless of life and death as they seem to be, they cannot live without a religion. And they give a vast amount of time and labor and money for their religion, poor as it is. It never enters their minds that they should be ashamed of their faith or of the sacrifices which they offer. They take it for granted that it is just as proper and natural and becoming for a man to worship, to be religious, as it is for him to eat or sleep. The birds fly in the air and the fish swim in the sea and the wild beast ranges the forest and the plain because it is their nature so to do. So man, in obedience to the higher laws of his being, must just as naturally worship, believe in the reality of spiritual powers, look for the guidance and help of a Being higher and mightier than himself.

So much can the poor Chinaman teach us, and so teaching can put us to shame if we are ever ashamed of our beautiful, blessed, and holy religion. It is one of the strangest, the most unreasonable, most unbecoming manifestations of character in our Christian land that anybody should be ashamed to say and to show, on all fitting occasions, that he is a Christian. The Hindus and Chinese all take it for granted that everybody in this land is a Christian. They think it all a matter of course that it should be so. Surrounded as we all are every day of our lives by the ten thousand blessings of Christianity, the arts, the inventions, the riches, the education, the freedom, the power, the immortal hopes of our holy religion, the Chinaman, the Hindu, does not see how we can be anything else than Christians. And they think it best for us, for them, and the world that we shall be worthy of the name and firm in our faith. Many times I asked the Hindu and the Buddhist if they would advise me to bring their religion to America and teach it to the people of this land. They always said, No. They took it for granted that everybody here must be a Christian, ought to be a Christian. They thought there must be something very wrong, very strange, very much out of the way, if in this land of ours any one can be found who is not a Christian.

The men of the East are right in so judging. In the minds of millions of the heathen on the other side of the globe the name Christian stands for everything that blesses the poor, comforts the sorrowing, beautifies character, builds the waste places of the earth, and gives hope to the world. They ascribe to Christianity the power, the arts, the inventions, the science, the riches, the culture, the civilization, the happiness, and the prosperity of western nations. Many of them already believe that Christianity is to supplant all other religions and eventually to possess all nations. The excuse which many of the heathen make for not taking it to heart is that it is too high and pure and exacting for them : they cannot attain unto it. And here in our own land we have better evidences of its divine purity and its redeeming power than the most intelligent heathen know. We see the humanizing, purifying, uplifting power of the gospel everywhere, even among those who do not obey its commands. It blesses all, the evil and the good, and every moment. Take away all which it has brought to our land, and our homes would be like the dark places of the earth which are full of the habitations of cruelty, full of specters and shadows and demons which men worship in fear and horror all the days of their lives. I have seen the dark habitations where millions live in the populous East; I have looked into the depressed and hopeless faces of the multitudes that throng the streets of the great towns and cities; I have looked out upon the fields where laborers toil under the shadow of grim idols and in perpetual fear that malignant spirits will disappoint the hope of harvest,— and I come home with a deeper feeling of wonder and sorrow than I ever had before, that anybody in this land, this dear, blessed land of America, should be ashamed of Christ, or should hesitate to say that in the gospel of Christ we are to look for the Desired of all nations and the Hope of the world. Multitudes of the heathen have learned enough of Christianity to know that those who receive its spirit and obey its instructions are bound to make it known to all mankind. If I could gather up the millions of voices of all the East and pour them forth in one supplicating cry, loud enough for all in my native land to hear, I would say, "Fulfill that just interpretation of the spirit of the gospel which the heathen have learned to make, accept and honor your high commission to disciple all nations, secure the greatest blessings to yourselves by giving the best you have to those who have them not."

XII.

THE COMMON PEOPLE OF THE EAST.

MANY travelers visit the East and come home and say they have been there and know all about it, when in fact they know very little about the undercurrent of thought among the rich and educated : much less do they know about the underlying life of the poor and ignorant that make up the great mass of the native population. They are to be seen everywhere in city and country, in street and field, in shop and house and home, in temple and bazar and boat. They flow, a living current, through the broad and narrow streets; they are crowded like cattle in the third-class cars of the railway train; they trot along the highways with burdens on their heads; they cut the wild grass on the banks of the roads and the borders of the fields; they climb the tall palms; they gather about temples and tanks and places of pilgrimage; they lie sleeping in the sun on the ground at noon, and they find the same lowly bed under the dews of night. Pictures of everyday life in the East must give the lights and the shades, the foreground and the broad spaces, to the common people. It is not once in a thousand miles of travel in India that one can see a great rajah mounted on his elephant with footmen and outriders clearing the way before him, or seated in his hall of audience, clad in purple, flashing with diamonds, girt with turbaned guards, and bringing to mind the glory and the guilt of the great moguls. But the poor are everywhere, darkening every landscape with their sad looks, offsetting the magnificence of temples and palaces and tombs with their poverty and misery. Excursionists and pleasure seekers, who have been around the globe on swift steamers and fast trains, have seen multitudes of dark faces and scanty costumes; but they learn very little about the real life that the people lead in their wretched homes, still less of the fear, the ignorance, the hopelessness, and the superstition that brood over the minds of millions in the East.

After many months of time and many thousand miles of travel, and much help from the best of interpreters, I could get only some faint glimpses at the inner life of the people in India. It is only such impressions that I propose to give. If there be dark shades in the picture which I hold up to view, I can only say that no truthful representation can be anything else than dark. Perhaps the darkness appears the deeper because the light is beginning to shine on the thick clouds which cast their shadows upon the homes and the pathways of the people of the East. It is much to save us from utter discouragement that wise men, who have stood face to face with the great darkness in those lands for years, are full of hope, and they are looking for the coming of a kingdom of righteousness and prosperity and peace to supplant the long, cruel reign of poverty and ignorance and wrong. It is much that the men who know the East best are most strongly assured in hope of the coming of a better day, and they see the signs of its approach all round the sky.

It is impossible for one who was born in America, and who has never been beyond the boundaries of his native land, to conceive the ignorance, the superstition, the poverty, and the degradation of the common people in the East. Poetry has dowered that far-off and mystic land with pearl and gold. It has clothed its mountains in the morning with purple, and covered its plains with the dazzling splendors of noon, and curtained all with the glory of sunset skies and starry nights. It has built halls and thrones and palaces of surpassing beauty for its princes. It has made the life of the poor one long holiday of basking in the genial sun and singing in the gentle moonlight, and taking such food and dress as kindly nature gives, without care or labor, as she gives to the birds that sow not and to the beasts that never gather into barns. The poets of fancy have done all that for the commonplace, everyday life of the East, and the poets of faith have done much more than that for the religious life. They have made the highest possible attainment of man to consist in sinking into a passionless, dreamless slumber — a sleep of endless years which shall never be broken by hope or fear, thought or desire, effort or aspiration. These poetical rhapsodists, who make Sakya Muni the great light of Asia and all the East, comfort the weary worker in the rice field and the famishing dwellers in mud cabins with the hope that they may come to that blessed Nirvana of nothingness, that everlasting sleep of Buddha, if they bear their burdens in patience and wait for the great consummation. Some have even gone so far as to attempt to show that the intense and fervid life of the West would be greatly improved if it could be rounded with the dreamless sleep of the slumberous East.

Now, laying aside all such ingenious fancies of the poets

and all similar fables of a glory long gone by, I tried hard and long to find out the actual life of labor and feeling and thought which is led by the millions of the East. I could not speak their language, but I could look on and listen and ask of those who knew best what I wanted to know. I taxed my kind friends, who had lived long in the country and knew the people well, with my importunities; but their patience was equal to the task, and they never came short in giving the information which I desired to gather. I traveled miles and miles in the crowded streets of the great cities and the close-packed villages of India and China and Japan, in company with men who had for years made a conscientious study of the inner and the outer life of the people in order to relieve the necessities of both body and mind. I asked questions all the time about the purpose of everything that I saw and the meaning of everything I heard. I must have seen millions of the common people face to face in the course of the year that I was among them; for the streets were always full, the lanes and footpaths were crowded, and the living tide flowed like the river that never rests.

I made a constant study of the people, their looks, their attitudes, their dress and their want of dress, the work they were doing, the burdens they carried, the tone of voice with which they called to each other, and the spirit or the listlessness with which they entered into their daily tasks. I saw them in the rice fields wading half knee-deep, preparing the ground for sowing, stirring up the sticky mass of earth and water with their own feet, or driving a buffalo with a rude harrow attached to the laboring animal, and the men and the beast equally black, besmeared, and naked. I saw women creeping on hands and knees in mud and water six inches deep, weeding the rows of rice, and the mud had been made by mingling sewage from the city with the earth of the field. I saw women with four rings in each ear, one in the nose, and a dozen on the neck, wrists, ankles, and toes, gathering offal in the streets, carrying sewage in large buckets miles into the country to enrich the ground where the rice grew. I saw men coming into cities and villages at evening, carrying on their heads bundles of weeds and coarse grass which they had been all day gathering by the roadside and in unoccupied fields. I did not need to know the language of the people to understand with what spirit they did such work.

I saw the miserable mud houses in which millions of the people lived, the mud floors upon which they slept, the hard blocks of wood which they used for pillows, the palm or rush mat which they spread over them for a blanket in the chilly night. In the narrow streets of towns and on the muddy banks of streams, I saw thousands of children with no clothing at all, looking as if they never knew what it was to play, staring at me with wild, wondering eyes as if I were some fabled monster that they had seen pictured on the walls of temples and tombs. I saw thousands of men working in their fields with tools so heavy and clumsy that it was a wonder to me that they could make the ground yield half a crop under such tillage. In many places when the grain was grown, it was a contest between the cultivators and the beasts which should have it. Men were raised up on scaffolding above the millet and the wheat, watching the grain, scaring away the birds by slinging stones or balls of mud.

The birds were very little frightened, for they knew that none of them would be killed. Even the deadly cobra might cross the everyday paths of the people and creep into the mud houses where they slept without danger to itself, for its life was esteemed more sacred than the life of a man. Riding in cars in India I ran my eye over millions of acres of land covered with full-grown wheat that was but two feet high, and wild deer were feeding it down with nobody to drive them away. Indian corn was sometimes growing beside the wheat, but the thin soil and the surface plowing produced only a yellow and a sickly growth, and many spindling stalks stood up straight and slim with no sign of ears. I was constantly surprised to find that so large a portion of the cultivated ground yielded so meager a harvest to reward the laborer for his toil.

I saw men climbing palm trees fifty feet high to bring down sap in a bucket, each man climbing forty trees to that height every morning and the same number at evening, and getting eight cents a day for the toil. I met men running on the public road at night, carrying the mail on their heads with a lantern in one hand and with the other shaking a string of bells to scare away the deadly serpents that lie in the track. The man runs at the rate of a quick trot for a traveling horse; he keeps on the road for many hours, and when he gets through, his pay for fifty miles of service would not get him the simplest meal at an American restaurant. I saw men dragging fine nets through muddy tanks and pools and deep ditches in the rice fields, hoping to catch minims an inch long and little bigger than a knitting-needle, and with that small fry to make their one meal for a day.

I visited the villages of some of the lowest castes — the scavengers and the gatherers of offal, the carrion-eaters and the outcasts. I tried to find out what they thought of life, and whether they had any hope of ever rising above the wretched condition into which they had been born. They always said they were made for just the life they were leading, and they were good for nothing else. It required great faith in humanity not to believe them when they said so. They did not want any school; they did not wish to learn to read: they only asked to be permitted to do the lowest and filthiest work for the least pay, and then be left to wallow in the mire with the beasts that perish. All over the East the feeling and the faith prevail with all classes of the poor and the depressed that they are fated to live just as they do. They were born with their destiny written on their forehead, and no hand of man can blot out what the finger of fate has written.

In Benares and Moradabad and Peshawar and Rawal Pindi and Calcutta I looked into the shops and saw the poor artisans sitting half naked on the ground, bending over a handful of burning charcoal, producing in some cases the finest work, but with the clumsiest tools and with the longest time spent upon the task. I saw weavers bringing forth from their rude looms the most beautiful fabrics of silk, embroideries that gave the most delicate shadings to figures of birds and flowers; and yet the men were working in dark, floorless cabins, and getting only a few cents for the day's labor. I met a few of them in a little, floorless room that served them for a schoolhouse. They crouched upon the ground and rested a few moments from their labor while I told them something about America and how much laborers received for a day's work with us and what kind of houses workingmen live in here. They listened with looks of mingled wonder and incredulity, and I was in doubt whether they understood what was said or believed it if they did. When I told them that the Bible, the sacred Book which the missionaries had brought to India, had given us all a great hope in this land and had brought us the best things we had in America, they did not look as if they thought the sacred Book would do as much for them as I said it had done for us. It never seemed to occur to them that their lot could be any better than it was.

The hopelessness of the life which millions lead in the East is written upon their faces. Notwithstanding their apparent contentment with their lot, or at least their submission to it, the common people looked to me saddened and depressed. They seldom laugh; do not even smile. I never saw children engaged in any kind of play which called forth effort and shouts and laughter, unless they had been taught the game and urged to play it by foreigners. They seem to have no sense of the ludicrous. Somebody tried to amuse the natives by translating some of the funniest things in Gough's lectures into Tamil. But the people could see nothing in them to laugh at. They read them as solemnly as they would read the funeral service. Neither in public speaking nor in private conversation do they say anything that provokes a smile.

Meeting such people by the thousand in the street, looking into their solemn faces, seeing the burdens they carried, the scanty clothing they wore, knowing how meager the subsistence by which they lived and the little pay they got for their labor and the impassable wall of caste by which they were hemmed in on every side, I could not help thinking that they must be unhappy. They seemed to me bowed down and broken-hearted by their hard lot, and only waiting, in despair of anything better, for death to come and take them out of the world. I tried every way I could to get into their inner life, to learn their daily round of thought and speech. I wanted to know what joys or sorrows they had, what hopes or fears they entertained, so that I could make up my mind whether they were really as unhappy as they looked to be, whether they had any desire or aspiration for a better lot than that into which they had been born.

Of course I could not go very far in my inquiries in that direction. My life had been so little like theirs that I could not stand in their place and look out upon the world as they saw it. I could not discover that the common people knew or cared very much about what was written in their sacred books as the symbols of their faith. They simply observed customs and superstitions which had come down to them from their fathers. The only reason they could give for anything they did or believed was that their fathers did and believed thus in their day. In my inquiries I was dependent upon interpreters whom the natives possibly might not always understand, or upon the imperfect English sometimes spoken by the low-class people themselves. So far as question and answer could bring out anything, I did not find them as unhappy or discontented with their lot as I supposed they would be, and even ought to be. I knew that I could not live submissively in their condition without having, either the loftiest faith in God and in the better life to come, or else a wild and frantic resistance to the chain that bound me. But they had neither the faith nor the feeling of resistance to their hard lot. They did, however, have sensibility enough to feel that their lot in life was hard and their pathway very dark; and they looked up with a vague and passive wonder that the world had nothing better for them. But in all the traditions, changes, customs, and religious faith of their land, they could not see one ray of hope that they could ever rise to a truer, nobler, better life. They must be poor, ignorant, and bowed down all their days, and when death comes they must welcome it as a release from miseries greater than death can inflict. They must go hence upon the pathway of darkness with the comfort that it can lead to nothing worse than life has been to them and their fathers. Neither the government nor the religion nor the philosophy nor the sacred traditions of the East has ever done anything to lift up the fallen or comfort the sorrowing or give peace and immortal hope to the dying.

Most of the people of those distant lands have, however, heard of late that a great light has risen upon the world in other nations, and that it shines with especial blessing into the homes of the poor and it brings divine consolation to the sorrowing and the broken-hearted. Most of them in some way have heard of a great and mighty Helper who has come to undo the burdens from the heavy laden, to give rest to weary shoulders and peace to stricken hearts. Some of them have been told that gracious news many times and with great plainness and simplicity. But their poor, darkened minds, accustomed only to look at shadows and the false shows of things, can scarcely grasp the meaning of the good tidings, or they think it too good to be true, or it seems to them so far off that it can never come nigh to cheer and to help them rise up and walk in the joy of a new life and the strength of a new manhood. Millions still cling to the despairing faith in which they were born. They still think that it must be the lot of the poor and ignorant like themselves to labor and hunger and suffer while they live, and to die without hope of anything better beyond death.

When I saw those people of the East by thousands and by millions carrying their heavy burdens without a Helper, wandering in darkness without a Guide, I thought it must be the most glorious and godlike mission ever given to the nations of the West to lift up those bound slaves of darkness and misery into the light of Christian hope and the joy of Christian liberty. With all our arts and arms, all our science and civilization, all our command of the resources of nature and the knowledge of the divine order of the world, we can achieve no higher victory, we can attain no higher glory, than that of extending the kingdom of righteousness and peace among the nations that have been wasted with war and darkened with superstition for ages. The first and the most obvious appeal which they make to us for light and hope comes from their poverty, their degradation, their subjection to castes and customs which have led them captive for ages. They are so poor that an American laborer would not think he could live a week as they live through all the year. They are so ignorant that the first and simplest facts of life and duty with us are great mysteries to them. Tell them things that our children learn without teaching, and they stare at you with looks of wonder and incredulity that seem to say, How can such things be? They believe things absurd and monstrous and impossible, but in the great facts of nature and reason and duty they have no faith at all.

And yet these degraded people of the East are men like ourselves — immortal men. They have minds to think and hearts to feel just as we have. They have the sense of right and the sting of self-reproach when they do wrong. They know what it is to suffer and they would gladly know better what it is to enjoy. The food they eat is of the simplest kind, the smallest in amount, and the supply is always uncertain. The cruel fiend of famine is always hovering about their lowly mud cabins, ready to come in as an unbidden guest and stare them in the face with cold, cruel eyes that make them go mad and die. Three millions so died in one small section of India in one year. Ten millions more in one province of China perished for want of food and from diseases that follow in the wake of famine. A slight change in the rainfall for a single season will at any time strew the fields and pathways of the East with the skeletons of multitudes who die of want and of the pestilence which comes to glean in the fields where death has already gathered the harvest of millions of sheaves and left nothing but stubble behind.

Looking in the faces of these poor people day after day and month after month, I never could cease to ask the question, What have these poor shadows of humanity to live for? What hope or aspiration or ambition can ever stir their poor hearts to gratitude or joy or thanksgiving? And what is life worth to men who know not what it is to be thankful? It is one of the sad evidences of long ages of hardship and oppression and despair in the East that in some of their languages there is no word for gratitude. The people do not know the sentiment, and so they know no use for the word to express it. What a hard lot it must be to toil along the pathway of life, every day carrying a burden which tasks the utmost strength, and yet with no hope that any kind hand will lighten the load till death comes and drops both the burden and the bearer into the same grave! Millions of people in the East know no better experience than that all their life long. Millions of mothers in the East, instead of rejoicing over the newborn babe, only think, with weeping that will not be comforted, that one more hungry mouth has come to claim a share in the food of the family that never had enough to eat, one more weight of sorrow and suffering has been laid upon the shoulders of parents who already had more than they could carry.

This great want and suffering in the lands of the East need not be, ought not to be. It is due to the ignorance, the vice, and the superstition of the people themselves. It is not because the country is too much crowded or the natural resources are too limited for the population. In the most thickly settled portions of the East, the ground, under proper cultivation, could be made to support many times more than the present population. Three hundred millions of acres of land in India are cultivated. Two hundred and ninety-eight millions more are not cultivated at all. The cultivated portion might be made to produce manifold more than it does or ever has done, if it were in the hands of a free, intelligent, and industrious people. The acre which now bears six bushels of wheat might just as well produce twenty-four. Trees in China, which bear the crudest and hardest fruit, causing sickness and death among the people, might be replaced by trees which would load the table with the best of food for old and young. Tools that weary the workman and waste his time and strength and material might be exchanged for machines which would increase the productions of industry a hundredfold. Agricultural implements which only scratch the ground and take ten men to do the work of one might be replaced by others which would increase the harvest tenfold and relieve the labor of human hands in the same proportion. The duration of life and activity is shortened, millions of lives are lost, by ignorance and reckless exposure and injurious food. Twenty thousand natives are killed every year in India by the bite of venomous snakes when not a single foreign resident is bitten, just because the natives are ignorant and careless and superstitious, and foreigners know how to take care of themselves and the serpents too. Millions of money of the poor are expended upon unprofitable pilgrimages, injurious and debasing festivals, attendance upon temples, altars, shrines, and idolatrous sacrifices. So the people are kept poor, the land is impoverished, and human life runs to waste. Let Christian character and education take the place of heathen ignorance and superstition, and all the waste lands of the East will blossom as the rose.

The people of the East do not ordinarily complain of their hard lot, just because they have never seen or heard of anything better. They think it has been written in the books of eternal destiny that they shall be just what they are from generation to generation — toilers in the dust and heat and mud, living in earth cabins and going back to the dust of the earth from which they sprang. Under the native princes of India the condition of the common people was far worse than it is now under the English. They were drafted into armies to maintain wars of ambition and robbery. They were compelled to toil on the temples and palaces and tombs of the princes, leaving their lands uncultivated, and they received no pay for the forced labor. They were oppressed with all manner of taxes, forced loans, and conscriptions. Their lands and flocks and harvests and villages were constantly exposed to plunder and robbery. There was no established law or justice in the land to defend the innocent or to punish the guilty. The man who could pay the largest bribe was sure to gain his case before the judge. Famine came, and there was no relief for the starving. Rulers often enriched themselves by storing up grain and selling it at an exorbitant price to the hungry. Pestilence came, and there was no medicine or nursing or hospitals for the sick and dying, often no burial for the dead. So it was in the days of the great moguls, Aurungzebe, Jehangir, Shah Jehan, whose temples and palaces and tombs remain as monuments of the riches they exacted from the poor and the victories they gained by crime.

Now under English rule there are order and justice and peace. The peasant reaps his own harvest, poor as it is, with none to molest or make afraid; the artisan enjoys the reward of his own skill and industry; the coolie carries his burden or runs on his message and gets his pay with no publican to snatch it from his hand in the name of the prince. Even the criminal is sure of a fair trial in the courts, so far as it depends on government and not on native witnesses, who learned the habit of lying under the old order of India's native princes. The punishment meted out to the transgressor is only the due reward of his deeds.

But still to the American traveler the condition of the great mass of the common people in India seems so utterly dark and wretched that it saddens his heart every day only to look at the multitudes — multitudes in the shops and streets and fields. Persons who travel from mere curiosity may indeed have their time and thoughts taken up with temples and tombs and monuments. They may think more of a curious piece of carving than of the living man who did the work. They may not mind much about the people, unless it be to get pictures of their dresses, their houses, their vehicles, or specimens of their peculiar works of art. But anybody who goes through the countries of the East supremely interested in the condition and character of the living men he sees there is sure to have many sad and serious thoughts on the way, and to come home constantly revolving the question, " Can anything be done to help those ignorant and degraded millions who belong to the same family with us, and who are born to the same inheritance of immortality?"

But we are not to look upon the hard lot of the common people in the East with anything like their feeling of enforced submission to destiny. They are not fated so to live, nor is their seeming contentment a wise submission to the inevitable. They can all be raised up out of their sad state by bringing them under the enlightening, humanizing, Christian influences which have given the American people their happiness, their resources, and their prosperity. It has taken a thousand years to make us what we are at the best. Under the superior advantages of this Christian age a hundred years may give the millions of India all the enlightenment and the prosperity which we have attained. Our ancestors of the Saxon race, in the wilds of Britain, were a more barbarous people than the natives of India are now. Christian education and example can do for the men of the East as much as it has ever done for the men of the West.

The great labor and hope of Christian missionaries in India and in all the East is to raise up the millions of those countries to a new and immortal manhood by teaching them the same word of truth which has given us our superior intelligence, our strength, and our prosperity. The missionaries believe in science, in education, in the useful arts, in all the means of promoting culture and the highest civilization; but they also believe that the Bible is the first great educator of heathen nations, and that when its sacred lessons are received to the heart and brought out in individual character, all other improvements in arts and in education and social life will follow. Christianity has a thousand times over proved itself to be the best enlightener of the ignorant and the best friend of the poor. The one living and immortal hope of the gospel of Christ will give the despondent and the heartbroken the highest incentives to improve their condition in this world and the best preparation for the world to come. The missionaries believe that the gospel of Christ, received as God's message of salvation to all races of men, will be the best means of undoing the heavy burdens, cheering the dark homes, lifting up the sad hearts of millions of the poor and the ignorant in the great East. Missionaries feel themselves called to that work of enlightenment and Christian instruction by commission from Him who first came to preach his own gospel to the poor and to bring in the acceptable year of the Lord. We on this side of the globe can share with them in that work and in its great reward. We should accept and improve the opportunity as the greatest honor and privilege of life. And surely we must feel that the call comes to us loud and urgent and clear when we look into the depth of poverty and ignorance and degradation into which the great mass of the common people of the East are pressed down to-day. With all our bright hopes and grand expectations we are just the people to help those who are so utterly lost to all the high attainments and experiences of humanity in this life and still more sadly and utterly lost to the immortal hope of the life to come.

XIII.

FAITH AND HOPE IN HEATHEN LANDS.

I HAVE spoken of the physical condition of the common people in the East; I have given some illustrations of their poverty and their destitution of the chief comforts of life, as seen by a traveler who passes through their countries and observes and inquires and listens as he goes. But the sad outward state of millions in the East is the direct and inevitable consequence of a deeper and darker degradation which is upon the soul. If the mind had not been overshadowed with the cloud of ignorance and superstition, their earthly hopes would never have been dark, and their burdens would never have been greater than they could bear. I tried hard to get into the inner chambers of their minds and look out upon the world as they saw it. But I seemed to myself, so far as I succeeded, to be like one going out of the sunlight into a cave without a candle or a guide. I could only grope my way a little distance from the light and then guess what was beyond. When I came back from such blind endeavor and found myself surrounded by the glorious light and liberty of Christian revelation, it seemed to me like passing from a night of cloud and storm to a morning of brightness and beauty on the sea.

In Southern India, in the dominions of the rajah of Travancore, I turned aside from the highway into the open field to look at a Hindu shrine which an old-time resident told me would show me something worth seeing if I wanted to know what heathenism is at home. The shrine was made like the open porch of a small house, covered with a roof, yet all open in front to the light of day. There were two human figures of life-size standing inside: one was that of a man, the other of a woman. The features of the female divinity were carved and painted into the most horrible expression of ferocity and cruelty. The front teeth protruded like the tusks of a wild boar. Between the teeth was the body of an infant child with the head sticking out on one side and the feet on the other. The monster was biting the body of the little innocent in two in the middle. In the left hand of the same figure was another infant child, and the right arm was uplifted with a dagger in the hand in the act of plunging the weapon into the heart of the child. At the feet of the grim idol were fresh flowers, which had been brought there as an offering that very morning. A little hollow in the stone floor had been filled with oil and burned in place of incense to propitiate the demoniac representation of murder and cruelty.

To the poor people who cultivated the adjoining fields and climbed the beautiful palms that overshadowed the shrine, that horrible image stood for the highest object of worship. They thought it a fit representation of the power that ruled over their destiny and determined the measure of their prosperity. The health and sickness, the life and death of themselves and their families were subject to the will of that horrible monster. Little children had been led there by their mothers as devoutly as Christian mothers lead their children to the house of God in our own land. The little dark-eyed heirs of Hindu superstition, naked and nameless, had been taught to kneel down with clasped hands and upturned faces before the image and present the flowers as an offering of fear and worship. They had been told that theirs would be the fate of the child between the teeth of the idol if they did not pray and bring offerings to the devourer of children, the fit representation of demoniac cruelty. It was as if the children of Jerusalem in the days of Christ had been taught to bring incense and offerings to Herod, the destroyer, rather than to the divine Child in the manger of Bethlehem. The glory of the gods of heathenism is to frighten the timid, deceive the ignorant, and destroy the defenseless. The princes in heathen lands take to themselves the titles and attributes of gods, and they too make it their highest glory to fill the world with the dread of their power and the terror of their name. Christ says, "Come unto me, all ye that labour and are heavy laden, and I will give you rest." Christ takes little children in his arms and blesses them.

All over India the imagination of children is filled and defiled from the earliest years with images and tales and traditions of cruelty. They are taught to believe that the whole material world about them is filled with horrible monsters, hideous and malignant as that grim idol, and always watching for opportunities to do them harm. They are terrified when they are most susceptible to fear; they are deceived when they are most willing to go where they are led. Their whole idea of prayer, worship, offerings, services, sacrifices, is to escape the wrath of evil beings that haunt the trees, the fields, the fountains, the forests, the dark places of the hills and the deep places of the sea. Children grow up into a world which they are taught to believe is under the control of malignant spirits, powers of darkness, that delight in bringing misfortunes and miseries upon men. The days of youth, which we try to make bright and beautiful to our children, are haunted with shapes of fear and horrible monsters of cruelty to the children of the East. When they are grown up to manhood, they set grim idols to overlook their fields and gardens. They pour water and oil upon stones that stand for vice and all manner of filthy things; they hang bits of bright cloth upon fruit trees and along the pathways of the fields and the highways of public travel. They go to the great temples and bow down in worship before the monstrous images of lust and cruelty. They do all such things and many more to escape the anger and the persecution of malignant beings that are supposed to live in the air and in the sea, and who come out of their hiding places only to plague and frighten and torture men. So the dark places of the earth are still full of the habitations of cruelty as they were in the Psalmist's day. Heathenism makes no advances toward light and liberty. It is no better now than it was two thousand years ago, but rather the worse for age and experience. It clings only to the past. It knows nothing of what we mean by progress and improvement. If in any case or to any degree it has put off its grossness and given a rational interpretation to its traditions and ceremonies, it is in consequence of light which has come from Christian nations. If it does not now expose its indecencies to public gaze under the name of worship, or confer protection and sainthood upon professional murderers and beastly profligates, it is because it no longer has the power to do it.

When the great hope of the gospel comes to the people of the East, they look back upon their life passed under heathenism as if it were a horrible nightmare dream, in which they were terrified by unreal dangers and were engaged in death struggle with foes that had no existence. In the bright dawn of their Christian faith they feel as if they had come back into the real life of God's beautiful world. They find it full of voices of gladness and they join the great song which the fair earth is ever singing to its Maker. Instead of demons and malignant spirits to torture and to terrify them, they have angels and ministers of grace to guide them in all their ways, strengthen and comfort them in the hours of affliction, and keep their habitations in peace.

In the city of Calcutta I visited the famous temple of Kali, where bloody sacrifices are offered to the cruel goddess every day. It is in an old and out-of-the-way part of the city, occupied only by natives wholly given up to idolatry. We were obliged to leave our carriage and make our way on foot through narrow lanes and over muddy stones before reaching the sacred shrine. We passed a small, filthy tank, the water of which looked like the drainage of a barnyard. Women dressed in beautiful silks were moving down the muddy stone steps with cautious and timid looks and dipping their hands and wetting their foreheads with the filthy water. They did it to wash away their sins, but to me they came up from the tank more unclean than they went down. But to them, the more vile and disgusting the water, the greater was its power to wash away the guilt of sin.

The temple which we were seeking was not large or lofty, but it is said to contain an image of peculiar power in granting the wishes of its worshipers. Like the image which I saw in the field of Travancore, the Kali of Calcutta is the embodiment of murder and cruelty. Around the waist is a girdle of bloody human hands, around the neck a necklace of human skulls, human bodies hang by the hair from the ears, a bloody tongue protrudes from the mouth, the face is red and bloated like a drunkard's. There was a kind of porch standing out from the main temple with a low roof supported by pillars of stone, and the porch was floored with a pavement of stone. Under that roof I saw a man and his two sons. They had with them a pretty young kid which frisked about and played with the boys while the father was holding a long and anxious consultation with a gross and brutal looking priest. I was in company with a professor of one of the Calcutta colleges. He had lived in the country many years and he knew the ways of the people well. I asked him what he supposed was the subject of the man's long consultation with the priest. He said that probably the man had lost a small sum of money by trade or gambling, and he wanted the priest to tell him some charm which would enable him to get it back again; or his ox had died, and he came to the priest to learn what he should do to appease the demon that was supposed to have killed the ox; or some member of his family was sick, and he wanted to know how he could drive the evil spirit that had caused the sickness out of his house and out of the body of the suffering one. For such things the Hindus in the great and elegant city of Calcutta go to the terrible goddess Kali, and the priest is supposed to reveal the secrets of her will.

At length the consultation ended. The priest, the man, and the two boys stepped down upon a lower platform where I was standing, and they took the young kid with them. There was an upright board set in the pavement with a slit cut in the top downward, two inches wide, giving it the appearance of a two-pronged fork. One of the boys seized the kid, dropped its neck down the slit with the head on one side of the board and the body on the other. The priest seized a cleaver, and while the kid was still bleating, its head dropped on one side of the board and its body on the other. The priest threw the bloody head on a heap by the wall; the father and the sons took the body and went away to their own home. They had performed what was to them the greatest act of faith in their religion. They had gone to the sacred temple of their god. They had consulted the priest, they had obeyed his bidding, they had sacrificed the pet kid, the playmate of the children and the pet of the whole family. And now they would wait and see whether the lost money could be recovered, the sick child would get well, or the demon could be kept from killing the rest of the cattle.

That is all that millions in the East know about the meaning or the worth of any act of religious faith or duty. There was no approach of a penitent, trusting, loving heart to the one almighty and all-forgiving Father. There was no incentive to a higher, truer, purer life. There was no outlook of hope for the future beyond death, no strength sought or given to bear burdens, resist temptation, to do good to others and live in peace with all mankind. The father went to his home with his mind filled with some lying tale which the priest had invented for the occasion. His sons were more and more confirmed in the superstition that they were surrounded with evil powers, dark, cruel, deceiving spirits of evil; that their house and fields and flocks were all liable to be possessed, bewitched, plagued by unseen workers of evil to man, and they must do everything in their power to win the favor of these most dreaded enemies of man.

Such is the whole idea of religion in the minds of millions of people in the East. Their faith in its power does not give them patience in trouble, hope in adversity, purity of heart and life under temptation. Their religion only increases their fears, their sorrows, their poverty, and their degradation. In all its modifications in India and Siam and China and Japan, it is a religion of fear — a strange, complicated, irrational attempt to defeat or deceive imaginary powers that are all the while supposed to be busy in bringing evil upon men. Their religion does not make them pure or just or truthful or humane. It is often said by the common people, the more religion a man has, the less he is to be trusted. Pilgrims who have made long journeys to visit sacred shrines are thought to be men for others to beware of. The great saints of the East are for the most part men who have made the people believe that, like evil spirits, they have the power to curse, to send blight and sickness and famine, and therefore their favor is to be propitiated by offerings. The man whom the people look upon as a saint is often the vilest, the most selfish and licentious man in the whole village; and they honor him and make him gifts just to escape his anger and save themselves and their homes and fields and beasts from his curse. Towards each other they are often kind and sympathizing and helpful. But it is not their religion which makes them so. The people would be much better if the priest would let them alone.

At Darjeeling, on the slopes of the Himalaya Mountains, I saw large numbers of tall poles like flagstaffs, fifty feet high. From the tops of the poles hung streamers reaching halfway down to the ground. The streamers were written all over in Chinese characters with prayers, chants, invocations. When the wind fluttered the streamers to and fro, it was hoped that the prayers would drive the evil spirits away from the homes and the walks and tea-gardens of the people who set up the poles to pray for them. On the same wild hills I visited a temple which was set around on three sides of the whole space within its one apartment with upright cylinders, three feet high and ten inches in diameter. The cylinders were filled with scrolls of prayers and set on pivots so that they could easily be made to revolve. A worshiper entered the temple, passed around the three rows of cylinders, and set them all whirling. Thus he made all the enclosed prayers his, and he offered them as many times as the whirling apparatus went round. Then he went down to his stone cabin under the shadow of the great mountains, feeling that he had warded off evil from his house and family and field for the day. He thought the whirling prayers would mystify the evil spirits and send them elsewhere in search of mischief. His praying by machine had not made him a better man: it had only comforted him with the belief that he had got the advantage of the evil powers which were ever busy in some way to do him harm.

In the great and busy city of Bombay, — a city which has grand public buildings, palatial residences, and the most elaborate and highly ornamented railway station that I ever saw anywhere in the world, — I visited a hospital for aged, diseased, and broken-down animals. It was a vast enclosure of pens and stalls and an open space like a barnyard in the middle. There were spavined horses and lame oxen and galled donkeys and broken-legged buffaloes and featherless chickens and domestic beasts of every kind. In one quarter there were three hundred dogs. They looked mad and mangy enough to be taken from the public streets and put under guard more from regard for the safety of the people than from pity for the dogs. When I came near them they growled and barked and yelped with such fury that I was glad to have a strong fence between me and their snapping teeth. There I saw a woman bring a handful of green grass which she had been a long way to gather by the roadside or in the open field. She knelt down and gave it to a lame ox reverently and humbly as if she were performing an act of worship. She had been taught to believe that there might be the spirit of a man imprisoned in the body of that ox. By giving the animal grass she hoped to propitiate the human spirit and gain merit for herself to ward off evil from her household. I could get no one to admit that the broken-down and suffering animals were kept and cared for from pity or kindness to them. It was all done in the hope of storing up merit that might inure to the advantage of the one who brought the grain, the grass, or the water to the beasts. Outside of the hospital thousands of animals were abused and tortured every day and no kindness was shown to them. When they were broken down with labor and abuse and were no longer able to work for the owners, they would be brought into the hospital, and the misery of their life prolonged in order to lay up merit for the men who had tortured them with blows and heavy burdens and hunger in the fields and on the high-ways.

When I was at Sholapur a child had just been bitten and killed by a cobra. The story was told to the wife of a wealthy Parsee. She expressed great sorrow for the child and great sympathy for the parents in their affliction; but when told that the snake was caught and killed, she forgot all her sorrow and sympathy for the human sufferers and expressed great horror at the awful sacrilege of killing the cobra. She thought that in the body of the venomous beast the spirit of a man, passing through millions of transmigrations, might be resting for the time, and that the killing of the deadly reptile might bring the vengeance of the human spirit upon the homes of the living. In that case, too, it was not pity for the snake which moved the heart of the woman, but fear of incurring the displeasure of spirits that are ever ready and waiting to do mischief to man.

In the city of Tōkyō I entered a great temple which was thronged with worshipers. There were gamblers and thieves and fortune tellers and hucksters of every name plying their trade while the worship of the priests and the people went on. Some came with a prayer written upon paper which they chewed in the mouth until they made a pasty ball of the prayer, and then they threw it at the image of the god. If it stuck fast where it hit, the thrower went away with the belief that his petition was heard and his desired good fortune would come. Some went nearer and pasted a leaf of gold foil upon the body of the idol, and then turned away with the hope that more gold would come to them than they had given to the god. I saw a woman throw a few small coins for her contribution through the rack into the treasury of the temple and then bow down to the floor three times before the great golden image of the ever-sleeping Buddha. Then she went to an old, blackened, and featureless image, rubbed her hands three times reverently over the face, put her hand into her bosom each time, and then she went out with a half-saddened and half-satisfied look. Her offering had been made and her act of worship was done. I asked an old-time resident in Japan what it all meant. He said the woman was suffering from some kind of illness, and she had been told that if she stroked the face of that ugly image three times and cast her gift into the treasury of the temple, the spirit of the god would come out of the dead stone and heal her pain. The face had been stroked so many times by worshipers that the nose and lips were nearly gone. The priests of the temple got the gifts, and it cost them nothing to praise the healing power of the dead stone. If the worshipers got better, they thought the god had healed their disease; if they grew worse, they thought it had been fated that they should die: and neither gods nor men could undo what the fates had decreed.

I visited the most popular and frequented of all the temples of Ningpo in China. There was a throng of people coming and going, and they looked apparently with equal reverence upon the imagery of hell and the pictures of paradise that illustrated the walls. The usual trading and gambling and soothsaying were going on, and a stranger could not distinguish between the prayers of the devout and the lying prophecies of the fortune teller and the mystic mumbling of the astrologer. The priest, who seemed to be the master of the temple and the overseer of everything done within the sacred walls, looked about him with an air of the utmost gravity and sincerity. To all appearance he was as well pleased with the game of the gamblers and the tricks of the fortune tellers as he was with the prayers of the devout and the gifts of the faithful. All paid him, and why should he not be equally pleased with all?

I saw women handsomely dressed in native costume, wearing silks that were the brightest and finest that the weaver and dyer could make. Their shining black hair was elaborately dressed in winglike folds and it was kept in place by gold bodkins and silver spangles. They looked serious, thoughtful, and sensible, and it seemed to me that they must know the emptiness of idol-worship. But they went around reverently, bending in worship before many images, setting incense sticks burning before many idols, and then they went out of the grim and ghastly looking joss house with as much decency and dignity of deportment as we would expect in persons leaving a Christian church on the Sabbath day. In that same temple at the same hour of the day I saw a man shaking a long round box in which were many divination rods marked with lucky and unlucky numbers. He was to shake till one fell out before the god. If it proved to be a fortunate number, the man went to his home with as much complacency as the women went to theirs, after the offering of incense and prostration before the idol, and both believed equally that they had sought aid in their human affairs from the powers above. After the act of morning worship, if worship it could be called, they all were happy in the belief that the demons of mischief and misfortune would not trouble them that day.

Every shop in the streets of Canton has a little niche or altar place cut into the pedestal of one of the side-posts of the door. The trader keeps joss sticks burning in that recess all day to drive away the demons that disturb trade and deceive men into making bad bargains. When he opens his shop in the morning, he takes up his counting-frame with which he does all his reckoning, and he shakes the sliding buttons violently backward and forward many times to drive the mischief-making spirits out. He is afraid that they may have got into the frame over night with the design to stay there all day and lead him to make false reckonings in his business. When the spirits are gone, he keeps incense sticks burning at the door to prevent the invisible mischief-makers from coming back and disturbing his trade. He takes it for granted that the spirits always have some evil intent and that they never visit shops or homes except to do somebody harm.

So all over the East the minds of men are possessed with the belief that the powers of the invisible world, whatever they are, hover about the paths and homes of rich and poor, prince and peasant, always with the intent to inflict evil. Great cost is incurred and great efforts are put forth and endless devices are resorted to in the endeavor to escape their malignity. By millions of people, every day, incense is burned, sacrifices are made, gifts are given, lots are drawn, temples are visited, idols are gilded and crowned with garlands, priests and fortune tellers are consulted, prayers are whirled in cylinders or floated on flagstaffs or burned in paper or mumbled in unknown tongues, to guard against the powers of evil which are supposed to beset and plague men's life everywhere and at all times. It is hard to say what can be the origin of this universal fear, but it looks as if the imaginations and consciences of men were evil, and they transferred the secret dread and the dark surmisings of their own hearts to the surrounding world and so filled the earth and the heavens with avengers of their own evil deeds or emissaries of the powers of darkness.

At Peking, the seat of the government which rules over more millions of people than any other government that exists or ever has existed on the face of the earth, I saw a large paper ship with masts and sails and spars and rigging and a hull big enough to hold figures of sailors and passengers of life-size. It was brilliant in color and artistic in finish and it must have cost much time and money to make it. And it was set on fire and burned to ashes in the broad street in the presence of thousands of admiring and applauding spectators. They looked upon it as a great and acceptable offering to win the favor of spirits that held the life and health of the living in their power. The same day and evening I saw hundreds of paper figures of houses and horses and servants and sedan chairs and carts and household furniture, bread and grain and garments and money, all burned in the open street. It was done in hope that the reality of the things represented by the paper figures would go into the service and propitiate the favor of spirits that were supposed to be hovering in the air, haunting the houses, infesting the streets, and ever ready to derange business, destroy property, waylay and mislead travelers, mildew the grain, poison the fountains, bring drought and plague and famine upon the land.

The wise men of China, the sages and the philosophers, who have been trained in the principles of Confucius all their life long, join in such offerings with the common people, and they teach and encourage the people to make them. I supposed that they might, as a matter of policy and for the sake of keeping peace among the people, yield to the customs which had come down to them from their fathers. It did not seem to me possible that they could actually believe in the fitness and efficacy of such offerings in securing the welfare of the country. But I sought information on that point from a man who knows the foremost men of the empire better perhaps than any other foreigner and who has lived in the country and made a diligent study of Chinese opinions and customs for a quarter of a century. He told me that, in his opinion, the most enlightened and progressive statesmen in China at the present time believed in the sacredness and the importance of that custom, and they encouraged the people so to believe by precept and by their own voluntary example. In the arts of diplomacy, in the management of difficult questions and the negotiation of treaties between themselves and other nations, the Chinese are said to be more than the equals of European statesmen. They are unrivaled in all matters which depend for success upon concealment of motives and methods of operation; they are quick and keen in their judgment of character; they are patient in adherence to the one aim they have in view; they will persist in their purpose in face of all hindrances, oppositions, and delays. At the same time they adhere to the old absurd rites, usages, and superstitions just as the lowest of the people do. My most intelligent friend gave it as his opinion that they do it as a matter of faith and not merely of policy or expediency. They have talent, education, experience, knowledge of the world, but they are heathen still, just like the common people about them.

These renowned Chinese statesmen and diplomatists have had intercourse with Europeans for years; some of them have visited Europe. They can read the English language and they have access to the science and history and the literature of western nations. Even if they read no language but their own, translations of books on the most important and practical branches of science are within their reach. And yet they are in bondage to the prince of the power of the air, like the coolie that toils in the rice field or runs in the riksha. They build up a blank wall on the opposite side of the street as high as their front door to keep the spirits, that move in straight lines through the air, from finding their way in. When they start on long voyages by river or sea they set fire to paper pictures of money and rice and houses and garments and all manner of good things, and cast them into the water as offerings to appease the spirits of the deep, lest they should be angry and rouse up the winds and waves, and send forth lightnings and thunderbolts, and hurl the ship to the bottom with the swift and terrible typhoon. They imagine that some mysterious and mighty dragon lies coiled in many a scaly fold beneath the thronged streets of great cities, and that if houses were set in line along the streets the monster would become angry, and with one whisk of his tail toss houses and temples and people millions of miles into the air. I overheard an excited conversation between a foreigner and an intelligent Chinaman in the streets of Fuchau. When I asked what was the subject of the controversy, I was told that the Chinaman feared some mistake had been made in building lines by the foreigner, and that in consequence the great dragon would turn angrily in his deep bed under the hill, and natives and foreigners alike would be buried in one common ruin. The Chinamen speak of such absurdities with as much earnestness and sincerity as we would expect to see in the look and manner of a man who was guarding and protesting against the most awful calamity. If something should go wrong in the family, if there should be sickness or accident or trouble of any kind, they would hire priests and astrologers to come to the house and stay there for days and weeks, feasting, incurring the expenditure of hundreds, even thousands, of dollars in vain ceremonies, reading, chanting unmeaning formulas of words, burning pictured paper, cutting right and left with swords, under the pretense of driving the spirits that plague the family out of the house.

Such is the faith and such the practice of the foremost men of China, the great scholars and teachers, the viceroys and governors of millions, the statesmen and philosophers trained in all the wisdom of Confucius and Mencius, men who have passed through all the examinations of the boards of education with success and honor. And if such be the leaders, the best educated and the most progressive of the men of China, what must the people be? How dark and dreadful the cloud of ignorance and superstition which casts its shadow upon their daily life! How the world must seem to them like a prison house, haunted with demons and hung around with pictures of fear and horror!

XIV.

HAVING EYES AND SEEING NOT.

THE traveler in a foreign country has his attention drawn first to things that look least like what he has been accustomed to see at home. So in the East the American cannot keep his eyes off from the wretched homes, and in all his letters and conversation he keeps talking about the poverty and degradation of the common people. He has never seen such raggedness and nakedness; he has never looked into so many hopeless and spiritless faces; he has never before met with millions from whose minds the light is so completely shut out. So he is apt to talk about the sad condition of the people as if there were little else to see. In my own case I did not stay long enough to get used to it or to have my mind so taken up with work for the relief of the poor and ignorant that I ceased from silent wonder or useless lamentation. But in five months' time and five thousand miles of travel in India alone I saw poverty and wretchedness and superstition enough to make me think and talk about it in spite of myself.

I do not suppose, however, that the masses of the people in the East feel the misery and the degradation of their lot as it seemed to me or as I represent it in these pages. They do not feel it as we would if we were taken out of our present homes and surroundings and put in their place. If in their condition we could remember our former state and yet have no power to recover it, we should feel that the doom of immitigable and endless despair were upon us. Yet the people of the East are the more to be pitied by us, and their call to us for help and instruction is the louder, just because they do not know how needy they are. They do not long for light to shine upon their dark path, just because they have walked in the night of ignorance so long that they do not know what the day is. They choose darkness rather than light, just as the Greenlander prefers a cabin of ice to a comfortable home. Sometimes, even, they think they are the wisest, the most enlightened, and the happiest people on the earth. The habitual cloud which rests upon their minds makes them think that all remote portions of the earth are inhabited by demons and deformed men who are constantly scourged by hail and tempest or wasted by drought and famine. They are like the sick man to whom the first symptoms of approaching death come with release from pain and he thinks it the sign of returning life and health. Life, light, instruction, increase the capacity for enjoyment, but they also correspondingly increase the capacity for pain. So, sometimes, when the light begins to shine in upon the dark homes of the heathen and to show them their wretchedness, they wish it had not come.

The call to us to do what we can in kindling the light of hope and salvation all over the East is the more urgent just because the people of those lands try to shut out the light and are content to walk in darkness. The common people of India are solemn, serious, dejected in their look and manners. To me they seem sad, as if carrying the burden of some great sorrow upon their hearts. I never saw them, young or old, engaged in any kind of spirited and mirthful play. I could not learn that they ever indulged in jokes or witticisms in conversation with each other. The juggler and the snake-charmer, the story-teller and the gymnast, the teacher and the school-boy, were as solemn as the fakir and the guru. I do not remember ever to have heard a native Indian laugh loud; seldom did I see one even faintly smile. They have no sense of humor. They see no meaning in wit that would make an American audience wild with laughter. They look as if they thought life too great and awful a reality to permit them to laugh at anything. The whole teaching of Buddhism especially, and, to a less degree of all the other religions of the East, is that life is a great calamity, existence is a burden to be laid down with a deep sense of relief when the time of the end comes. How can they be cheerful when their religion has taught them that they have nothing to be thankful for? How can they be merry when the opening of the mouth in laughter may give an evil demon an opportunity to rush in and torture them to madness? How can they see brightness and beauty in the world about them, when every grove and hill and fountain is believed to be the home of spirits whose delight is to destroy their harvests and bring sickness and sorrow upon their homes?

Yet I was not quite sure that the common people always had such sad thoughts in their hearts. I do not think that even the best of them were quite living up to the dismal demands of their religion of demons or their philosophy of despair. I never felt quite sure that I understood the inner life and spirit of the people. Foreigners who had lived in the East thirty years, and who spoke the languages about them well, were still perplexed and mystified in their attempts to get into the secret depths of the oriental mind. The most intelligent traveler has little chance of becoming thoroughly acquainted with men and things in the East, unless he stays long and studies hard, and then he will sometimes feel his ignorance more deeply in the end than when he began. Oriental modes of thinking and living are so different from our own that we find it quite impossible to put ourselves in their place and look out upon the world with their eyes. To them, the broad landscape and the distant mountains and the wide river and the boundless deep are inhabited and controlled by beings which to us have no existence. Their minds are haunted by fears and inspired by hopes which would only provoke our ridicule, if we did not pity their ignorance and wonder at their superstition. The meaning which they give to language, the motives which inspire them to action, the sources from which they draw their pleasures, and the basis on which they build their expectations are so far out of the range of our common thinking and feeling that it requires the study of a lifetime to understand the East. Men of equal talent and opportunity engage in that study for years and come to very different conclusions, just because the subject itself is so dreamy, mystical, and uncertain. The books of the East often mislead the student quite as much as the manners of the people mislead the observer. If we put western interpretations upon what we find written in their books, we shall be as far out of the way as we should if we put trowsers upon men who wear turbans in India or tall hats upon men who wear tails in China. If we believe everything that is told us at first, we shall find ourselves misled so often that we shall be in danger of believing nothing in the end.

The people of China are just as great a mystery as the Hindus, just as fast bound in ignorance and superstition, just as much enslaved to custom and tradition. And yet they have a strange and unconquerable vitality. They are not as much bowed down and crushed by their work, however hard it may be; they do not look as much as if they were ever lamenting their hard lot and wondering at the great mystery of life. They have a singular mingling of cunning, of deep and dark deceptiveness, together with an air of childlike simplicity. They have great ingenuity but no invention. When, by any accident, they light upon a new art, a great invention, they are not apt to know it. They find their way to the door of the great world-wide temple of art and improvement, but they never step inside. They have great individuality and self-esteem, but no capacity to adapt themselves to men and circumstances out of their usual line of thought. They talk a great deal about wisdom and truth and honor. Yet they are foolish and treacherous and unclean in their lives. Their classics are loaded with precepts about prudence and integrity and the qualities which belong to the superior man. Yet they have little sensibility to the value of truth; they do not dare to trust each other, and in four thousand years they have not produced a man whose sayings can be quoted for wisdom and whose doings can be commended for righteousness among all nations. So far as they have any religion at all, it sits very lightly upon their consciences and their hearts. An old resident in China told me that he had been studying the Chinese mind for thirty-four years, and yet to him it was still an impenetrable mystery. After five months among the solemn-faced and sad-looking Hindus, and two months more among the indolent and sleepy Buddhists of Burma and Siam, it was a pleasant relief to me to get among the active, hard-working, irrepressible Chinese. But then I thought, what have these poor coolies of the great Central Flowery Kingdom to gain by their hard work? What have they to rejoice over as the fruit of their labor? They are just as ignorant and debased and superstitious as the solemn-faced Hindus. They are just as much in need of the message which brings glad tidings of great joy to all people. They are even more unconscious of the darkness and degradation in which they live.

The people of the East are all exceedingly religious, and they are not ashamed to show their religion wherever they go. In the street and in the house, in the field and on the highway, in the workshop, the ox-bandy, and the railway car, they all show in some way what they believe and what manner of life they lead. In India they paint the horns of their oxen red and blue; they hang bits of bright-colored cloth on the trees by the roadside; they set up figures of men and horses, serpents and sea-monsters, to overlook the fields and drive away drought and blight and famine; they make offerings of fruit and flowers and oil before the idols, beside every fountain and under every green tree; they shave the head and they let the hair grow long; they wear peculiar garments and they go naked; they bathe in sacred water and they cover their bodies with the most abominable filth; they give up their streets to bulls and cows and monkeys; they let their houses be infested with bats and birds and lizards and centipedes; they give up a part of their scant breakfast to be taken from their hands by intruding crows and parrots and sparrows; they look with sacred awe upon the life of the toad, the tortoise, and the deadly serpent. All these things, which are to be seen everywhere, are services of religion among the people of India. The sacred ashes and the vermilion lines on forehead and arms and body; the sacred cord and the bead roll; the hair matted with mud and the body besmeared with worse coating from the sewer and the dunghill, — all tell the faith in which they live and the gods whom they trust to deliver them when they cry. A man would no more think he could go into the street, the shop, or the field, without some act or sign to show his religion, than the tradesman would think he could sell goods without a sign, or the sailor would venture out to sea without a compass or a chart.

To the man of the East religion is his daily bread to strengthen him for his work and his nightly sleep when his work is done. It goes with him for a constant companion on his journeys, and it is the first to salute him at his own door when he comes home. The white and the variously colored turbans and the manner of arranging the folds on the head; the loose garment for the body and the tight girdle for the loins; the call of the coolie for work and the cry of the beggar for alms; the dull singsong with which porters and messengers trot along the road, and the monotonous refrain with which palanquin carriers cheer each other in the night, — all have some religious meaning and are full confessions of faith in the legends of Hindu life and the tales of Hindu gods. When he rises in the morning and when he lies down at night, when he eats and when he goes hungry, when he dresses himself with care and when he goes naked, at his birth and marriage and death, the Hindu proclaims his faith in Siva and Krishna and Vishnu; he declares his adherence to the traditions and customs of his country for a hundred generations.

So it is impossible to talk about the people of India with intelligence and truth without having much to say about their religion. The peasant life in the field and the shop life in the city, the home life in the house and the boy life in the school, the priest life in the temple and the sailor life on the sea, are all accompanied with religious rites and are mingled with confessions of religious faith. If their religion were only good and true, if it enlightened the mind and purified the heart and ennobled character, we should say they were wise in making so much of it. The religion which lifts a man up to God, makes common things sacred and sacred things real, which gives strength to bear every burden, courage to meet every danger, and faith to gain the final victory over death, is not a thing to be hidden in the heart when the world needs to know its truth and feel its power.

A very slight glance at the landscape as one moves leisurely along in the Indian train is sufficient to convince the traveler that pity for the poor is not one of the virtues inculcated by the saints and sages of Hinduism. The beggar is indeed sometimes helped in answer to his miserable cry, but he is sure to get his pitiful dole of charity only when he assumes to be a saint or prophet and to have the power to curse those who refuse to answer his call for gifts. Let him do that, and the poorest will give out of their poverty to escape the evil which the holy man has the power and the will to inflict. Let such a pretended saint, the vilest and the filthiest of the tribe, go to a Hindu village and require the people to bring him a contribution of money or cloth or provisions, and let him threaten them with his curse if they fail to comply with his demand, and they will bring him the best of everything they have. Even then the lying beggar, who assumes the character of the filthy fakir, will confirm his claim to sainthood by rejecting a part of the gifts, as if he would be defiled by the touch. If a cup of cold water is given to quench his thirst, he makes a cup of the hollow of his hands and commands the draught to be poured into it that he may drink without touching his lips to the vessel which others have brought. If in his haste and extreme thirst he should swallow the smallest fly or worm or waterbug or living creature of any kind, he would make a great outcry of grief and horror for having committed a mortal sin, and he would claim that he had laid himself liable to ages of punishment in the next world for the great wickedness he had done in taking animal life.

Villages in great numbers may be seen right and left of the road as we pass over the vast plains of Southern and Northern India. They are mostly a rude huddle of thatched and mud-built huts. It seems extravagant to call them houses or habitations for human families to dwell in. The thatch looks old and weather-worn, the huts have no windows, the mud walls are crumbling to the earth, and it seems a wonder that they are not all washed down to the level of the mud out of which they have been built when the rainy season comes and the clouds pour down water enough in a few weeks to last the whole year. The rude coverings for the people are no more pleasant and comfortable inside than the exterior would lead one to expect. Millions live in a low, narrow kennel, with no ornament, no furniture, no ventilation, no floor but the ground, no window to look out from or to let the light shine in; nothing to see inside but the bare mud walls and the faces of the family that are of the same color with the mud. The village is generally sheltered by a few trees that first attract the eye in the distance and show where the people live. The palm, the banyan, and the mango become as familiar to the traveler as the hills, the plains, and the mud cabins of the people. To one who has been accustomed to the bright homes and the pleasant villages of America, the villages of India seem like a cloud on the landscape, and the cloud looks darker in the distance when once we have been inside the mud cabins and seen for ourselves how comfortless and dreary they are. So long as the natives have nothing but mud huts for homes, it will be hard to lift them to a higher civilization or a purer life.

When the common people of India come under the instruction of the missionary and they receive the healing and inspiring truths of the gospel into their hearts, one of the first outward results of the new life is seen in the effort to improve their wretched habitations and make them more like Christian homes. I have visited the houses of Christian natives, and the first glance inside was enough to tell me that something better than Hinduism had touched the hearts and quickened the minds of the occupants. Neatness and order had taken the place of filth and confusion; separate apartments had been made for different members of the family; the ground outside had been set with trees and flowers and made attractive to children, that they might be kept from the vice and the vulgarity of the heathen village and the common street.

One object which arrests the attention of the traveler in Southern India and Ceylon may seem at first thought to conflict with the statement that there is little pity for the poor and the toiling in heathen lands. It is called a burden-bearer. It is a convenience for coolies and porters of every kind, but it would have no value in countries where living men and women are not made packhorses to carry all manner of burdens. Sometimes it is a broad brick or stone wall built beside the public road, eight or ten feet long and as high as a man's head. Sometimes it is only two upright posts of wood or stone and a cross-piece reaching from one to the other and of the same height as the wall. It generally stands under a banyan or a tamarind tree and beside a fountain or tank of water. The weary coolie, staggering under the load on his head, is glad to lay off his burden on this support without stooping to the ground, and then rest for a while, bathe himself in the tank, and sleep under the shade of the tree. When he rises to resume his walk, his load is already lifted to the height of his shoulders. So the wall or framework is called a burden-bearer. To build one is thought to be a work of great merit; and the builder hopes to reap the reward of his labor and expense in a future state of being. The man whose next birth might make him the brother of the swine may purchase for himself the privilege of being born into a higher caste of humanity, by building one of these rests for the weary by the roadside where multitudes are always passing. If he goes farther and plants a tree for a shade and digs the ground for a tank, in which the weary may wash, he will be all the more sure to purchase for himself a good estate in the next life. It is not supposed or claimed in either case, however, that the builder is influenced at all by pity for the poor and heavy laden. He only wishes to make a good bargain with destiny and purchase for himself a better lot in the next life.

Under English rule in India broad, smooth highways have been constructed through large portions of the country, so that the place of porters is often taken by beasts of burden. Bandys and bullock carts move slowly along, the wheels creaking aloud and the cart groaning under the heavy load of humanity and household goods. The driver sits under cover at the tail of the oxen and a cloud of dust marks the course of the caravan across the plain. It often looks as if it were moving day between villages, and whole families with all their earthly goods were on the road. The covered bandys are filled with the motley mass of living humanity, old and young, men, women, and children. The clatter of pots and kettles and earthen jars is louder than the clamor of voices, for the travelers are generally very still. They move very slowly, for nobody is ever in a hurry in these old countries of the East, where centuries of history pass over the peoples and races and leave them just as they found them. They see no reason for quickening their steps, for there is nothing better in the future to run after, and there is nothing bad in the past that they can get away from by hurrying. The days of all are written in one great book of destiny and it is not for man to contend with fate. Take what time is given: nobody can get any more. Sleep in the sun, dream on your journey, dig while you can, and die when you must. The gods will have their own way with us all, and we are no more in their hands than the dust which the hot wind blows along the road where the rumbling wheels and the trampling feet stir it up. Neither the faith nor the philosophy of the drowsy East can go farther than that. The newcomers upon the scene of action find all places full, and they look so much like their predecessors that the departing leave no vacancy and the coming make no crowd. Thousands can be spared and nobody be missed, and thousands come to fill their place, and yet the country never is full.

So the stream of life flows on, age after age, in the great and populous East, and so it must flow on until the coming of new life from nations that have heard the glad tidings of peace on earth and good will towards men. Let that message come to the degraded millions of the East and it will make the world and all things therein new to them; it will lift the heavy burdens from weary shoulders; it will bring the light of peace and kindness into the habitations of cruelty; it will drive the imaginary hosts of demons and spirits of evil from the homes and paths of men; it will bring angels of mercy to guard their dwellings and direct their steps in all their ways; it will take away the great horror which broods over death, and open to the vision of the dying the prospect of a land where pain and sorrow can never come; it will bring out the oppressed and the enslaved into the glorious light and liberty of the children of God. The poor pariah of India, scoffed at and spit upon by the proud Brahmin, the naked coolie of China carrying burdens in the street or toiling in the muddy rice field, will look up with surprise and joy at the great discovery that he too is a man, made in God's image, endowed with the infinite inheritance of immortality.

When the ancient East is filled with a population who rejoice in the divine truth of the Christian faith and live in the divine character of Christian love, there will come a new and great era of riches and power and glory to those lands that have been for ages devastated by famine and war and darkened by superstition and idolatry. It is for the dawn of that day that we offer our prayer when we say, "Thy kingdom come." It is to hasten the answer to that petition that we send our missionary brethren to preach the glorious gospel of the Son of God to those who sit in darkness and in the region of the shadow of death. It was to see them in their chosen fields, and if possible to speak to them some word of sympathy and encouragement in their toil, that I went on a journey of many thousand miles and I became familiar for many months with the lights and shadows of eastern life. It is a great happiness to come home and to say to all who will hear that our brethren in the foreign field are faithful to their high and sacred calling and that the blessing of God is upon their labor. Slowly, surely, the dawn brightens in the dark places of the earth and every sign shows that the full day is drawing near.

XV.

LIGHT IN THE EAST.

THE prudent mariner, pursuing his voyage in mid-ocean, diligently observes the stars, the clouds, the winds, and the sea. It would be very rash in him not to look to the heavens to find his place on the deep below, or not to regard the signs of change which are hung out in the brightening or the lowering sky. If at any time he suspects that his ship has fallen into some hidden current and is drifting out of its course, or that there is some variation in the compass and that the needle no longer points to the pole, or a sudden fall of the barometer indicates that some awful convulsion in the atmosphere is at hand, he doubles the watch, braces every spar, sets sails and rigging in order for whatever may come, and so escapes foundering on the open sea or wreck on the lee shore.

We are all out upon the great sea of life, ever moving on to that undiscovered country from whence none ever returns. Millions of others are associated with us in the voyage. We influence them and they influence us in the course we take. If one wanders from the true way, a thousand others may follow and disappear in darkness. If one holds high the beacon light of hope and steers through storm and sunshine with undeviating course for the port of peace, others will follow his lead and share with him a safe arrival in the blest harbor,

> Where no storms ever beat on the glittering strand,
> While the years of eternity roll.

So it becomes us all to be diligent and discriminating students of the time in which we live, that we may know the currents of opinion and custom by which we are borne along, the material and spiritual forces which are forming individual and national life, and which will determine what is to be the condition and character of the human race on the earth in the ages to come. Such a study is always interesting and profitable, but especially so to one who is visiting the great historic scenes of the past and is constantly raising the question, whether the ages of darkness and division and conflict are to be repeated in the future, or whether the human race will ever come into one harmonious and happy brotherhood, walking together in the light of peace and love, living by one law, and both promoting and rejoicing in each other's welfare as members of one family.

The traveler who makes the circuit of the globe must be very thoughtless if he does not raise such questions many times in the course of his long journey. And he must be a very unintelligent observer if he does not see signs of the breaking day in the dark clouds of the East. He has only to keep his eyes open and his mind attentive, and he will discover tendencies to such unity among nations as never existed in any past age. He will look forward to a time when one manner of law shall be accepted and obeyed by all races of men, and one foundation of faith shall give rest and peace to all human hearts. Some of these tendencies are material, some are intellectual, some spiritual. If we look at them separately in the light of our time, we shall find many arguments and evidences with which to answer the prophets of evil who are continually saying that the former days were better than these upon which we have fallen: —

I. — INCREASED FACILITIES FOR TRAVEL.

THE most apparent and powerful of all material influences which are now drawing the nations into one family and giving light for the guidance of all feet in the safe way are the increased facilities for travel and for the transmission of intelligence all round the world. The railway, the steamship, and the telegraph are binding the tribes and races of men together in bonds of iron which are not fetters of enforced bondage, but nerves of living thought and commanding power. I stepped into a telegraph office in Hongkong at nine o'clock in the morning and wrote words which were in the capital of one of our southern cities before sunrise the same day. They had traveled faster than the sun, and had completed half the circuit of the globe in the time that I took to climb the hill above the city and look down upon the shipping in the harbor. When men can talk with each other at that distance apart they are not likely to keep up the old heathen notion that all people are barbarians but themselves.

The traveler on the Pacific steamer will find sitting at the same table with himself one man who has just come from Australia or Honolulu, another who is going to Yokohama, Shanghai, or Canton; still another whose destination is Calcutta, Bombay, or Constantinople. If he stops at any one of the leading hotels in any of the great cities of Europe, he will find in the same house persons who have recently been in St. Petersburg or Stockholm, Rome or Athens, Damascus or Cairo, Singapore or Peking. They talk with each other at the table and in the public conveyance. They make known their nationality and the knowledge they have gained by travel in different countries. So the whole round world is bound together by ties of personal acquaintance and common interest which reach every clime of the inhabited earth and every member of the human family. So long as this open intercourse of thought and travel is maintained it is impossible for the world to go back to the old classic ages when the most intelligent people called all others barbarians, and they fancied that the remote parts of the earth were inhabited by pigmies a span high, or by monsters who could wade the deep places of the sea without wetting their armpits and use the tallest pine for a walking-stick. There are some people in the world who entertain such opinions still, but we do not look to them for lessons in philosophy or for leadership in the progress of the human mind.

All the means and instrumentalities of western and Christian civilization are fast becoming the property of all the millions of the East. The works of the useful arts, the manufactures of industry, the machines and inventions for daily use in the shop and field and home, and the cultivated products of the earth, travel as fast and as far as the men that work in the shops, ride in cars or ships, or till the ground in their own chosen land. Whatever is made or grown in any country is as sure to go where it is wanted for the use of man as the clouds are sure to gather on the mountains or the rain to water and fertilize the earth. And as this free communication of the products and industries of nature goes on increasing, the prejudices and hostilities of the early ages must abate and the wastes of war must cease. When men are brought so near each other that they can send morning messages of salutation round the globe, and speak to each other so that the voice of each shall be recognized across the ocean, they cannot afford to call each other foreign devils and barbarians. The brotherhood of nations becomes a necessity when continents have become only separate apartments in one house, and the fire that warms and the food that supports and the harvest that enriches are the same to all.

There was a time when the poet could truly say: —

> Lands intersected by a narrow frith
> Abhor each other. Mountains interposed
> Make enemies of nations, who had else
> Like kindred drops been mingled into one.

But the narrow frith is now most apt to be spanned by an iron bridge or crossed every hour by a steam ferry. The mountains have been tunneled for the railway train. And the people living on each side are so mingled together by trade and talk and travel that they forget their prejudices and hostilities and live as friends and neighbors. Railways and telegraphs keep the peace between nations better than standing armies or city walls or ships of war. The proposed tunnel under the British Channel, connecting France and

England, instead of exposing England to invasion from the continent, as military men fear, will be the strongest bond binding the two nations on either side of the channel to keep the peace. China keeps her walls and refuses to dredge out the bars of her rivers because she is striving to live in an age long gone by. Her best protection will be to throw down her walls, clean out her rivers for free navigation, and stretch out lines of railways through all her provinces. If the present government cannot live in the hearts of an intelligent people and in the growing light of the world, it will have to die and be buried with the sages whose lessons have lost their meaning to the thinking mind and their value in the better organization of human society.

The knight errant of the Middle Ages going up and down the world to find somebody to fight with him, the feudal barons living in castles on the Rhine and in the Black Forest and desolating the country round with robbery and murder, the free towns of Germany and Italy keeping up desperate war with each other for years upon the slightest provocation, could never exist in an age when telegraphs communicate intelligence with the speed of the lightning and railway trains cross a kingdom in a single night. When steam cars were introduced into England, some "fine old English gentlemen, all of the olden time," thought them vulgar, a plebeian conveyance, fit only for men who earned their living with their own toil and paid their honest debts without help from government pensions or rent from entailed estates. Lords and ladies of the realm must ride with a coach and four and with liveried servants and lackeys for outriders and coachmen. And so for a while the peers and the princes would not ride in the train. But the progress of the age was too mighty for even them. They could not be content to ride six miles an hour in a coach, when their servants were riding sixty in the cars. And now kings and queens, emperor and kaiser and czar, must take the train like common men, and the steam horse carries one as swiftly and as willingly as the other.

Still later, when the railway trains first began to disturb the sleep of ages in India, the low-caste natives looked on the strange, loud-hissing, fire-breathing monster that drew the cars with silent and stupid wonder; the high castes stood aloof with affected indifference and proud contempt; the Brahmin thought them fit only for coolies and pariahs, the refuse and the offscouring of humanity. The latter would not soil his boasted divine descent from the head of Brahma by riding in the same train with the vulgar herd who sprang from the feet and were fit only to be trodden in the dust. The coolies were afraid to get aboard, though they could ride third class at a small fraction of a cent a mile. Among all the legends of the mighty doings of their millions of gods, they had never heard of anything that seemed to them so awful an embodiment of power and terror as the traveling steam engine. The miracles of Brahma and Vishnu and Siva were only stories told by the gurus and believed by the people, but nobody had seen them with his own eyes. But here was a fiery monster that swept across the plain faster than the typhoon, the sun was darkened by the cloud of its breath and the earth shook with the sound of its coming. They would not trust themselves in the train of such a loud-hissing demon any more than they would dare defy the thunder-god of the clouds or the storm spirits of the deep. The Brahmins said it was nothing in comparison with the wonders that men had seen of old when Krishna danced with the milkmaids and Hanuman built a highway through the sea. Yet it was as much from fear as from affected contempt that they refrained for a while from defiling themselves with the wicked and demoniac invention from the West.

But the trains kept running all the same, leaving rajahs and Brahmins, coolies and pariahs, to get aboard or stay behind, just as they chose. The first act of condescension on the part of a great rajah was to send an order for the train to wait at the station till it suited his pride and indolence to come. But to his unspeakable astonishment he found that his order had no more influence upon the train than it would have had upon the moon or the tide. The train had been gone an hour when he arrived at the station an hour late. Now, at last, the Brahmin and the great rajah have learned that they are not lords of the nineteenth century and that all the world was not made for them. They have made up their minds to submit to the inevitable. Both ride in the same train with the coolie, who once was obliged to step five rods from the road to let a Brahmin pass. Even the proud rajah runs to get aboard when the station master gives the signal for starting.

I saw one of the proudest of the princes of India, a great maharajah, on the platform of the station at Patna. He was clothed with purple and fine linen. He was belted with gold bands and blazing with diamonds. He was surrounded with a retinue of servants and minor chiefs. If he spoke to them, they approached him bending the whole body and clasping their hands as if worshiping Brahma himself. One kneeled to place the long pipestem between his lips and to hold it while he took a whiff. It would be servile for his highness to put forth his hand and take the pipe himself. Another kneeled to adjust his slipper, which was slightly out of place. He seemed to have no more care of himself than an infant a week old. But suddenly the steam whistle gave the signal to start the train. The servants did not bow or clasp hands at that call. They ran with the utmost speed to get their places in the third-class car, where they rode. And his high-and-mightiness, the great rajah himself, had to run too, with no one to carry his pipe or pick up his golden slipper if, in his unprincely haste, he should chance to drop one from his foot. His car was in the same train with the vulgar herd, and he must go with them or not go at all. It was a great fall for the proud princes of India, who reckoned their descent from Aurungzebe and Jehangir and Shah Jehan. But I thought it a sign of the rise of the millions of the people, and I rejoiced for their sake, and I wasted no pity on the princes.

Self-interest in the end overcame the fear of the ignorant, the contempt of the conceited, and the pride of the princes. And now sudras and Brahmins and rajahs ride in the same train; high-caste and low-caste sit on the same seat; men, who would not voluntarily come within five rods of each other fifty years ago, are so closely packed in the flying train that all regard for caste distinctions must be given up. All must yield to the pleasure and the profit of riding so fast and so far, so cheaply and so comfortably, instead of plodding along the dusty roads in the hot sun for days and weeks to reach some sacred shrine to worship or some sacred river to wash in. The holy place will make the pilgrimage holy, in whatever way the pilgrims travel, and the holy water will wash away all sin and all defilement contracted from contact with the strange arts and devices of the West. The railway humbles the proud without intending it, and it lifts up the lowly by carrying them as fast and as far as the richest and mightiest can go. So the railway gradually breaks down the barrier which caste had built up between people of the same race as high as heaven and as deep as the grave. All improvements in the practical arts have the same tendency in the old lands of the East, where everything has been done in the same way for ages and it is thought to be a sufficient reason for any custom that the fathers of a long past generation did so. The East will never be free till the iron yoke of caste and custom is broken from the necks of high and low.

So, too, all over the world, railways and telegraphs and steamships are breaking down the walls of separation between castes and classes, tribes and nations, destroying the old factitious distinctions which have lifted up the proud and trodden down the poor for ages. Everywhere the rising order of things is putting each individual man in his right place as a member of the one great family and household of faith, truth, and humanity. Railways and telegraphs and steamships are indeed not Christian institutions. They may fall into the hands of men who use them for very unchristian purposes. But they are direct outgrowths of that intellectual and spiritual quickening which

Christianity has imparted to the human mind. They never would have been invented by a heathen people. Heathenism lives only in the past: it has no future. Two thousand years ago heathenism was talking and writing about a golden age and a silver age, both even then long gone by and never to return. Its great misfortune was to live in an age of iron. It did not then know, and it does not now know, that the age of iron is the age of progress and of power, of invention and of improvement of every kind. The world can get on much better without gold than it can without iron. Railways and steamships and telegraphs, printing presses and mowing machines, power looms and cotton gins, all belong to the age of iron in which heathenism has no hope.

When heathenism was high and mighty, towering in its pride of place over all the great nations of ancient times, it never lifted up the people, it never poured light upon the path of the wandering, it never brought rest to the weary or comfort to the sorrowing or hope to those whose dwelling was in the region of the shadow of death. When art and eloquence had reached the highest pitch of cultivation in ancient Athens, there were twenty slaves to one free man in the proud democracy which claimed to be the eye of Greece. When the Pharaohs in Egypt carved obelisks and built temples and tombs that are still the wonder of the world, the life of one of their human subjects was less sacred than the life of the beetle in the dunghills of the Nile. So, now, heathenism can only boast of temples and tombs and statues and shrines which were made a long time ago and which stand now as the blind, bewildering, stony dream of an age which never can come again and which, if it could come back, would only bring war and darkness and death unto the nations. The age of travel and of swift communication over all the earth, the age when thousands, millions run to and fro and gather knowledge of all things best worth knowing, is the Christian age, the age which is shedding its morning light in many lands and which will shine with ever-increasing brightness unto the perfect day.

II. — PROGRESS IN THE USEFUL ARTS.

ANOTHER sign of light in the East is progress in the mechanical and useful arts. The rapid diffusion of all tools, implements, inventions of everyday use, is doing much to bring the nations together and especially to lift up the common people of the oldest inhabited countries from ignorance and degradation. The great works of ancient times were done to glorify kings and conquerors, to gratify the pride and ambition of the princes and oppressors of mankind. One pyramid of Egypt exhausted the revenues of a whole kingdom and it cost the lives of a hundred thousand laborers. And when it was done it was worth nothing, either as a work of art or of utility. It did nothing to improve the outward condition or the personal character of a single one of the millions that dwelt in the valley of the Nile. It made a tomb for one dead Pharaoh, when his death would have been a blessing to multitudes had not another come after him just as proud, cruel, and oppressive as he had been. The Coliseum at Rome was built out of the spoils of conquered nations. It served no other purpose for centuries than to brutalize the population of the imperial city and hasten the downfall of the empire. The mighty walls and imperial palaces of Babylon were all built for one man, "for the house of his kingdom and for the honor of his majesty." The great stones of Baalbec were cut out of the mountain and moved across the plain to their places in the temple of Baal to gratify a despot rather than to worship the god. The beautiful Parthenon of Athens, the renowned Temple of Diana at Ephesus, were all expressions of an age when millions were made slaves that one man might be dreaded as a tyrant or worshiped as a god.

In India to-day the story is the same. The beautiful tomb, called the Taj Mahal, at Agra, at the sight of which enthusiastic travelers go into raptures of admiration, the great mosque and palace of Delhi, the cave temples of Elora and Elephanta, the grotesque towers or gopuras of Madura and Tinnevelly, represent enormous cost in labor and skill and time, but they never did anything to bring light and instruction and hope into the hearts and homes of the people. They lifted no burdens from the shoulders of the weary, they plucked no sting of sorrow from suffering hearts, they shed no light upon the pathway of the future for the parting souls of men. They were forced sacrifices to tyrants, who lived in lust and luxury, or, even worse, they were the willing offerings of debased and darkened worshipers to gods more base and brutal than themselves. So with the great works of heathen nations both in ancient and modern times. Their whole aim and influence were to perpetuate and glorify war, to strengthen oppression, to establish the thrones of iniquity, and to confirm the reign of darkness and superstition. To regard them with anything like feelings of admiration or pleasure, we must forget the object for which they were built and the miseries which they brought upon millions. In our most favorable judgment we must look upon them as splendid monuments of wasted toil and perverted art.

It is one of the hopeful signs of our time that the art, the skill, the invention of ingenious men are now directed to the improvement of the people, the increase of the comforts of life and the means of subsistence to all that dwell on the face of all the earth. The simplest and most common tool, instrument, or engine, which relieves human muscles and improves and multiplies the products of human industry, is a greater blessing to the world than Cleopatra's Needles or the mighty Coliseum at Rome. We wonder as we gaze at these great works of ancient and modern heathen nations; but we are glad to think that the world will never have any more of them. The world has now better uses for its men and its money than to build tombs costing millions for the burial of one despot, or to cut temples out of the solid mountain for the worship of demons. It is not for the want of wealth or skill or power that Christian nations in modern times do not repeat the architectural follies of ancient heathenism. Many single individuals in America, out of their own private resources, could surpass all the monumental structures of the Pharaohs and the Cæsars. Surely the man who originates a railway system, which supports a hundred thousand men and increases the wealth and comfort of millions, is deserving of more honor than the man who spends as much in building a tomb to perpetuate a name that had better be forgotten, or a temple for the worship of a god that has no existence.

I saw advertisements for the sale of the Waterbury watch, filling whole columns in newspapers and large spaces on the outer walls of buildings, all over India. I heard the hum of the American sewing machine in the byways and broad streets of Bombay and Calcutta and Rangoon. I saw American lamps for burning American petroleum hawked about the streets on wheelbarrows for sale in Yokohama and Tōkyō and Shanghai. I heard the clatter of the American typewriter in Che-Foo and Tientsin and Swatow and Aintab. I heard American dentistry praised as the best in the world, and I traveled with an American dentist who was on his way to practice his profession in the city of Peking. I afterwards received his printed circular, announcing his arrival in the great imperial capital and his readiness to extract the molars of mandarins or fill the cavities of Confucianists in the most approved style of American art.

I was glad that the genius and the skill and the invention of my countrymen were put before the people of the East in so practical and useful a form. I was much better pleased than I should have been if I had fallen into the company of an ingenious and enterprising Yankee, who had adopted the Chinese dress, shaven the front of his head, and cultivated a pigtail, and was proposing to teach the people of that land how to build temples and tombs and pagodas equal to those built in the best days of their fathers. We do not need to go to China to build pagodas or to decorate pottery or embroider silk or carve ivory. For two thousand years the Chinese have known and practiced all that better than we can teach them. But they do need somebody to teach them those homely and practical arts which relieve labor and lift up the poor out of poverty and increase the value of life to every man that lives. The building of temples and palaces and tombs, the adornment of vases and urns and ivory, has never made the people of the East rich or intelligent or happy. They have done all that for ages and in the most exquisite manner, and they are still ignorant and impoverished and degraded. They need men from the West to teach them the divine, the Christian art, which adorns and improves everything it touches — that divine, Christian truth, which re-creates and beautifies man himself in the image and after the pattern of Him who made man at the first. The Chinaman needs to learn that the restored image of God in the soul is the perfection of all beauty, outlasting temples and monuments made with human hands and growing brighter and more glorious forever.

I am well aware that some persons among us, who make high pretensions to fine taste and æsthetic sensibility, put a very low estimate upon the value of the practical arts. They speak of them as only vulgar, material, mercenary, fit only to stimulate the passion for money getting, and exalting the man who has made his millions above the man whose riches are of the mind and soul. Such critics would go into ecstasies of admiration over a peach-bloom vase which had cost twenty thousand dollars, or a piece of Satsuma ware which was said to be five hundred or a thousand years old. But I cannot forget that the eastern artists who made the pottery have lived in hovels and mud cabins and eaten rice for a thousand years. Their fine taste and their wonderful skill in making things not necessary for human use have not raised them out of the dust and degradation in which they were born. They have never devised, invented, or discovered any means or instruments by which the burdens on their shoulders could be lightened or the clouds upon their minds could be scattered.

In America the common mechanics who make watches and sewing machines and steam engines have elegant houses and liberal education and a great hope of better things for themselves and for all the world. They do not ask either to be pitied for their poverty or to be praised for their ingenuity. With God's help and a good education they can take care of themselves and let their work praise them. I have heard of a brilliant popular lecturer who talks with great freedom and volubility upon the beautiful decoration which the poor Japanese artist puts upon a vase or a teacup, and then exclaims, with well-affected astonishment and indignation, against the absurdity of sending missionaries to convert such ingenious men to Christianity. As if men who make fine patterns in pottery and cloisonné ware could be anything else than pure in heart and upright in life! And yet I have been told by a physician, who had lived and practiced his profession there many years, having more than a thousand patients pass under his eye in a week, that those ingenious and tasteful artists who make the most prized ornaments of our parlors and sleeping chambers are among the most loose and licentious people that he had ever seen or heard of on the face of the earth. With all their fine taste and wonderful susceptibility to the harmony of colors and the grace of form and outline, they are poor and ignorant and superstitious; they have all the vices which Paul charged upon the heathen in his day, and they have been living in that way ever since the apostle's time. Physicians ascribe the smallness of the stature and the slenderness of the frame of the Japanese to the enervating vices which the people have practiced for ages.

The American mechanic and day laborer who makes tools and machines and engines of practical utility and daily service in shop and house and field has a clean house and comfortable apartments to live in, books to read, and sources of daily information concerning all things said and done all over the earth. His wife is as intelligent as he is, and his children have the opportunity to fit themselves for the highest positions of honor and usefulness in the world. The young children of the eastern artist go naked; his wife digs up the field with a heavy mattock, or she gathers offal in the street to enrich the few rods of ground which she cultivates. The difference between the personal character and the outward life of the eastern artist and the American mechanic is due to the fact that the Japanese has taste without principle, sentiment without purity, a quick susceptibility to form and color, but deadness of conscience that lets him live like a beast and die as the brute dies. He gives his skill and the labor of his life to works that please the eye but never purify the heart. A houseful of his most beautiful and costly decorations would never make the owner virtuous or happy. All the beautiful paintings and statuary in all the churches and palaces of Italy never did as much to elevate the people and purify their lives as the spelling book and the New Testament. When the chief distinction of Rome was its treasures of art and it was the gathering place of artists from the whole world, it had more ignorance and superstition, more crimes of sensuality and violence, than any other city in Europe. When the Italian government took possession of the city and brought with it railways and telegraphs, schools and libraries; when the vile Jewish Ghetto was cleaned out and streets were straightened and old ruins gave place to comfortable houses, — artistic and sentimental people said that the dear old city had lost its charm, its sacred haunts were desecrated by modern improvements, its picturesque beggars and lazzaroni had learned to read and to wash themselves, and some of them had actually begun to work, and the whole city was becoming so disgustingly clean and decent that artists and antiquarians would soon have to give it up and go home!

Yet I am inclined to think that the homely, practical arts have more to do with the progress of the world and the elevation of the human race than the finest paintings and statuary of Europe or the most elaborate vases and embroideries of Japan. The work of the intelligent American mechanic, though despised by professional men of taste, is really of a higher order and is more elevating in its influence upon the laborer himself, because he is working for the common good of all mankind. The products of his skill and toil go to increase the resources upon which the whole family of man must depend for subsistence and instruction and improvement in the great age of the future, when all people shall be righteous and all labor shall receive its due reward. All the beautiful ware in the East might be sunk in the depths of the sea in a single night and nobody would go without a breakfast on that account the next morning; nobody would find a dark shadow upon his path for the day; nobody would find that the substantial means of human happiness and improvement were lessened in any considerable degree. Put a few of the plainest and commonest of the instruments and inventions in the useful arts out of existence in a single night and there would be cries of woe and looks of despair in millions of homes. The instantaneous destruction of all the friction matches in the world would bring greater distress upon the human family than the crash of all the picturesque pottery and the burning of all the pictures in all the galleries and palaces of Rome.

All inventions and arts which tend to the improvement and happiness of all classes and conditions of men have come from Christian nations; from men whose minds have been quickened into life by the divine impulse of Christian truth — men who have learned the worth and the divine descent of the individual man from the Bible — men who are animated by the great hope that a universal reign of righteousness and peace is to come on the earth. The Pyramids and the Coliseum, the Taj Mahal of Agra and the world-renowned temples of a thousand columns and a hundred thousand gods, the decorated vase and the delicate tracery of enameled and inlaid ware, have all come from people who were shut up to one narrow round of thought and life, and who had no hope of ever rising above the dead level of servitude and superstition into which they had been born.

And, therefore, I was glad when I saw American tramcars running in the streets of Tōkyō and the American windmill pumping water on the bluffs of Yokohama. I was glad when I heard the click of Connecticut clocks keeping good time for the Orientals, who are always late. California canned fruits and Oregon salmon and Boston baked beans in hotels all over the East made me think that home was not so very far away and that the time was fast coming when one might compass the globe and find himself at home and among his own people and hearing the familiar sounds of his mother tongue all the way. And the fact that America is so often represented in the East by the homely articles of practical and everyday use did not make me wish that my country had more works of fine art and more ruins and traditions of ancient time.

The Bartlett pear and the Jersey peach and the damson plum were introduced into China by a missionary who was the son of an American farmer. When a boy he learned to break colts and plant fruit trees and hold the plow in western New York. He went to China to plant the tree of life, where the thorns and briers of superstition and ignorance had usurped the ground for ages. When I saw him picking fruit from trees and vines which he had planted with his own hands in his garden, when I rode with him on a wheelbarrow of his own making through the streets of Che-Foo, with a horse twenty feet ahead to draw and a Chinaman before and behind to steady the vehicle, I thought him a good illustration of the typical American who lives in all climates, masters all trades, and gives an inspiration of hope to all people. The Japanese jinriksha, which runs in every city and country road of Japan, is the invention of an American missionary whose salary failed him in time of war and he was obliged to turn his hand to mechanical work for a while to secure the means of living. The Japanese persimmon, which grows in great abundance and makes a delicious fruit in California, was introduced by an American missionary who was out of health and who went to California to recover. He made thirteen thousand dollars out of persimmon planting, and then, having recovered his health and thinking that he could not afford to spend his time in making money, he went back to his chosen work in Japan. In such cases it was the earnest, practical, inventive genius of men educated in Christian lands that brought profit out of loss and turned a personal affliction to the advantage of thousands and millions. Such are the results which flow from the quickening of the human mind wherever Christianity prevails all over the world.

Under heathenism there is neither material nor intellectual progress towards a higher and better life. The art of decorating pottery and painting screens and working wonderfully in ivory had been in China for two thousand years, and the people still lived in mud houses, children went naked in the streets, and their parents worshiped the spirits of the air and the dragons of the deep. Women dug up the field for planting instead of turning the soil with the plow; men pulled grain up by the roots instead of reaping it with sickles or mowing it with scythes; children learned the ways of their fathers and plodded on in the journey of life under the same weary load of ignorance and superstition from generation to generation. Christianity comes bringing first the kingdom of heaven, and, as fast as that is received, all useful and practical arts and occupations follow in her train. Homes are brightened and beautified, minds are enlightened, hearts are cheered, and the people look up as if they saw the day of their redemption from the bondage of ages drawing nigh.

III. — ADVANCE IN SCIENTIFIC KNOWLEDGE.

THE wide and rapid diffusion of scientific knowledge is another sign of light dawning on the darkness of the East. Knowledge of the common facts and phenomena in the world about them is fast bringing the people of the East into the common life and faith of Christian nations. Science is fast taking away from them the horror and the mystery with which they had long been accustomed to look upon the great forms and forces of nature. As education advances, the gods of wind and thunder and rain, the gods of seas and earthquakes and famine, give place to the facts which they learn in the everyday lesson of the school and the common observation of the world. When the American astronomers set up their instruments for the observation of the transit of the planet Venus at Kōbe, it was an open proclamation to all the people of Japan that science is the same on all sides of the globe and that all people who would live by the laws of nature, the prime facts of the material world, should be united in faith and hope and duty. The Japanese were taught most effectually in that way that science is neither eastern nor western, but the same to all men and all ages, and extending as far as the clearest vision or the mightiest magnifying power of man can reach. The powers that rule in the heavens and in the earth, the forces that direct the course of the seasons and the productions of the earth and the means of subsistence to man and beast, are the same to all nations, through all ages. The main facts with which science has to do are the same all over the world, to all nations. Science is not theory, it is not speculation. Theory and speculation may stimulate and direct inquiry, but they are not science. Science is the knowledge of the great facts concerning the mode of the divine work in the world, what men call laws of nature, the putting forth of the infinite power in guiding and upholding all things from age to age. Just as far as the people of the East learn that great fact which lies at the foundation of all science, they must cease to be heathen. They may not be Christians, but they can no longer be heathen. It is the highest study and science of man to find out the work of God, whose goings forth through the whole creation are from of old, whose ways are everlasting. No system of heathenism in the world can retain its hold upon the minds of a people who understand and accept the simplest facts of physical science. There is an attempt just now on the part of educated young men in India to bring the two together. They accept science in the school and they submit to heathenism at home, and the two contradictory attempts at faith have a strong tendency towards utter unbelief.

The two greatest facts in physical science are light and gravitation. Nobody knows what either is, save that it is a mode of the manifestation of the one infinite Energy, the uncreated Mind, that rules all things. No matter how many theories men may devise to explain light and gravitation, the facts are the same to all nations, to all time. And men must live by them in Japan and China and India as well as in Europe and America. The pyramid and the pagoda must be built in compliance with the law of gravitation not less than the church steeple and the chimney of the manufactory. The sunlight, which lifts millions of tons of water from the ocean into the air, and the ranges of cold mountains, which condense the invisible vapor into clouds and rain to fill all the rivers and water the earth, work as willingly for the dwellers in the valley of the Mississippi and the Amazon as for the Chinaman, who thinks the sun shines only for him and that the mountains were made only to separate his own Central Flowery Kingdom from regions where the rest of mankind dwell in cold and darkness. The knowledge of these simple and common facts in elementary science is fast taking the ignorant conceit out of the minds of men in the East and bringing them to acknowledge their common relation to the rest of mankind. The most cultivated and thoughtful of the public men and all the children in the schools are learning that they belong to the same family with us, that we all alike have one Father in heaven, and the true life for us and them is to live in obedience to the same laws of nature which God has put into the world, and the same laws of duty which he has written with his own finger upon the living tablets of all hearts.

Science is not religion, but it must always agree with true religion because one is as much a fact as the other, one comes as truly from God as the other. Both teach obedience to the laws of life and duty which God has made.

Both inspire reverence and humility and worship. The true Christian looks with wonder and gratitude upon the lily of the valley which God has clothed with beauty surpassing the robes of kings, and upon the great mountains which God has raised up and set fast with his infinite power. And the true man of science looks with equal wonder and gratitude upon the manifestation of God in his works and his word.

As fast as the people of the East find that their long-established religion does not agree with the plainest facts of science and of everyday life, they conclude that theirs is no religion at all. It is only a mass of fables and superstitions that have no existence save in the perverted imaginations of men. So when the missionary from the West brings them a religion which harmonizes with all the laws of nature and all the most rational convictions of their own minds, they see beyond all doubt that the religion from the West must be true and from God, and that therefore it must be fitted equally for men of the East and of the West and for all mankind. The stone unsupported falls to the earth: and so the dumb stone confesses the power of gravitation, which is only one of the manifestations of the power of God. Then, again, if we turn to the spiritual world, we find that conscience approves the right and condemns the wrong, and so the living soul confesses the law of duty which God has written upon the hearts of all men. One is a fact of science, the other of religion. And one is just as truly a fact as the other. The germinating seed shoots up a tender stalk out of the dead earth, and so confesses the quickening power of the sunlight. The soul is lifted up to God in prayer, and so confesses the need of divine help and the hope of securing it in answer to its humble request. One is as much a fact as the other. The growing plant stretching towards the sun for life and strength and the living soul reaching forth to God for help are equally facts in the realm of science and faith.

The thoughtful people of India and China and Japan are beginning to see and to confess these great common facts of science and religion. Such are the reasonings which they adopt when they are disposed to reason at all. Thus they find that their old traditions and superstitions have no foundation in the reality of things about them in the world or in the rational convictions of their own minds. Sometimes, in their surprise and mortification at finding all the most sacred traditions and teachings of their fathers false, they rush from the extreme of believing without evidence, which is superstition, to the extreme of resisting all evidence, which is skepticism. But the more considerate and conscientious see that there is, there must be, a religion which comes from the same source as the laws of nature, and that religion must be in harmony with all the great facts of science that are in the world. They accept the religion of the Bible and the science of the Christian teacher because both are equally true. They take their place willingly and happily in the great family of man, because they have learned to believe that one supreme and everlasting God has made of one blood all nations of men to dwell on all the earth, and has so determined the times and the seasons and the boundaries of the habitations of all that they should equally and gladly seek after him. The most advanced science of modern times agrees with the special revelation of the Bible in bringing the East and the West to the same conclusion.

So our missionaries all over the East teach science and Christianity as both coming from the one infinite Source of truth and fitted to draw all men unto Him. Both agree in bringing forward the day when truth and righteousness shall prevail over superstition and ignorance and error, and the one great Father of all mankind shall be equally loved and obeyed in every land. The missionaries believe and teach that true science consists only in tracing the workmanship of God in the whole surrounding creation. And they also believe and teach that the revelation of God in the Bible is given to help us understand God's work wherever we can find it and enrich ourselves with the treasures of truth with which God has stored the whole creation. When the heathen accept that twofold teaching their land will yield its increase without recurrence of famine, their habitations will be filled with light, and their hearts will be lifted up with immortal hope.

IV. — DIFFUSION OF THE ENGLISH LANGUAGE.

ANOTHER sign of light dawning in the East and of growing unity among all nations is the rapid diffusion of the English language all over the world. I spent five months in India, traveling from Ceylon on the south to the utmost northern boundary of the great empire of two hundred and fifty millions. I passed eastward from Bombay to Calcutta, taking time to observe and inquire all the way. I left the country for Burmah with the full expectation that English will be the language of business and culture and education and public affairs in all India within fifty years. In a hundred years, nine tenths of the common people will make little use of any other tongue. Even now I was told that five millions of scholars are studying English in the schools at any one time, and as many millions more are learning it in the intercourse of trade and social life. In five years another class larger still will take the place of those now studying English in the schools. In any great city of India speak to any well-dressed native in English and the chances are that he will answer you back in the same tongue. I was riding in an ox-bandy in the streets of Madura. My coolie driver had forgotten where the station master had told him to take me, or perhaps he did not know when he was told. I could not talk with him any more than I could with the ox which he drove; but I saw a man in full native dress, carrying an umbrella, and having the air of an educated man. I asked him if he would kindly tell my coolie where I wanted to go, and I did not first ask him whether he could speak English. I took it for granted that he could, and he was apparently pleased to have me presume so much upon his good education. He gave the directions as I desired in the trilling accents of his native Tamil; and then in English as good as my own he expressed his pleasure in doing me the favor. My coolie driver turned the head of his ox the other way, and I was soon at the door of the house where I wished to go. At all leading hotels and business houses, stations on railways, and ticket offices of railways and steamboats; at all great public meetings in cities, and in the transaction of government business, the

English language is spoken, and in many cases it is well spoken too. I never heard a native use a slang word or any of the vulgarisms which we are apt to hear in our everyday speech, and which, very much to our shame, are sometimes admitted into our schoolbooks for children to read and sometimes are recited and declaimed on platforms by professional readers and students of oratory. The educated natives of India have not yet learned to read our slang or dialect stories and poems. They do not see the wit or the wisdom of such writings when they hear them read by others, and it is to be hoped that they never will.

In the public schools of Japan the English language is required to be taught by law. One needs no prophet's vision to foresee that English will be the ruling language in that island empire fifty years hence. The brightest and the most ambitious of the young men in the open ports and commercial cities of China are all eager to learn English as a passport to wealth, position, and employment. The best educated of the native preachers in all the East must needs learn to read English, or they will have no resources to fall back upon in their preparations for the pulpit. Constantinople has long been a babel of tongues. One of our venerable missionaries, who is himself a learned linguist and who has been heard preaching in twelve different languages within the same week, told me that he had heard twenty different languages spoken during a half-hour's walk in the streets of that great cosmopolitan city. And among them all English is fast coming into use as the fittest to be the universal medium of communication on that great highway of nations between East and West.

A brother of the king of Siam, who is trying to establish a system of popular education in his own country, asked me many questions about the organization of common schools in America. He invited me to visit a large government school which was kept within the enclosure of the royal palace for the sons of princes and nobles. I went, as he suggested, and the first class I found were reciting in English. I met a Siamese nobleman at his house on the riverside. He asked me half a dozen questions of the greatest difficulty about the books of Moses and the oldest records of the sacred Scriptures. In the course of the conversation he brought out a volume of Chambers' Encyclopædia to verify a statement which he had made. Judged by our standard of dress he was ragged, and his hands did not look as if they had touched clean water for many a day; but the strong spirit of inquiry which is going round the world had touched his dull mind and quickened it into life. The Gospel by Luke in English was lying on his table. In Robert College at Constantinople, in the Syrian College at Beirût, and the Batticotta College in Ceylon, in all the high schools and colleges in India, the students read, write, debate, declaim in English, just as students do in our own country.

All this indicates the dawning of a great light upon the dark lands of the East. We can hardly understand how poor and beggarly are all the resources of their native literature for the purpose of a modern practical education. Their languages have no moral or physical science; no chemistry, geography, history, mechanics, engineering; no anatomy, surgery, physiology, or materia medica; no international or constitutional law, no national records sifted from fable and the enormous exaggerations of eastern chroniclers, no polite literature purified from the indecent and monstrous tales of heathen gods and mythical heroes of human birth. Of course they have no theology which sets forth the character and the works of one infinite, all-wise, all-beneficent Creator and Governor of the universe. The youth who grow up in heathen lands with nothing but native literature to read, — if they can read at all, — nothing but heathen schools to teach them the first elements of knowledge, can have no idea of the world as it is or as it has been in the past. They can see nothing about them but one thick cloud of mystery too dark for the keenest eye to penetrate, one inextricable network of fable in which they strive in vain to find meaning or connection, inspiration to duty or assistance in work. As they grow up to manhood they still grope their way along the journey of life blind, and led by leaders as blind as themselves, and they find no outlook of life and hope at the end. The boy of India or China, well educated and well read only in the schools and literature of his native land, knows nothing of the shape or size of the earth, nothing of the planetary system or of the number or distance of the stars; nothing of the properties of light, electricity, magnetism; nothing of the arts which build steamships, railways, and telegraphs; nothing of the history of Europe or America; nothing reliable of the history of his own land. So far as he has any theory at all of the world and the things therein, it is founded in fable, it is overloaded with contradictions and absurdities, it begins and ends with mystery and darkness; and there is nothing in the literature of his native language which can lead him out of the labyrinth of confusion and contradiction to the light of day.

The English language, with all its immense accumulations of science, literature, history, poetry, biography, theology, opens upon such minds like a new revelation. Sometimes they are amazed and confounded in contemplation of the thick darkness in which they and their countrymen have wandered so long. Sometimes they are lifted up with vain conceit, and they press on in the pride of having escaped from their former ignorance and superstition until they are involved in the deeper darkness of utter unbelief. They find so many of their oldest and most sacred traditions utterly without foundation that they hastily conclude that there is nothing to believe, and so they embark upon the dreary and desolate ocean of skepticism. But wisdom is justified of her children. Truth will make its way, even though some use the knowledge which it communicates in the endeavor to defeat its mission and deny its power. The men of the East are but children as yet in the mastery and right use of the great facts of science and philosophy. It is not strange that some of them get bewildered and lose their heads when they find the door open and free admission into the treasures of thought and reasoning and investigation and theory with which the English language is stored. They will settle down to rational faith and practical work in the end. They will acquire habits of sound reasoning and patient investigation and rational faith in place of the old eastern habit of baseless assumption and dreary rhapsody and enormous exaggeration. Then the East and the West will join hands and move on with even step towards the great future of light and liberty which truth will bring in for the enjoyment of all nations.

I believe that the English language is the chosen and sacred medium which divine Providence will use to bring the eastern nations to right conceptions of truth and duty, right understanding of the world as it is and of the destiny which awaits man in the future. Its progress in our day is a clear indication of the coming of an age when all the nations shall have one language, one faith, and one law of duty and of love to God and to each other. Ingenious men are at work in the endeavor to invent a universal language which will serve as a medium of intercourse among all nations for all ages. It is all labor lost. The inventors are behind the time. The language is already found, not invented by men, but the natural outgrowth of the providential lead and teaching by which English-speaking people have encompassed the globe with their commerce and their colonies, their inventions and their literature, their missions and their power, their truth and their faith. The exhaustless physical forces of the earth are most completely in their hands; all arts, sciences, and machines are at their command; they are endowed with energy and vitality which enable them to live in every climate between the poles, and they must be foremost in bringing the great Christian age of the future which is every day drawing nearer and nearer.

Students and statisticians who have given especial attention to the subject say that a hundred years hence there will be seven hundred millions of people speaking the English language, and they will be scattered all over the globe; they will find homes and property and influence in every land. And in that day, if they retain their present tireless energy and practical sagacity, it will be easy for them to bring the remaining millions of men to the adoption of their speech and the acceptance of the one universal religion which has given English-speaking people their peculiar power in the past and their immortal hope for the future.

It is a great blessing to have the English language for our mother tongue, with all its stores of truth and sacred teaching for our inheritance. It is an immense advantage to have our earliest impressions, our taste and style and modes of speech drawn from the exhaustless treasure house of English undefiled, our beloved old English Bible. It is a blessing for which we can never be too thankful not to have had our youthful minds stored with the monstrous fables and the polluting tales which make up the mass of native popular literature in the East. And it becomes us to show our gratitude for our better speech by doing our best to keep it pure and to use it well. It is an awful shame for the man of genius to use the peculiar talent which God has given him in storing our popular literature with the coarse, vulgar, profane jests of the barroom, the street broil, the miner's tent, and the new settler's cabin. Let teachers and makers of schoolbooks never bring before their classes for exercise in reading and the cultivation of taste any composition which is not chaste in style, pure in thought, and fit for the approval of the most delicate and judicious minds. Let parents see to it that their children never defile their lips with the coarse jests and vulgarisms of which bad boys are proud and which bad men are too willing to teach. The French were once proud to say that theirs was the court language of Europe. Let it be our earnest effort to make ours fit to be the language of the court of heaven, fit to be the blessed speech of that land where nothing can enter that defileth or maketh a lie.

V. — THE KNOWLEDGE OF GOD.

THE greatest and the most distinctive sign of light dawning in the East is the fact that the people are beginning to know God, the true, the only living God, and Jesus Christ whom God hath sent. They are just waking up to the great discovery that there is one true and undefiled religion, equally fitted for all people, all lands, all time. It was the old heathen idea that every people might have a religion of their own, Hinduism for the Hindus, Buddhism for the Buddhists, Mohammedanism for the Mohammedans, and Christianity for the Christians. I asked an old Buddhist priest in the incomparable pagoda at Mandalay if he thought his religion true. He said, "Yes." Did he think it good? "Yes." I said, I am a traveler in search of good things and true to carry home to my country. Would he advise me to go back to America and tell my people that I had found a good and true religion in Burmah, and that they would do well to believe and adopt it as their own? "Oh, no," he said: he would not advise anything like that. He would not have the worshipers of Jesus change nor the worshipers of Gautama. Let each observe the religion into which he has been born. I met a company of Hindus at a sacred shrine near Batalagundu, in Southern India. I pointed to a rude stone image and asked if it were a god. They said, "Yes." Did they worship it? "Yes." What! worship that dead stone which was once in the field like other stones and now has been only carved a little and shaped and painted with vermilion on the head by the hands of a man? do you worship that? "Well, not exactly that; but the image helps us to worship the god that is in the stone." "Would you advise me to take an idol like that to America and tell my people that it will help them to become great and wise and happy if they will learn to worship the god in the stone?" "Oh, no; let the Christians be Christians and the Hindus, Hindus." They thought it kind and courteous so to speak. But never in India or Burmah, Siam or China, could I get a heathen to advise me to take his religion home with me and teach it to the people of America. They would even admit that it would be a calamity to the world if Christians should abandon Christianity and adopt any form of heathenism that exists or ever has existed in all time.

I spoke to a heathen audience of two hundred and fifty men at Nagercoil, in the principality of the maharajah of Travancore. They made no disguise of their faith. They wore the marks of devotion to their gods on their foreheads, arms, and breasts. I stated the characteristics of a religion which would be equally good for all people, all lands, all time. I did not quote the Bible, I did not name Christianity. The meeting had been organized after our manner by the choice of a chairman, and many leading persons of the city occupied the platform. A heathen judge presided, with the sacred ashes on his forehead as a sign of his devotion to the god Siva. At the close of the lecture he said to me that he knew I meant Christianity all the time, for that was the only religion in the world to which my definitions would apply, and that in fact was the only universal religion. I said, "Would you make that statement to this assembly of your countrymen?" "Oh, no," he said; "I could not. If I did, I should lose everything I have in the world. I should become an outcast. My office and my income would be taken from me, my wife and my children, my dearest friends and neighbors would desert and despise me, and the lowest of the people would think me only worthy to be scorned and spit upon." "But is not the true religion, the religion which makes men children of God and heirs of immortality, worth suffering for? The best things we have in America have cost somebody a great deal, but we think them worth all the cost." "Ah, that is the way you Christians talk. Perhaps my great-grandchildren will say as much. I cannot."

Nevertheless many thousands, who are still heathen like that courteous and kindly judge, are coming slowly to the conviction that there is one and only one true religion; not one for the East and another for the West, not one for the Hindus and another for the English and the Americans, but one for all people that dwell on the face of all the earth; and that religion is Christianity. They see, as they never saw till Christian teachers came with the Bible in their hands, that there must be one infinite, almighty, and everlasting God, and the test of the true and universal religion must be that it sets God first, highest, and best in all things, and it brings man — every man, however high or lowly be his condition — into direct, living, personal connection with that sole, infinite, eternal God. That is the greatest thought that has yet found its way into the eastern mind — every man responsible personally and for everything to God, every man cared for kindly and tenderly by the one almighty Father, every man lifted up with the hope of glory and life everlasting. That one thought sweeps away at once all the idolatries, mythologies, fables of the sacred books, traditions, and sacrifices of the great eastern world. When the heathen have given up all that, they must become utter unbelievers or they must become Christians. They must take it for granted that the one true religion, being a revelation from the one true and eternal God, must be consistent with all the laws, forces, and phenomena of the material world, for God made the world and all things therein. If he speaks to man in the revelation of the Christian Scriptures, that written word must agree with all the revelations of God in the world which he has created and which he upholds and governs every moment. And besides, the revelation of God must answer the deepest necessities of the human soul, it must set before every man the noblest and the truest life, it must hold out in hope and bring within the reach of all the most glorious and everlasting destiny. Anything less than that would not be a fit message from the almighty Father to his beloved and yet wandering child.

Neither the Brahmin nor the Buddhist nor the Confucianist ever finds anything like that in his sacred books. They find many things absurd, irrational, impossible, but one infinite, eternal Mind, whose will is the one infinite force of the universe, they never find. So when the one great idea of the God of the Bible dawns upon them it is as if a new sun of life and truth and love had been shot into the chaos of their old mythologies and contradictions. The heathen are very slow to take in the one first great truth of the Christian Scriptures; but when they do grasp it they hold it fast. They know little about the doubts and perplexities which trouble even Christians in our country. Having once received the Bible as God's word and Christ as a divine Saviour, they rest in that faith with a peace and a firmness that delight and surprise the Christian teachers who have taught them the way of hope and salvation. So light is dawning slowly upon the great darkness of the ancient East, and the full day is as sure to come as God is to keep his promise to them that trust his word and labor for the coming of his kingdom in all the world.

XVI.

VIEWS FROM CAR WINDOWS.

IT is not easy to give specific directions beforehand to one who is about starting on a long journey in the East and who wishes to bring home a fair impression of the aspects of the country and the condition of the people. Probably the best way for him to get well informed will be to look carefully at everything seen, listen closely to everything said, ask countless questions, but give few opinions of his own, go through the land in its utmost extent and see as much as possible of the outdoor life of the people, make the acquaintance of foreigners who have lived longest in the country and who are there for every diversity of purpose, get them to tell everything they know and to express every opinion which they entertain, and then form theories and draw conclusions after getting home. For one experiment in that line of observation let me suppose myself to be passing leisurely through the country by rail, seeing everything I can from the car windows, making a little stop here and there in towns and villages in order to get closer to the people and make a few guesses at their home life and thought. I will make no attempt at critical inquiry, and I will spend few words in moralizing upon things seen by myself or things said by others. So far as I can I will give the reader the use of my eyes in looking at things seen by the way, and the experience of my sensations in traveling a hundred miles by rail in a tropical country.

Early in the morning we start out from Madura, a city of seventy-five thousand inhabitants in Southern India, and we design to go a hundred miles and more to take a look at Tinnevelly, Trevandrum, and Tuticorin, where the railway system of India begins and runs northward to Peshawar, at the opening of the Khyber Pass, some three thousand miles from the starting point. We load ourselves and light baggage into an ox-bandy for transportation to the station. The carriage is a small cart with a cover of matting and the body resting on the axle without springs. It has no seats inside or out for passengers, it is not high enough to stand up in, and it has neither door nor window to look out of. We make ourselves as comfortable as we can on the board bottom without asking for straw or unrolling our quilts for bedding, for the distance is but a mile to the station and the bed of the street is smooth, without pavement or curbstone. The coolie driver mounts the shafts and gives a twist to the tail of the ox as a sign for starting. The animal knows very well what that means, for he has felt it many times before, and he knows better than to wait for whip or spur. He starts off at a rolling, lubberly trot, and the coolie calls out to the people in the crowded street to take care of themselves lest they should be run down by the rapid motion of his lumbering team. But the people mind little what he says, for they know well that there is not the least danger that anybody will be run over by fast driving in a Hindu city.

The broad street is full of people — coolies bearing burdens and moving swiftly along with bare feet and panting breath; women, with arms, ears, nose, ankles, and feet covered with jewelry, gathering the droppings of the cattle to carry home to dry for fuel; children entirely naked; women with a child astride upon the shoulder or hip; oxen with painted horns; buffaloes plastered with mud; idlers sitting in groups on the ground; shopmen drawing strange figures with chalk on the mud walls or the smooth bed of the street at their doors; here and there a native gentleman carrying a white umbrella, wearing a white turban of many folds upon his head, clothed with a white tunic that comes down halfway between the knee and the black and bare feet. He carries palm slips prepared for writing in his hand and a writing stylus in his girdle. He has the air of office and authority, and the naked urchins lying in the dust of the street get up and give way for him to pass. The elephants of the great temple have been out for a morning walk and they pass us with their long, lumbering step on the way home. They are followed by half a dozen sannyasis, or fakirs, covered with filth and displaying their indecent and disgusting appearance in the street as an act of morning devotion. Grain lies here and there in thin beds upon the ground to dry, and wild birds come down to help themselves with nobody to drive them away. Rooks and crows are looking about the shops for a breakfast, and a stray ox makes his way through the crowd as if he were his own master.

These glimpses at eastern life in the street may be caught from the opening of the bandy behind, and much more might be seen of people and of manners if the covering were off. But we reach the station in due time; I pay the coolie two annas (about six cents), the usual fare for the ride, and he takes it with the same look of oppressed and injured innocence which the Hindus wear whether treated harshly or kindly.

The station master, as everywhere else in India, speaks English, and I ask him any questions I please with the certainty of receiving a prompt and intelligent answer. I pay three rupees and eight annas, about a dollar and sixteen cents, for a ticket to Tinnevelly, one hundred and eighteen miles. It is second class, and yet the price seems low. I enter the car assigned me by the station master when the train arrives, and when I look about me the fare seems high. There is a closet, and cloth-covered seats long enough to lie down upon at full length, and hanging shelves to stow away bundles and baggage, and the whole compartment is given up to two persons all the way. And again I say we have got all we paid for, and the man who complains of the cost must be hard to please in India or anywhere else. We start off, and after we have felt the monotonous rumble of the carriages over the rough road for three hours, and have run less than forty miles and have stopped long enough at each station to drop off cars and make up a new train, we review our estimate of prices and accommodations, and we say it is cheap traveling for the coolie, who rides third class for a third of a cent a mile, and it is high fare for the English official who takes the first class and pays twice as much as we do in the second and goes no faster and gets no better accommodations than we, except that his cushions are a trifle softer and he is more likely to have the whole of his car to himself.

Views from the car windows, as we move on at a leisurely rate, give a fair impression of the general character of the country and the occupations of the people all over India. Cactus hedges, with their sharp-pointed and ugly-looking leaves, saw-toothed and spear-shaped, line the road on each side all the way. The plant sometimes shoots up a tall central stalk and puts forth blossoms that have as little beauty as the leaves. When full-grown it makes a fence which cattle will not attempt to jump over or break through. And indeed a regiment of soldiers would need to send forward a company of sappers and miners with axe and spade to clear the way before they could safely attempt to pass. I have ridden along the crooked and narrow paths of Palestine between rows of these cactus hedges, and I needed to keep careful watch lest the sharp spines should pierce through my boots or give an unnecessary spur to my frisky horse. Where the soil is rich and the hedge grows luxuriantly, it covers a broad space, and demands more every year till at last the railway companies are obliged to root it up and put wire in its place.

Paddy fields stretch away long distances to the right and left of the road, greatly relieving the bare and houseless aspect of the country. Here and there men and women are wading or creeping half knee-deep in mud and water between the rows of rice, pulling up the weeds. When the grain is pretty well grown the laborers crouch so low at their work that they cannot be seen, except when one is looking in the direction of the rows. Low, narrow, crooked ridges, made like dams to stop the flow of water, divide the fields one from another, and they serve as roads or paths for the people who have occasion to travel across the country. An English engineer tells me that he has traveled a great many miles on these narrow, uneven footways between the fields when making his surveys of the country. A Chinese missionary told me that in his tours about the province of Shantung he had completed forty miles a day traveling in a wheelbarrow on one of these ridges with a horse before to pull and a coolie behind to keep the one wheel in place on the narrow track. The rice plants look like green grass or half-grown wheat, some of it pale yellow as if growing on thin soil; other plats are dark green and very luxuriant.

The ground is prepared for sowing rice by covering it with water, and then men and buffaloes go in with bare feet and rude plows or harrows and stir up the soil until it is made into thick mud, sticky as putty and black as the beasts and men that work it into a suitable state for the seed to sprout and send up its slender blade of green into the hot air. The rice is sown first in a small bed and very thickly. When it is eight or ten inches high it is pulled up by the roots, tied in small bundles, and carried away to be set in rows across the larger fields. When first transplanted it looks very thin and not likely to grow. But continual supplies of water and the hot sunshine bring it forward rapidly, and soon it covers the whole field with the dark green which goes before the russet brown of the harvest. In all Southern India and the flat lands along the great rivers of China and the picturesque hollows among the hills in Japan, the rice grounds are always pretty to look at; but I should not want one of its broad fields of mud and water to look out upon from my door. I should expect that chills and fever would be the price to be paid for the enjoyment of the view. The rice grounds in Japan have a very tasteful and garden-like appearance, and they give diversity and beauty to the landscapes of hill and valley with which the island empire abounds.

When the soil in southern India becomes dry and sandy, as it often does, cotton takes the place of rice; but the crop, as seen from the car windows, looks like a pasture of low brushwood growing wild. The small white floss just breaking out of the dry pod would make a stranger think that a flock of sheep had been running among the bushes and that the sharp and hooked ends of the twigs had caught little wisps of their wool. The amount of cotton is so small that laborers must work very cheaply to make it pay for the picking, to say nothing of the cost of cultivation.

Broad level carriage roads are made all through the more thickly settled portions of India. They are all the result of English rule. Under the dominion of the native princes a royal road would sometimes be made for a king or a conqueror to pass, but nothing was done to supply convenient and serviceable highways for the people. The great roads can be seen from the car windows, stretching away for long distances across the plains and sometimes climbing the hills to the cool retreats where the officials of government find a summer home. They are lined on both sides with rows of great wide-spreading banyan, acacia, and tamarind trees, and they make a very pleasant break in the landscape, which would be bare and dreary without them. The main trunk of the banyan is sometimes so large as to take three men with outstretched arms to measure its girth. The main branches drop down fibers or rootlets no bigger than a fish line, and they grow twenty or thirty feet through the air in search of the ground. When at last they reach the earth they send out roots, and the small cord grows into a trunk, and the branch from which it springs draws new support and nourishment from the stem, and sometimes it becomes bigger and stronger than the original tree from which it sprang. Along the highways coolies are required to keep the descending lines cut off several feet before they reach the ground, lest the tree should become so large as to cover the whole breadth of the road and cut off all travel. Large bundles of the filaments, that have been thus cut off and intercepted in their growth, may be seen hanging in the air under the parent tree and waiting for a chance to fasten themselves in the earth. One tree left to itself would make a forest by the continued extension of its branches. One growing in the Botanical Garden at Calcutta is already large enough to shelter an army of ten thousand men, and it is still shooting out stems and branches in every direction.

The branches of the broad banyan are the favorite haunt of snakes and monkeys, and the two tribes of tenants are constantly contending for the right of occupancy. The snakes are still and sleepy; the monkeys chatter and caper from branch to branch as if they never slept, and the happiest time for them is when they can run the most freely and make the most noise. The only time when they agree by common consent to be still is when they see a cobra coiled around a branch and taking a noonday nap. They enter into council as to what shall be done, talking more with looks and gestures than with tongues. At the conclusion one of the bravest and strongest is delegated to act for the rest. Proceeding upon his perilous commission the appointed monkey steals up silently till he comes within grasping distance, then he seizes the deadly foe by the throat, drags him down to the earth, and grinds his head upon a stone till his teeth and jaws are all worn away and the fangs destroyed. Then the triumphant monkey throws the conquered and toothless cobra to be made sport of by the children of the tribe, while the older members of the council set up a chorus of joy and laughter.

The native people suffer all manner of tricks and depredations from the mischievous monkeys rather than molest their tormentors or even drive them away from their gardens or markets. It would be thought a great crime to put one of them to death; and I never met with but one foreigner even who would confess that he had killed one of the four-handed climbers of the houses and the trees; and he said that the dying creature set up such a piteous and human wail after receiving the death shot that he felt as if he had committed murder, and he resolved never to fire upon the cunning and tricky tribe again. As you drive along the highways under the overarching trees, the monkeys run across from side to side overhead on the green branches, they stare down upon you, and chatter as if laughing at your funny appearance and wondering where such a queer-looking monkey as yourself could have come from. They imitate your motions and make strange grimaces to each other, and then burst out in a loud chorus of jabbering voices as if they never saw such a ridiculous sight before. If you are so much of a philosopher as to see your great ancestors in the long-tailed race it may take a little of the conceit out of your wisdom to see that these funny creatures are so much like yourself and yet are brutes. Nevertheless the long rides over the level roads and under the archways of the banyans would be more wearisome and lonely if it were not for the queer and cunning occupants of the treetops who look down and laugh at you as you go by.

The mango, with its rounded and thick-leaved top, is a conspicuous figure in every landscape of Southern India. When the trees stand at considerable distance from each other in their natural growth they have the appearance of a park or pleasure ground, realizing the oriental idea of a paradise. They seem to have been purposely set at diverse and irregular intervals to avoid the uniformity of straight lines or the artificial air of cornfields and peach orchards planted in rows for the convenience of cultivation. The fruit of the mango tree is about three inches long, yellow, oval, and flattened down at the sides. Inside is a large stone shaped like the stone of a prune but much larger. The best method of eating the mango is as diverse and as much disputed as the method of eating an orange in Florida. The most delicate and æsthetic way is to remove a slip from each flattened side with a sharp knife, as deep as the stone and as long as the fruit, and then scrape the yellow and juicy pulp from the cutting with a spoon. In that way you get no stain upon your face or fingers and you do not endanger the white linen of the friend who sits nearest to you at table. The more luxurious method is to remove the yellow jacket of the fruit with a sharp knife, leaving only a small ring at each end for a handle, and then with head bent low over the plate and both hands grasping the mango, proceed to business as men eat boiled corn from the cob in New England homes. When the rhapsody of appetite is over the face of the eater is not presentable to the company, and he needs a liberal use of the finger bowl before proceeding to the next course or shaking hands with a new guest. When a modest man with a full beard adopts this style, he prefers to eat his mangoes alone.

The mangosteen mingles with the palm and the mango in clothing the nakedness of the landscape through which the railroads run, and it is sometimes called the king fruit of all the East. I should be disposed to dispute its title to the crown, and yet I think it worthy of high honor among the trees. The fruit is about the size and shape of a medium Baldwin apple. It is dark brown outside and it has a rind a third of an inch in thickness. The covering has a dark yellow, very astringent juice, which puckers the lip that touches it and blackens the knife which is used in cutting it. It is said to be good as a mordant in causing colors to set, and it has a great amount of tannin matter. It has a sharp, stinging, bitter taste. Inside of the brown covering, packed in the neatest form, are five or six lobes of white, clean, exceedingly pleasant fruit, so juicy and limpid, so nicely flavored and finely packed that one wonders how such a shiny and precious deposit of nectar could find its way through such a bitter and astringent covering. The same root and tree and stem, the same sun and rain and soil minister nourishment to the bitter bark and the globe of sweetness packed inside. What mysterious chemistry can make the change in the common elements of earth and water and air as they pass through the living trunk and stem of the tree it is beyond our science to discover.

So sometimes, once in a thousand or a million times, we find a man with all manner of roughness and bitterness of manners and hardness of speech; but when we make our way into the inner sanctuary of his heart we find sweetness of temper, kindliness of disposition, good feeling towards everybody. But we do not think such a character one to be commended to the young nor to be admired in those who have it. Men are not apt to be better than they look to be. If the gentle angel of charity and peace keeps the house of the heart, the cheery voice of his singing will be heard by the passer-by, and the light of hope which keeps burning in the sanctuary of the soul will shine out through the windows of the eye and the features of the face to show wanderers the way of peace and the path home. The mangosteen is beautiful to look upon and pleasant to the taste, but it is not the best model for the makeup of character in the everyday man. The mysterious chemistry which stores up sweetness in the heart of the brown and bitter shell cannot be relied upon to enrich in the same silent manner the sanctuary of the soul with the more precious jewels of gentleness and peace. In the case of the man, the outer casket must be in harmony with the treasure which it keeps.

Another look through the car windows discovers a new shade upon the landscape. Vast fields of the castor-oil bean plant, with its broad and rounded leaves, relieve the eye when it has become wearied for many miles by the sameness of rice and cotton and cactus hedge. It would seem as if all the doctors and druggists in the world might be supplied with castor oil from the fields which are given to the cultivation of the plant in Southern India alone. The plant grows twenty or thirty feet high, puts on a purple tint towards the top, and surrounds itself with a coronal of bluish-green leaves, which are broad enough to shield the head of the coolie from the sun. It does not improve our appetite for the cakes and patties, which are brought out for sale at every station, when we are told that castor oil is an important article among the supplies for a native kitchen. Tall grass or reeds, with fine, flossy plumes, offset the broad leaves of the oil plant, and both are relieved by a kind of grain which puts forth a great abundance of yellow blossoms and reminds one who has traveled in the Holy Land of the mustard which grows on the plains of Akka and Gennesaret high as the head of the horseman and giving shelter and nesting places to millions of small birds among its branches.

Most of the country which we see from the car windows, as we pass along the chief lines of railway, is under cultivation, and yet it surprises the traveler from America to see how large a portion of the land in this thickly-settled country of India produces nothing for the support of man or beast. English statistics say that only half of the whole country is under cultivation. And then the half which is cultivated might be made to produce five times as much as is now raised if it were in the hands of an intelligent and energetic people. Native plows only scratch the surface two or three inches deep; there is little or no effort to return to the soil what has been taken from it by the crop; water and the sun are the only fertilizers, and famine follows inevitably when the heat is excessive and the rain fails at the same time. It takes four laborers in India to do the work which is easily done by one in America; the wages paid the four is less than half we pay to one, so that the means of living are eight times in favor of the American. In India the poor have nothing laid up in store against the day of want, and the rich are little inclined to give of their abundance to relieve the starving. The high-caste man counts it no part of his religion and he feels no prompting of his conscience to comfort the sorrow or to relieve the suffering of the low-caste man, whose fate is written on his forehead and who must live and die by the changeless law of his being. Under English rule great improvements have been made in agriculture; the products of the field, poor as they are now, are much greater than they were in the days of the great moguls; in time of drought and famine relief is provided for many thousands whom princes and Brahmins would have left to starve.

All the broad highways in the neighborhood of cities and between villages are lined with natives walking and carrying loads on their heads. Some are men, with a plow or a bundle of grass or a fagot of sticks for their burden; some are women carrying a few vegetables which they have raised in their gardens to sell at the bazar; some are children ten or twelve years of age, each with a small baby strapped upon the back, the baby's head bobbing about at every step of the child carrier, the baby often asleep with its face turned directly to the blazing sun, and then again just as often the eyes of the infant will be wide open and staring at the fierce light with a gaze which ought to make it blind, as it often does. The prevalence of ophthalmia and all manner of diseases of the eyes in the East is easily accounted for by this constant exposure of young and old to the intense light of the sun with no covering to protect the sight. The Hindu turban, with its many folds, is a good cover for the head, but it affords no shade for the eyes; the Mohammedan fez protects neither; it is especially out of place in every land where Mohammedanism prevails, and it is useless and ugly everywhere. It is a very strange thing that the natives of these eastern countries have been living here for thousands of years, suffering unutterable things from the intense light and heat, and have never devised any broad-brimmed covering for the head as a shelter from the sun. The genius of invention and adaptation is utterly wanting among the millions who bow towards Mecca in prayer or repeat the names of Rama and Buddha in their devout meditations. In cities and villages we see the blind everywhere, led by the hand or making their way with a walking-stick through the crowded street or moaning and stumbling along the public road; and nobody among the natives seems to suspect that half the blindness might be prevented by the adoption of some suitable covering for the head. When any such covering is recommended by wiser men from the West, they can only say that the customs of their ancestors forbid all change and they would rather go blind than break caste. Ismail Pasha, as I saw him in 1870, was dressed in European style throughout, except the red and rimless fez on his head. I asked why he did not wear some kind of head covering with a rim for the protection of the eyes from the sun; and I was told that it would cost him his crown as viceroy of Egypt if he should appear in public with a hat on his head in place of the fez, for the people would understand that he had renounced Mohammedanism and they would rise in revolution. The streets of Cairo and Alexandria and all the villages of Egypt are thronged with red-eyed children who are fast going blind or becoming subjects of chronic ophthalmia, just because the custom of the country forbids them to wear any fitting shelter from the fierce light of the sun. I have looked over the heads of thousands of people, filling the street from side to side in a Chinese city, without seeing a single head wearing any kind of covering at all. In such a country I was not surprised to find many blind. I found a man at Hankow who had traveled three hundred miles on foot with a boy for a guide because the man himself was stone blind when he first came to the mission hospital to be cured. The surgeon succeeded in his operation upon one eye and then told the man to go home and come again at the end of some months, and then if all was right he would try upon the other eye. When I was there the man had come back for the second operation and he had brought forty-eight other men with him, all seeking help from the wonderful physician who could give sight to the blind. Anywhere in China it would be easy to get together many times forty-eight persons who need to have some healing operation upon the eyes.

Looking from the car windows in Southern India we see large herds of black cattle and buffaloes wandering about the pasture lands and the jungles. The buffaloes are often very large, with only a slight sprinkle of coarse hair and strangely twisted and crinkled horns. Sometimes the horns hang down on each side of the head like the ram's, and like his are coiled about in a ring. Sometimes they stand out from the head nearly in a straight line with each other and measuring four feet from tip to tip. Sometimes one stands up and the other points as directly down to the ground. Their long, pointed horns, red nostrils, and keen eyes make them look dangerous; but the great lubberly animals are very kind and docile, obeying their masters very meekly and permitting a little child to lead them. They are much more manageable than their smaller, red-eyed, and vicious-tempered brethren of the same name that wallow in the pools of the Pontine marshes in Italy. Occasionally one is of a light brown or yellowish color, looking like an albino among his black brethren or like the so-called white elephant of Siam among the black monsters that pile ship timber at Rangoon and carry princes in Bangkok. The buffaloes are all exceedingly fond of mud and water. They delight to lie down in the tanks and mud puddles and leave nothing but the nose out. The coolies gratify them by plastering them all over with mud or permitting them to lie down in the pools and cool themselves in the heat of the day.

We often see buffaloes in the fields preparing the ground for planting rice. They wade about with the men in the soft mud, both are equally black and besmeared, and it is not always apparent which is master, the man or the beast; but both belong to the country, and no landscape in Southern India would be complete without them. The buffaloes and the oxen have undoubtedly been here as long as the men, and they have done their part towards making the country habitable for their masters. They draw carts and bandys, they travel at a trot on the highways, they tread out the grain on the threshing floor, they supply milk for the family and fire for the cooking, they behave themselves peaceably in towns, and they relieve the landscape in the country. India without buffaloes would be like Lapland without reindeer.

On some roads the public bandy takes the place of a post coach and runs all night with relays of oxen instead of horses. The driver sits on the shafts and twists the tails of his team instead of applying the whip or goad. The bulky beasts move along the road at a slow, swinging trot from sunset to sunrise, and at break of day I have found myself fifty miles away from the starting place of the evening before. The passengers lie at full length inside on a bedding of hay or straw, and the jolt of the heavy wheels over the broken stone of the macadam road makes very little difference with the amount of sleep secured by an old Indian traveler. The oxen are changed every six miles, and the tail-twisting torture of the coolie driver is not so severe as to require attention from the Society for the Prevention of Cruelty to Animals.

We often see women washing their dark faces and their bright-colored cloths in the tanks and pools where the water is already so muddy as to be of the same color with the traveled road or the plowed field. Yet the faces look brighter for the bath and the cloths come out cleaner than they went in. They take great pains in washing their long, coarse, black hair. They plunge their heads under water again and again, wring out their hair, and then repeat the dip in the muddy bath a dozen times over. Sometimes we see them going through the process of purification at a well. In that case they draw bucketful after bucketful and one performs the kind office of dashing it on the head of the other. They are so dark already that one cannot easily tell whether they are whiter after the washing than before. When they have poured fifteen or twenty bucketfuls over the head or have gone as many times under water in the tank or river and they think their tresses are sufficiently clean, they apply a large amount of oil, either cocoanut or castor, making the hair glisten in the sun like a newly polished boot. After that profuse anointing they will on no account let a drop of water touch the head till the time comes for another bath and a new anointing with oil. When they go out in the rain they are very careful to shelter the head from the falling drops by carrying a palm leaf for an umbrella; but they do not mind wetting other parts of the body or the small amount of clothing that they wear. It is to be said in behalf of the native woman of India that, when she has made her toilet in her own way and wrapt her one cloth of seven yards' length about her in graceful folds, she looks very shiny and trim, and she may well seem very charming and attractive in the eyes of the other sex as well as her own. It is a constant surprise to western people that the native woman of the East can seem so well dressed when she has nothing on save one plain breadth of cloth.

When the train arrives at a station there is always a great

number of people waiting to get aboard or to see who arrives or to break the monotony of their dull and passive existence by the sight of something that has life and power. They are apt to talk loud, very fast, and make a great deal of noise. The station master moves about among them as if he were in authority over all the multitude, as in fact he is. He comes out with a pen lodged above the ear and with paper in hand as if he were ready to write down the names of all that come and take note of all that go. He assigns passengers to the car they are to ride in, takes the tickets of those who stop, and gives the signal for the train to start. If you have bought a ticket for the second class and the seats in that are all taken when the train arrives and you happen to be a respectable looking stranger, he will put you into the first class and tell you to make yourself comfortable there until there is a vacancy in the second; but that means, Stay where you are to the end of your journey.

The station master is every way a more important man in the railway management than the conductor or guard. Nobody has the right to start or stop without leave from him. He speaks English and gives all needed information to natives and foreigners alike. He keeps the station grounds ornamented with flowers and vines. The bright purple, gold, and flame-colored blossoms make a striking offset to the picturesque costumes of the station loungers, who move about in white, red, green, and scarlet garments, as well as in the dusky livery of the sun concealed by no garments at all. Beggars mingle with the crowd and hold up their mutilated hands or their distorted limbs to move the pity of the passengers. They get a small coin now and then from a native, but the European always says it is given not from pity for the poor but in hope that the gift will make merit for the giver and secure him a better lot in the next world. This is one of the contradictions of the native faith. In all the superstitious fears which they entertain and in all the acts of worship which they perform they assume that the gods, or the powers of the unseen world — whatever they may be — are hostile to man; are busy, for the most part, in bringing evil upon the human family. Yet it is assumed that a deed of kindness, done to relieve the miseries which the gods themselves have sent, will bring great reward to the doer in the other world over which the gods preside. So it is not pity to the poor and suffering, but profit for himself that moves the doer of the kindly act.

Whenever the train stops coolies come alongside of the cars bringing water for the thirsty passengers to drink. They carry a cup, but they set it on the end of a long rod lest they should defile it with their touch and thus make it unfit for a higher class to drink from. In other cases the man who wishes to drink makes a dish, or trough, by putting his two hands together; the coolie pours the water into the hollow, and the conscientious man drinks with nothing but his own hands to defile the draught. Near every village there are private wells and a public tank to supply water for the whole town. The tank is seldom what we would call a reservoir, with walls built up around and a deep excavation inside to hold the water. It is more nearly what we would call a pond, made by throwing a dam across a stream or a dry hollow between hills so that the water in the season of the great rains may be kept from running off. As one passes through the country by rail, the tanks look in the distance just like ponds or, in some cases, like large lakes many miles around, and holding water through all the dry season sufficient to supply the fields and gardens of thousands of people.

Everywhere natives may be seen at all hours of the day bathing and washing clothes in the large tanks, and they do that all the same when it is only a small basin to supply water for the huts of a single village. Often there is a small tank filled with the most filthy water in connection with a sacred temple. Offerings of various kinds of fruit and flowers are thrown into it and left there to rot, till the sight and smell of the water become intolerable to anybody but devout Hindus; and yet they are all the more eager to drink the water and pour it over their bodies just because it is so filthy. The sacred tanks connected with the temples of Madura and Benares and Calcutta are as bad in look and smell as the water settled in the hollow of a barnyard or the sewage from the worst parts of a great city; and yet the Hindus dip themselves in such filth to make their souls and bodies clean in the sight of the unclean gods that preside over the temples and homes of the people. Tanks, or reservoirs, in Southern India often cover many square miles of country. Beautiful park-like trees grow on the margin. Soon after the rains, when the basins are full, thousands of trees may be seen standing in the water itself. Their shining green leaves and their shadows on the surface and their reflection from the depths of the broad lake beautify a landscape which would otherwise be barren and naked.

The water from the wells is drawn up in buckets of skin attached to a rope which is sometimes a hundred feet long. An inclined plane, equal in length to the depth of the well, is dug in the earth, and oxen descend the plane pulling at the rope till the skin bucket comes to the top and empties itself into the trough. Then the oxen are made to back up to the mouth of the well again and thus be in readiness for another draw. The oxen are sometimes kindly covered with an awning to break the direct rays of the sun. A coolie driver keeps them at their work, and he goes up and down the inclined plane every time the bucket rises from the well and goes back for another draught. Little rivulets run off among the fields and gardens from the well, and the fresh water makes everything green where it goes. The well is a fountain of life to the garden and the field. When the tanks are empty and the wells dry up, the half-grown grain is changed to stubble and famine looks in at the peasant's door.

When the rainy season is past, the river beds are mostly bare. The train passes a bridge a half mile in length, supported by trestlework and covering a broad channel down which the flood, gathered from the plains and the distant hills, comes rushing for a few weeks on its way to the sea. The flood soon subsides and leaves a broad, winding stretch of sand and pebbles glittering in the sun for the rest of the year. What water remains lies in pools or creeps along in a shallow rivulet as if to hold the right of way for the mighty river which is sure to come in its appointed season and gladden the hearts of millions who wait for the sound of the flood and the shining of the sun on the waters as wanderers in the desert wait for the day.

Men and women come down to the pools or the low-lying stream to wash clothes and dry them on the hot sand. Sometimes an acre of ground will be covered with white and red and scarlet and blue garments. A well-dressed Hindu woman wears but one piece of cloth. It is six or eight yards long and one yard and a quarter wide. She wraps it in graceful folds about her waist, shoulders, and body, lets it hang loose in some parts and tucks it in tight here and there to keep it in place, and she is neatly and becomingly dressed without the use of pin, button, hook, or string. When fifty such full dresses are stretched out at full length on the sand to dry, they cover ground enough for the camp of a company of soldiers. The Hindus are not characteristically a cheerful or a light-hearted people. The nearest approach to a scene of life and youthful laughter that I ever saw in India was a group of a hundred women washing by the riverside when the water was low and the main bed of the stream was bare. It is quite refreshing to the weary traveler as he wakes up and looks out of the car window in the morning upon the bright colors on the sand of the river bed and he hears the merry voices of the women mingled with the rumble of the train as it moves slowly over the bridge.

It would detract from the picturesque appearance of people in the East if they were to adopt our close-fitting style of dress. But the change must come if the East is ever to take its place with the West in the grand march of civilization and the varied practical industries of life. The fez and the turban, the showy girdle, and the long, loose robe appear well in a holiday show, but they are not fit for active work in the fields and workshops of the world. In the city of Cairo I received many calls from a famous Maronite dragoman, who proposed to conduct us through the desert on the way to Jerusalem. He always came dressed in flowing robes, wide and showy girdle, and the brilliant Damascus khefiyeh. When we were well out in the desert he appeared in high boots, trowsers, and a roundabout coat.

"How is this, El Hany," said I, "that you have laid aside your Oriental dress now that we are here among Bedouins?"

"Ah," said he, "loose robes and wide girdles will do for the city and days of leisure, but when we have hard and active work to do we must lay aside petticoats."

Mornings are not all beautiful and glorious in the East, as they have been represented by poets who dreamed under the misty mantle of German fog or the murky shroud of London smoke. And yet to one who has tossed and tumbled all night on the board bed of an Indian sleeping car, the breaking of the day is always bright and the lifting of the veil of night from the landscape seems like a new creation. The rising light falls in golden waves upon the green foliage of the banyan and the bo trees that line the public roads and stretch far away across the plain to the distant hills. The sky above is blue and dark, but it never shows the transparency, the ethereal brightness of an October morning in our New England clime. The broad-leaved plants about the stations, the plantains and bananas, mingled with castors and crotons and cocoanut palm and palmyras, shine with dewdrops, as if they had been especially decked and adorned by the night to greet the stranger at his coming. A hundred flowerpots stand about the station in tasteful order with leaf plants cut and scalloped and spotted and pointed, in every variety of form and color, yellow and brown and scarlet and crimson and purple, and all newly sprinkled with fresh water to bring out the hue and form of each; and all tell the awakened sleeper that the dull and somber world of the great East has not been left forgotten or unadorned by the one all-creating Mind.

Crows and rooks and magpies lend their voices to swell the music of the morning, and they make up in noise what is wanting in harmony to welcome the rising day. The gentle cooing of the doves in the tops of the palms answers back to the merry twitter and the mischievous pranks of the sparrows that dart in and out of the car windows and claim a part of the passenger's lunch as he moves away on the train. All these, not seen clearly enough to be criticized in hastily passing along, make the mornings in the East seem beautiful to the traveler who has spent the long night in heat and dust and weariness. He is glad to have any change which will break the monotonous rumble of the train and divert his attention from his giddy head and his aching limbs. To him the air of the morning seems so fresh and invigorating, everything so full of life and beauty, the whole creation so full of voices lifted up in praise and gladness, that for the moment he forgets the darkness of the land and the sad lot of the people. The rude villagers, coming out of their mud cabins to stare at the train, the naked children sitting astride on the hips or shoulders of their mothers, the little brown babies strapped to the backs of older children, and their heads bobbing about at every step of the carrier, the black-haired coolies eating rice with their fingers under the mango tree — all seem for the moment to the traveler to be happy in the morning sun. In the glow of his gratitude for the new day he does not dare to ask the presumptuous question why all these millions and millions of the great East, for ages and ages, have been born to such a sad condition in this world and to so little hope for anything better in the future.

But the day moves on and the lot of the people looks darker when they are seen in the clear light crowding about the station in their "untended raggedness," or creeping across the fields to hide themselves from the fierce heat in their mud cabins. Then he asks with deeper earnestness how these ages of darkness, which still brood over all the East, can be made to give place to light: how can this worship of dead gods under every green tree and beside every filthy tank be made to give place to the worship of the one only living and true God, who made the heavens and the earth and all things therein? And then, looking across the fields to the city which he is approaching on the other side of the river, he sees the spire of the Christian church and a schoolhouse under the palms and dark-skinned boys with turbaned heads and sandaled feet and close-girt loins, gathering, with satchels over their shoulders and moving along with the light step and the loud laugh of western boys; and then he hums to himself the dear old hymn, —

> "The morning light is breaking,
> The darkness disappears."

The light *is* breaking in all the darkened East, and it

foreruns a brighter day than the people of those lands have seen in all their history. When it reaches the high noon of cloudless splendor the people of that great continent of ignorance and superstition will wonder that their fathers wandered so long in darkness and never saw the clear shining of the full day. Then the cave temples and the grotesque gopuras and the vast halls of a thousand columns and the colossal images of sleeping gods will stand in ruins to show how great were the sacrifices that men offered in support of religions that darkened the minds and debased the hearts of the worshipers. Then too the millions of a free, prosperous, and happy people will bear grateful witness to the truth of Christ which has set them free from the bondage of ages and the blindness of ignorance and superstition.

XVII.

THE POWER OF THE GOSPEL.

MISSIONARIES in the South Pacific Ocean went to islands inhabited by people so savage and ferocious that the boat's crew of a man-of-war did not dare to come near the shore for fear they would be clubbed and eaten by cannibals. The messengers of peace were obliged to leap into the sea and swim to land with the Bible bound to the top of their head. They found people living in the "stone age," which wise men say was finished some hundreds of thousands of years ago. Their hatchets and hammers, their knives and bowls and basins, were all made of stone. Among a population of twenty thousand there was not a yard of cloth, there was not a path that a stranger could travel without peril to his life, there was not a cabin or a cave where he could sleep with any surety that he would not be murdered before morning. Children were put to death by their own parents, the aged and the helpless were buried alive or cast into the sea, the shipwrecked mariner, thrown upon the shore, was killed and eaten; if a newborn child were permitted to live, a priest was sent for to pray over him that he might grow up to be a murderer and an adulterer, a liar, a thief, and a libertine, glorying in the commission of every crime. Beautiful valleys were set with stones to mark the spot where men had been killed and eaten to make a holy day feast for chiefs and warriors. When men met each other on solitary paths or public assemblies, they looked upon each other as the lion looks upon his prey, impatient to gratify the universal craving for human flesh. A man was esteemed great and honorable in proportion to the number of men that he had killed and provided for cannibal feasts.

With those wild beasts of men the messengers of peace and good will made their home. Some died of hardship and hunger, some were murdered; others came eagerly and promptly to fill their place. With ceaseless toil and study they found their way into the dark minds of those brutal men. They gathered up the words of their meager and unspiritual language, and they made it express the thoughts of God and the highest truths of faith and culture. They put an end to feasts on human flesh, they made it safe for strangers to travel wherever they pleased, they caused the people to put away lying and licentiousness, cruelty and robbery and murder. At the end of twenty-five years there was not a cannibal or a heathen on the whole group. The people now build houses and wear clothes suitable to the climate. They learn and observe the principles of justice and purity and truth. Homes are peaceful and sacred, children are trained up in the ways of righteousness, the sick, the aged, and the infirm are tenderly cared for, the people live together as one brotherhood, children of the one almighty and all-loving Father in heaven.

Now a company of shipwrecked mariners is thrown upon the shore, and one of the number climbs a hill, slowly and cautiously, and looking down into a quiet valley he sees the spire of a church and, near by, the roof of a schoolhouse among the palms, and he hears the voices of children at play about the door, and he shouts with wild and unutterable joy to his companions at the foot of the hill: "We are safe! The missionary is among these people, and now we have nothing to fear." His companions respond to the shout with equal joy. They had feared that their fate would be to furnish forth a cannibal feast for the barbarous natives, and now they are sure of a welcome from men who have learned the story of the Good Samaritan and are trying to follow the steps of Him who went about doing good. They make their way to the first village, and are received with open arms; they are distributed among the cottages; for months they are provided with the best that the island can give. And when at last a passing ship is hailed and boats come off to take the rescued mariners aboard, they go with gratitude in their hearts and with the blessing of converted cannibals to gladden their passage home. So, too, elsewhere in the great Pacific, the gospel has repeated its miracles of power and of love, making new creatures of men in whom the first elements of humanity seemed to have become utterly extinct. The head-hunting Dyak and the man-eating Fijian and the war-loving Maori have learned the beatitudes of mercy and peace, and they have made their island homes seem like gardens of God in the sea, and have exposed themselves to torture and martyrdom while carrying the message of life to other islands which are still filled with the habitations of cruelty.

There is only one power in this world which has ever accomplished such a change in the life and character of a brutal and grossly savage people. Law, secular education, science, philosophy, civilization, moral culture, fine art, free speech, social reform, have never done it. Nothing but the divine constraint of the love of Christ, as set forth in the simple story of the gospel, has ever lifted men out of such awful depths of degradation, and given them the mastery of the brutal appetites and passions that had cast them down. No class of social reformers or secular teachers has ever gone to a lonely island of the ocean, found a people living in the utmost barbarity and ignorance, and raised them out of that condition to a high degree of order and civilization by teaching science and the natural laws of life without any reference to the gospel of Christ. When they have done so in one instance, it will be soon enough to question the peculiar fitness and power of Christianity to do the best thing for the improvement of the human family and to bring in a reign of righteousness and peace on the earth.

Philosophers studied the Hottentot to find the connecting link between the man and the monkey. The Christian Boers of South Africa did not think that their Hottentot slaves were fit subjects for Christian sympathy or instruction. Charles Darwin thought the Fuegians were still in a transition state, and not yet sufficiently developed into humanity to comprehend the simplest lessons of spiritual truth. He thought it would be as vain and foolish to attempt to Christianize them as it would be to attempt to teach dumb animals to speak. I have heard intelligent and professional men in our own country declare with great earnestness and every appearance of sincerity that negroes have no souls. Within the remembrance of many now living, the highest judicial authority in this land of America solemnly declared that black men have no rights that white men are bound to respect, and that, too, under a constitution the freest and the most equitable of any ever adopted by any people on the face of the earth. And yet, under the instruction and personal influence of the missionary, the Hottentot has made the great discovery that he is a man made in God's image, and destined, like his white brother, to live forever. The Fuegian, half naked and shivering in his land of fire, has shown such a capacity for spiritual truth and has developed so much manhood under gospel teaching that Darwin honorably confessed that the missionary was right, and himself mistaken, in his judgment of the man, and Darwin testified the sincerity of his confession by contributing to the support of the Christian teaching, which, he said, was better than his philosophy. The negro is slowly rising to equal rank with scholars and statesmen, and we can already see the dawn of the day when the Dark Continent shall be filled with light.

When the missionary first made his way through the mountains into the Bechuana country in South Africa, there was not a tool or an implement or a fabric of foreign manufacture in the whole land. The veteran pioneer, in preaching the gospel to those dark tribes, saw the day when two hundred and fifty thousand dollars' worth of English goods were required every year to answer the demands of civilization which the work of the missionary had created. The Zulu sold his children for cattle; he slept in a kraal, which was little better than a dog kennel; he crept out in the morning and sought to stay his hunger by living, like the jackal, on the leavings of the lion, or by feeding, like the vulture, upon carrion. Messengers of the gospel, ambassadors of the Prince of Peace, forerunners of light and civilization, came from beyond the sea, settled down among that dark people, worked their way slowly into their language and their life, and now the Zulu lives in framed houses, wears the garments of civilization, reads books and supports schools and churches, sends to Boston for tools, furniture, and agricultural implements, and stands ready to take his place in the forward march of nations.

The Kaffir child in South Africa was nursed and kept alive in infancy by his mother. When he grew up to strong manhood he made that mother carry burdens for him like a pack-horse, he set her to dig up the ground with a heavy mattock like a slave. When she became prematurely old, and could no longer carry burdens for her son, he exposed her in the forest or on the hillside to be devoured by lions. Now that that unnatural son has heard the story of the love of Jesus, his cruel and ungrateful heart has been melted into tenderness by the voice which said from the cross, "Son, behold thy mother." The Christian Kaffir takes his mother to his own home and cares for her tenderly in her old age, as she cared for him in his infancy. Science, philosophy, secular education, social reform, never did such things for an ignorant and brutal savage. Nothing but the divine and new-creating spirit of the gospel has ever been able to cast out the demons of cruelty and ingratitude and lust from the hearts of such men, and bring them to the practice of gentleness and purity and love.

The Turkish government sent an army of six thousand

men to exterminate a city of robbers in Northern Syria. An American missionary got the news of what was going on, and he rode over the wild Taurus Mountains to offer himself as a mediator between the city and the soldiers. He requested the Turkish commander to stay proceedings until he could go into the city and confer with the headmen. The request was granted simply because it came from a missionary and an American, who could be safely trusted by Moslems, when they did not dare to trust each other. The missionary went into the doomed city, saw the headmen, gave them such advice as he thought best, and secured from them the pledges that he wanted. He then went back and said to the Turkish officer that he would be responsible, personally, for the peace and good order of the people whose lives were threatened. The Turkish commander accepted the guaranty of the missionary's word and withdrew his troops without firing a gun or burning a house. Probably there was not a Mohammedan in all the empire whose solemn oath the Turkish general would have thought it safe to trust. He took the bare word of the Christian missionary, and left the doomed city to rest in peace. From that day to this the wild mountaineers have called the missionary their savior. A second and a third time he came to their help, once when they were dying of a disease brought upon them by their own vices, and once when many of them were made houseless by a fire kindled by their own carelessness and permitted to rage by their own passive submission to destiny. Afterwards, whenever the missionary rode over the barren mountains to have a little talk with that wild and turbulent people, every man who met him would be his bodyguard and every house he entered in the city of robbers was his sanctuary. Whatever Moslems and heathen may say against missionaries, they all trust them with unquestioning confidence in time of need, and they all believe that a divine power goes with the disciples of Jesus for their protection and to give them success in the work they have come to do in their Master's name.

The United States government brought seventy Indians to St. Augustine, in Florida, as prisoners of war. Every one of them had taken the life of men, most of them more than once. They were handcuffed and chained together and soldiers kept guard over them with loaded arms. They wore long hair, they had wampum and war paint on, and their wild looks, as they passed along the streets, made the spectators shudder and glad to see that they were chained. They were imprisoned in the old Fort Marion and a Christian captain was put in charge of the gates and walls and of all inside. The Indians never shed a tear of sorrow, they never laughed, they never sighed or groaned under pain, they never feared the face of men. They would not condescend to speak a word of English in the hearing of their guard, although some of them knew the language well. They thought it a dishonor to touch hand to any useful work; they would rather be burned alive than have it said that they were willing to wear the white man's dress or to go the white man's road. And yet, with quiet energy, with invincible courage, with enlightened common sense, that Christian captain commanded the fear, won the confidence, and melted the hearts of that terrible band of stolid, cruel, and implacable men. I have sat at table and knelt in prayer and joined in sacred song with those fierce warriors whose hands had been red with blood and who had been proud to wear the scalps of murdered men. I have met with them in the casemate of the fort when the voices, which had been trained to the war whoop, were lifted up in praise so loud and strong that the arches trembled as if under the recoil of heavy guns.

The power which wrought that mighty change in those bloody men is the same as that which goes with the missionary of the cross to the ends of the earth. And that one experiment of the Christian captain at St. Augustine, in touching the hearts of his savage prisoners with the love of Christ, has done more than any other one thing towards teaching our government to adopt a new and better policy than force in settling the Indian question. Soldiers and civilians worked at the problem for a hundred years, and the only sign of success was extermination, and that at a fearful outlay of men and money. It cost a million dollars and the lives of twenty-five white men to kill one Indian. When the missionary went out to succeed the soldier, and the Bible took the place of bullets, fourteen fifteenths of the money and all of the men were saved, and the Indian too. The government, with millions of money and any needed number of soldiers at command, utterly failed in rescuing the Indian from the degradation of savage life and in clearing the national name from dishonor. The presence of one Christian missionary has been a better guaranty of peace among warlike tribes than a thousand soldiers under the command of the best leader that ever led the battle or the chase. Under the influence of Christian instruction, the roving hunter has settled down to a quiet life and permanent habitations, the bloodthirsty brave has abandoned the warpath and taken to the plow, the lodge and the wigwam have given place to the comfortable home, the schoolhouse, and the church, and the unprotected traveler comes and goes in peace and safety, where, a few years ago, the stagecoach carried a battery of arms for self-defense, and the daring hunter was more watchful to avoid the warpath of the red men than to find the track of the buffalo.

We find an Island Empire of thirty-eight millions of people in the far East. They are quick in movement, versatile in art, courteous in manners, but they are reduced in stature and weakened in physical force by the long practice of low and wasting vices. They make the impression on the traveler, who does not understand their language and who stays among them only for a little while, that they are kind and gentle, and that their homes must be habitations of purity and peace. But a physician who has lived among them for half a lifetime, and who has ministered to thousands of patients every year, says they are the most dissolute people that he has ever seen or heard of on the face of the earth. They have been governed by one unbroken dynasty of kings for twenty-five hundred years. With an outward show of courtesy and civility they disguise a deep, inbred treachery and cruelty. They have no pity for the suffering, no gentleness for the feeble, no tenderness for children. The newborn child is kept alive or thrown into a pit and buried, just as the caprice or the convenience of the parents may prompt at the time of the birth. They are reckless of life, they account suicide honorable, they build monuments to murderers, they are destitute of humanity, their punishments are too horrible and revolting to be described. Their religion, their traditions, their superstitions, their social usages, have come down to them from ages so remote, they have been wrought into the history and character of the people so closely, they have been confirmed and strengthened and consecrated by such long and uniform practice, that it would seem impossible for such a people to change. There is no precedent in all history to warrant us in saying that such a people will cast off the chains which have bound them for ages and start out to take their place among the progressive nations of the earth, with new faith, new science, new education, new customs, new arts, and all in one generation. Yet that is just what Japan is doing in our day. The people seem to have stepped right out of the dark ages of heathenism and superstition into the full light of the nineteenth century. And the one all-quickening, new-creating power which has given new life to that people is the power which goes with the missionary on his errand of mercy and peace to the ends of the earth. It is the power which makes the cannibal a Christian, raises up the Hottentot to the highest rank of humanity, makes the Fuegian a surprise to the philosopher and a living monument of God's mercy to the world.

The history of Japan for the last twenty-five years seems, more nearly than anything else we find in history, a fulfillment of the ancient word of prophecy, "A nation shall be born in a day." A despotic government has voluntarily proclaimed a constitution; the right of suffrage has been given to the people; provision has been made for assembling two houses of legislation with concurrent power and responsibility in enacting laws; carriage roads have been built; railways, telegraphs, and telephones have been brought into use; public schools, normal schools, schools for education in law and medicine, colleges and a national university have been established; the best educational books have been imported by the thousand and put to use; daily newspapers have been started and supported; banks, post office, coinage, lines of steamships, exchanges, laboratories, philosophical apparatus, tools, engines for all manner of work in the arts, have been introduced; the costume of western nations has been adopted by the leading classes, and, last and most significant of all merely secular changes, it is required by law that the English language shall be taught in the public schools of the empire.

All this sudden and sweeping revolution in public law, order, and education in Japan has sprung from the belief on the part of leading men in that land that the religion of the gospel is the greatest power on this earth for lifting up decayed nations and giving new life and hope to millions that have long wandered in darkness. The thinking and inquiring men of Japan believe that the source of the great power and riches and prosperity of Christian nations is their religion, their adherence to the instructions and the leadership of Jesus Christ. They believe that the Christian nations, alone, have any hope for the future, and they themselves must give place to the advance of the one universal religion of the gospel, if they are to have any part or standing in the great future, the glorious age, for the coming of which the Christians are working and praying in every land. They have come to the conclusion that Christianity has quickened mind, stimulated invention, increased power, multiplied riches, advanced science, improved education, intensified effort, awakened hope and high expectation, among all western nations. Aback of steamships, telegraphs, railways, telephones, aback of all inventions in the arts, all discoveries in science, all advance in civilization, they see Christianity. They believe that the supreme power that rules in the world is on the side of the men who believe in the Christian's Book and are faithful in the endeavor to lead the Christian life. If they are to join the onward march of the nations to a great future, they think they must believe in that Book and become Christians too. They say that often ignorantly, because they have been bewildered and half blinded by the great light which has broken in upon them from the West, and they are like Peter on the mount of the transfiguration speaking and yet not knowing what to say. The great hope of missionaries in Japan is that when the bewilderment of sudden waking from centuries of sleep has passed the people of that land, like the disciples on the mount, will see no man, no human policy or philosophy, as the source of their new life, but Jesus only. Of one thing many of their leading men are already quite sure. They are ready to give up their despotic government, their gross idolatry, their popular traditions and sacred customs, and even their national language, if they can only get the power, the progress, the grand advance, and the great hope which the gospel gives to all who receive its word and walk in its light. Many of the foremost men of Japan, who have no desire or expectation of becoming Christians themselves, still think it would be greatly for the good of the country if the common people should receive the gospel and conform their lives to its instructions.

This has all come to pass in our day: not directly before our eyes, but within twenty days of our doors and within reach of direct and constant communication. Our own personal friends and brethren are in the midst of this most rapid and mighty social, intellectual, and moral revolution which has ever taken place in all history. They know whereof they affirm when they tell us what God is doing by their hands in the Sunrise Kingdom of the great sea. They themselves are no small part of the living force which has shaken one of the oldest and mightiest of the strongholds of heathenism to its foundation. They need to be wise men, cautious and conservative, prudent and well balanced in judgment, not to be carried away from their sound discretion by the swiftness and the force of the current with which everything about them is moving forward. They are very well aware that reaction and opposition, delay and difficulty, may come, and their hopes in some instances may be disappointed. But the most cautious and conservative feel sure that the new day which has dawned so swiftly upon the Sunrise Kingdom will not go backward but will advance to the high and cloudless noon. When one goes over to the Island Empire and stays a few weeks, moving about among the missionaries and the people and catching the spirit which is breathing the new life of a new and mighty youth into an old and dying empire, and then comes home and tells the story to Christians in his own country, and they listen with little emotion and much incredulity, it seems to him that the word of the Lord by the ancient prophet had come true again, "I will work a work in your days, which ye will not believe, though it be told you."

But it must be believed. The Church in this land of America will drift far away from the foundations of practical faith if we do not believe in the mighty works which Christ is doing in our day in Japan. The signs and wonders which exalted Capernaum and Chorazin to heaven in point of privilege, and for rejecting which the favored cities of the sea were doomed, were not greater confirmations of the divine mission of the Son of God than the lifting of a hundred cities and a thousand villages and millions of people into the light which shines to guide all wanderers into the way of peace. That work is just as real and satisfying a demonstration of the infinite power and divine authority which confirm His Word and His Commission to His Church, as it would be if He should appear in visible person and raise the dead to life before our eyes. It is more blessed to believe in the work wrought by His Spirit and Word upon the living souls of redeemed men than it would be to believe in the reality of His risen body when he stood before us in the open light of day for all eyes to see. This wonderful movement in Japan is the last grand confirmation of the divine authority of the great missionary enterprise, demonstrating, for the encouragement of the Church and for the confusion of all skeptics, that the gospel of the Son of God has power to raise up and quicken nations that have been held under the dominion of darkness and death long as the mummy of the Pharaohs has slept in the catacombs of the Nile.

This work in Japan is as strange and mighty as that done by the gospel in Fiji and Samoa, in Papua and Hawaii, in Kaffirland and Patagonia, and it gives brighter promise of better days to come and greater things in the future. The people themselves are not a mere handful, like the decaying islanders of the great sea or the savage tribes of the barbarous shore. They are more in number than the population of the British Isles. A thousand years ago they were more civilized than the inhabitants of Britain, and now, like their nearest and more numerous neighbors on the continent, they are full of irrepressible and invulnerable life. They are more inventive, more adaptable, more inquisitive than the Chinese. Since they have been touched by the all-quickening spirit of Christianity they are ready to go wherever the light leads, they are eager to grasp the results of all research and discovery and invention, they step forward, uncalled, to take their place in the grand march of the nations toward a reign of righteousness and peace on the earth. Let them be converted to Christianity and they will strengthen millions of their neighbors in the populous East. Let them be enlightened in Christian science and trained in Christian virtues and fired with Christian faith and they will kindle beacon lights on the hilltops of their island home bright enough for three hundred millions of the Chinese to see on the table-lands of Mongolia, on the cloudy mountains where the Yang-tse-Kiang takes its rise, and on all the plains of the eighteen provinces from the Tiger's mouth of Canton to the crumbling towers of the Great Wall on the north.

If this strange and mighty work of God in Japan does

not touch the hearts and enkindle the hopes of Christians in America, it must be because they have forgotten the words which Christ spoke when he gave his Church the great commission to disciple all the nations. But that final word of the ascending Christ, who gives us all our hope, must not be forgotten. It were better that the most skillful hand among us should forget its cunning, the most eloquent tongue should be struck with palsy, than that we should only stand far off and gaze and wonder at God's great work among the heathen, and have no part in that work ourselves, feel no joy in its advance, put forth no effort, give no gift, make no sacrifice to carry it on.

XVIII.

WORK ALREADY DONE.

A WIDE and rapid glance at the most diverse portions of the great missionary field of the world will discover abundant evidence that the gospel is now, not less than of old, the power of God unto the confutation of all human error and folly, the good news of God for all the discouraged and heartbroken, the revelation of God in Christ bringing life and immortality to light. It is God's chosen instrumentality for the accomplishment of all that needs first and most to be done to bring in the reign of righteousness and peace in all the earth. Wherever men have gone forth into the field, relying upon Christ's promise, evermore unto the end, to give his presence to cheer and his power to help, they have been successful in gathering in the harvests of eternal life. Success has sometimes been long delayed, and then it has come with the suddenness of the descent of the Spirit on the day of Pentecost, and with a fullness that confirmed the feeblest faith and filled the weary laborers with unspeakable joy. The work is no longer a doubtful experiment, but a glowing and glorious success, never more so than now. No new explorer, however ardent and daring, can henceforth find a field harder than any ever found and made to yield fruit before. No difficulties can arise greater than any which have been already met and overcome. No race or tribe of men can be found in depths of ignorance and superstition deeper and darker than the state from which fallen men have already been lifted up to the light of life and clothed in the seemly garments of righteousness and peace.

Full provision has been made for a united and swift advance by every division of God's host, in every quarter of the contested field. The preparatory work has cost long years of waiting and the heartsickness of deferred hope; it has cost hard labor and much suffering, millions of money and many precious lives. The lessons of experience have been dearly bought, but they have proved to be worth more than the cost. On the greater part of the missionary field the preparatory work has been done, and well done. Often it has been hard to hold an advanced post, and harder still to move on and win more. But, taking the whole field as one, there has been little giving up of ground once gained, no surrender to superior force, no proposal to close the campaign with anything less than conquest, no suppression of the Christian war cry, "The whole world for Christ!"

Every zone of the earth has been explored and inhabited by missionaries of the cross. They have gone to their fields of toil as truly in the name of the divine Master as John went to Patmos and Paul went to Rome. They have learned to live in all extremes of heat and cold, rain and sunshine, plenty and famine. Everywhere they have been the forerunners of civilization, they have created the call for commerce, they have been the first to make education possible and necessary among rude tribes and the lowest races of men. Missionaries have adapted themselves to every means of subsistence, every mode of travel, every style of dress, every kind of habitation, every form of practical work. In the time of need, the missionary has been the architect, building the church, the college, or the private home, and adapting each to the climate of the country and the habits of the people whom he was lifting up to a better civilization and higher life. When the pestilence came and brooded over the land and thousands died and millions mourned, the missionary has been the physician, visiting the sick, comforting the sorrowing, burying the dead. When famine followed the drouth and the plague, and the skeletons of the starving people lined the public roads and lay unburied in the streets of the villages, the missionary has been the philanthropist, feeding the hungry and clothing the naked and bringing back hope to a despairing population. When war has broken out between tribes and nations, and towns and fields have been ravaged by contending forces, the missionary has been the mediator passing between hostile ranks and restoring peace. When fire has desolated cities and villages, or flood has swept away the harvest, the missionary has been the first to bring help from afar to rebuild the burnt houses and repair the waste in the fields.

Missionaries have made their movable home with the roving tribe and they have dwelt in cities with men of settled habitations. Their labor has always been to lift up the poor and the degraded from the dust and the dunghill into bright homes and habitations of order and purity and peace. When circumstances required they have lived as they could for a time, to get nearest to the people whom they were seeking to save. The rounded kraal of the

Zulu, the cave house of Shensi, the abandoned temple of Buddha, the ice cabin of Greenland and Labrador, the mud-walled dwellings of Lebanon and Syria, the empty tomb of the Nile, the deserted palace of Indian princes, the marble courts of the Turkish pasha, the paper-partitioned apartments of Japan, the common shelter for men and cattle in Armenia, and the underground hiding from the heat in Mosul and Bagdad, have all been taken for resting places by missionaries in our day; they have been brightened with Christian hope and blessed with Christian prayer and praise.

Wherever missionaries have gone, the most ignorant and degraded people have been inspired to build better homes for themselves and provide better things for their children. When the cleansing power of the divine Word has come upon the spirit, it has made the people wash away the filthiness of the flesh, clothe themselves in clean and becoming garments, put away all envy and evil communication out of their mouths, and dwell together like brethren in peace and unity. Our brethren living among the heathen have endured their rude manners, their vile habits, and gross speech without sending home pitiful lamentations for the loss of the delights of civilization and the sympathy of cultivated society. Every day they have been wearied and sickened by the sight and sound and smell of things that cannot be named in decent speech. Every day their spirits have been stirred within them, as was Paul's at Athens, by seeing the great mass of the people about them wholly given to idolatry. They say they could not live and breathe in the foul and reeking atmosphere of heathenism, if they did not feel that they were doing something to scatter the darkness and bring in the healthful and purifying light of day. Christian women, educated in our country, with all the sensitiveness of the most refined and cultivated society, go through the streets of heathen cities every day, seeing the unutterable abominations of the people, and yet not giving way to nervous prostration, not crying out with wild exclamations of disgust and horror, maintaining a firm, serene, well-balanced mind, and doing all that as a life work, asking no release and only glad to live long in the land for whose redemption they have given themselves at the call of the Master.

With all the depressing influences that weigh down the Christian exiles in the strange land, they hold the post of duty which has been assigned them by the Prince and Captain of salvation. They keep the fire of faith burning in their hearts and they are not prone to speak words of discouragement and despondency. I have met personally with more than seven hundred of them in the field, and they told me their trials and conflicts with the utmost frankness, when I asked them to do so, but not one of them ever spoke as if laboring in support of a hopeless cause, not one of them expressed a desire to be released and called home. With a debilitating climate to impair their energy and the deep shadow of heathenism to depress their spirits, they do much hard work and they only cry for help and opportunity to do more. They have mastered difficult languages and found their way into the inner thought and life of the people that speak them. The natives of far distant lands hear the missionary tell, every man in his own tongue wherein he was born, the wonderful works of God. By reason of the intelligent and persevering labor of missionaries, the simple story of the cross is told to-day in twenty times as many languages as were heard in Jerusalem on the Day of Pentecost. Sometimes the stranger from beyond the sea compels the natives to confess that he speaks their language better than themselves. Many times the missionary, whose field of labor has been assigned him among debased and savage men, has caught words and sounds from the lips of the living, and made grammars and dictionaries and the whole apparatus of education in a language which never before had been reduced to writing. In copious and cultivated languages, like the Arabic, the missionary has become a master of higher authority for correct usage than natives who have made verbal criticism the pride of their life. In the most difficult and enigmatical languages, like the Chinese, the missionary has made dictionaries that cause the surprise and command the homage of professional scholars who have studied the classics of their native tongue seventy years.

The best book as yet written on that still dark and difficult subject, China and the Chinese, was written by a missionary. The only commentary on the Koran that I have ever seen, the best manual of original authorities on Buddhism, the best and almost the only translation of the Chinese classics, are the work of missionaries. The best record of the original customs of Polynesia and Madagascar, the thirty thousand volumes of scientific books sold in China every year, are the work of missionaries. The one lifelong observer of the action and eruptions of volcanoes; the indefatigable collectors of historic records and relics in archæology; physicians who have had the largest experience in the treatment of all manner of diseases; the most reliable witnesses to the religious belief and practice of all nations; the most careful observers of the manners and customs of people in the least frequented parts of the earth; the best authorities in regard to the plants that grow and the animals that live and the minerals that are found and the phenomena of nature that attract attention in the most distant quarters of the globe, — are missionaries. The men who do most to enrich science and promote education and enlarge the area of human knowledge, as an indirect result of their life's labor, are missionaries.

The writers of universal geographies; the compilers of world-wide statistics; the students of comparative philology; the popular delineators of the manners and customs of all nations; the speculators in comparative mythology and religion; the collectors of specimens of rude art and implements of a supposed age of stone or bronze, — all depend upon missionaries for the materials which they work upon, the warp and the woof of the theories which they spin. In the cloistered halls of learning, in the cabinets and laboratories of colleges, in the quiet studies of private life, ingenious speculators write books and propose theories, for which they get great fame as authors and philosophers, and yet they are indebted for the most important facts they use to the incidental observations of men who are preaching the gospel in the jungles of India, the mud cabins of China, or under the shadow of palms on the isles of the sea.

Many of the most valuable contributions which missionaries make to general knowledge are gathered by them as a mere diversion outside of the one supreme purpose for which they go to the ends of the earth and offer the labor of their lives as a willing sacrifice for the good of their fellow-men. One good man, at whose house I was hospitably entertained, and with whom I rode through the streets of a Chinese city on a wheelbarrow of his own construction, had done so much to teach the people about him better modes of managing their grounds and crops that he was actually afraid that he might be remembered more as a gardener and a fruit grower than as a missionary sent out to plant the tree of life beside all waters and over all hills and plains in the Central Flowery Kingdom of the East.

I met a missionary physician and surgeon who, I was told, could receive fifty thousand dollars of professional fees for a year's practice in London or New York, and yet he was giving himself, with all his skill and experience, to the blind and the palsied, the lame and the leprous, in Canton, for the bare means of living and the love of doing good to his afflicted fellow-men. I had many conversations with another missionary physician who had fifty thousand patients pass under his eye in a year, and who yet in the night and morning hours, when off duty in medical practice, mastered a very difficult language, translated the Bible for forty millions of people to read, and made a dictionary which for them is what Webster or Worcester is for us. I met another missionary physician who translated the Bible into the refined and copious language of the Arabs, and so completely mastered the tongue that once he was in peril of his life because a band of roving and murdering Druses took him to be a native and, as proof, insisted that no foreigner could speak Arabic as correctly as he did. I know another missionary physician who made a concordance of the Bible in the same language, and who mingled so much physical force and hardihood with his scholarly habits that he would mount his wild horse in the morning, ride over the steep and slippery paths of the mountains the distance of two ordinary days' journey, perform a critical surgical operation, and be back at sunset of the same day to sleep in his own house for the night.

I have met missionaries in the foreign field who had a large acquaintance with history, science, and general literature, and who spoke eight or ten languages, sometimes using them all the same day, preaching, as one did, in twelve different languages in one week, and yet such scholarly men making it the one chief aim of their life to teach the simplest truths of the gospel to men that know them not. A distinguished comparative anatomist went all the way from England to Egypt to study the habits of poisonous serpents and to satisfy himself whether the profession of the snake-charmer were an imposition or a reality. He did not know the language of the people nor the subtle ways of the charmers. He could not take the first step in his proposed investigations without the help of the missionary. He secured the desired assistance from one whom I have seen going on his rounds of daily service as a missionary physician in Cairo. The kind doctor made all needed arrangements, got the snakes and the charmers to appear on exhibition, and stood by to ask questions and interpret answers. The time came for the professor to return to London. He had formed no theory of snake-charming and he was obliged to go, begging the missionary to continue the observations and send him the result. In the course of time the learned professor appeared before the Philosophical Society with an acute and exhaustive article on snake-charming, and he received much honor and admiration for the manner in which he handled the difficult and delicate subject, and, in the meantime, the faithful missionary, who supplied the professor with all his material, was ministering to the sore-eyed children and the naked fellahin of Cairo, and did not hear the faintest echo of the applause which greeted the professor's essay in London.

An American ambassador made a famous treaty with China, and he gained so high a reputation as a diplomatist that the Chinese government sent him to all the courts of Europe to negotiate treaties for them; and yet every article in the American treaty which gave it any special fitness or value, and every negotiation which gave the ambassador any reputation, was the work or the suggestion of an American missionary who had made the language and the people of China a laborious and conscientious study for years, and who did not appear as a member of the embassy at all. The ambassador was a brilliant talker, a highly-gifted and accomplished man, but he knew nothing especial about China, the government, the people, or the country. He had no especial fitness to make his way through all the intricate mazes and contradictions of Chinese ignorance and culture, cunning and simplicity, to the attainment of his object. If it had not been for the help of the untitled and unofficial missionary, he would have been obliged to come home and confess that he had gone to the ends of the earth on a fool's errand and had come back no wiser than he went. The missionary does not indeed ask for titles or honors from the government of any country, but it is fair and becoming that the world should know how much the good understanding between nations is due to his knowledge of men and his sagacity in difficult negotiations.

Such are some of the outside and incidental labors of missionaries in the various countries where they make their home. In the direct fulfillment of their great and divine commission their labors have been much more abundant and effective. They have taught the heathen to observe all things whatsoever Christ commanded. They have preached the divine Word wherever they could find standing room or anybody to listen — in the jungle, under the shade of the palm and the banyan, at the door of the tent, in the open street, in the bazars, amid crowds of attendants on festivals, in front of shrines and tombs, as well as in the chapel, the schoolhouse, and the church. They have opened reading rooms and gathered libraries, organized the church and the Sunday-school, and adopted all our various social gatherings of people for worship and instruction so far as they have been adapted to the time, place, and people. They have not tried to make Western people out of Eastern, nor to put our dress and manners upon people who would only look the worse for wearing either. But they have been ingenious and inventive in finding out the best ways of securing access for the truth to the minds and hearts of high-caste and low-caste, Brahmin and Buddhist, Armenian and Moslem, Confucian and Taoist. They have established schools and colleges and theological seminaries and taught all branches of science and literature that are known in western nations.

They have educated native preachers and catechists, trained Bible and Zenana women to the delicate and difficult work of going from house to house promoting peace and teaching the words of life; they have found out how to live and work and dress in all extremes of heat and cold, and they have won the confidence of people who gave them no welcome at their coming and who only looked on them with distrust and suspicion. They have been loved and revered and almost worshiped by the very people by whom, at their first coming among them, they were reviled and ridiculed and stoned. They have grown wise by experience, courageous by exposure to peril, patient by long waiting for the fruit of their labor, and they have been eyewitnesses to the fitness and the divine power of the Word which they preach. They have seen men of the grossest minds and darkest hearts and most implacable dispositions renewed in spirit, made gentle and forgiving towards each other, and started upon a true and noble life. Upon the minds of thousands and millions who are not thus converted the missionaries have made the impression that they preach and practice a religion of purity and of love, and that it is destined to displace all other religions and to gather all nations into one faith and one family.

Our brethren who have gone forth into the great world field, and are gathering harvests to eternal life, desire our sympathy and they deserve our confidence: the commission which they bear is from the highest source and it ought to receive our most cordial and generous support. Every day, in every Christian home throughout our land, let prayer be offered that our missionaries may be endued with all wisdom and prudence, with the spirit of counsel and of might for their great work, and that they may be enriched with all utterance and all knowledge, and that their lips may be touched with fire from the heavenly altar to tell the wonders of God's redeeming love in languages that never bore the message and to people that never heard the story. In every private home, in every public service of the sanctuary, in all believing hearts, let continual prayer be offered that our brethren in the field may be clear and conscientious in their great office as ambassadors of the Most High, that they may be clothed with the meekness of saints and the majesty of kings, that the Spirit of the living God will pour into their hearts the courage of heroes and the faith of martyrs, and so enable them to stand against the principalities and powers of darkness, and having done all to stand, until the Church, triumphant in the Redeemer's might, shall win the well-fought day.

The great Christian campaign for the conquest of the world is now well begun. There have been skirmishings and reconnoiterings and taking of outposts in many lands and all over the field. But the ground has been well explored, the strength of the enemy ascertained, the weapons of the warfare have been tested; after many mistakes and failures, the best methods of attack have been found out and a salutary fear and trembling have been impressed upon the foe. Now is the time for a swift and resistless advance along the whole line. Every member of the Christian Church in every land should heed the call which comes from the Captain of the host, saying, "Go forward." The responsibility of those at home is the same as that of the foremost in the field.

We all serve the same Master, we are all enlisted for the same campaign, and we look for no rest or release till the end of the war. There is no neutral ground for noncommittal, no half-way covenant between the church and the world. If we stand wholly for Christ, his banner over us will always be light and love; we shall ever hear his voice loud and clear in the call to glory and virtue, to joy and victory. And when the final day comes and we all stand in our lot before the throne great and high, and we see the scar of the cross in the hand that offers the crown, we shall be glad to remember that we have served in the ranks of the sacramental host and have borne an honorable part in the toils and the sacrifices of the great campaign.

XIX.

FORWARD.

IF we take a wide and rapid survey of the great missionary field of the world, from the safe distance of home, the impressions which we receive and the conclusions to which we come will depend greatly upon the object we have in view and the previous habits of mind which we have been accustomed to entertain. If we have never taken any personal interest in the work itself, and we pride ourselves a little upon our character as independent observers, we shall often seem to be standing on the shore of a great and wide sea, over which the night of ages broods and thick clouds of ignorance and superstition gather. On the waves of that great deep, millions of mariners wander in unseaworthy hulks, without a compass, a chart, a pilot, or a helm. The storm rages and the hulks dash against each other in blind conflict and are broken in pieces, and the living mariners go down to their fathomless grave in the deep. A calm comes on, and the hulks lie rotting on the sea, like the poet's ships in his dream of darkness, and the living mariners go down as before to their deep burial beneath the waves. The miserable wanderers in the dark know not which way they are drifting, and they see no beacon light to warn them of danger or to reveal the safe shore. We hear their voices from afar, lifted up like the cry of nations, but they speak strange tongues, and we cannot tell whether it is a song of triumph that they are singing or a dirge of despair. The shore at our feet is strewn with wreck, and we gather up a gilded idol, an enameled vase, a piece of embroidered silk, a delicate cutting in ivory or stone, and we set them in our chambers and parlors and museums as curios of men who live far off, work in the dark, and never know what it is to walk in the light of life. We pity them, perhaps sometimes we pray for them, but not with a hope. They are so far off that we cannot go to them; they are so many that we cannot count them; they are wandering in such deep darkness that we should be lost ourselves in the endeavor to find them out and show them the way of peace. If there were but one or a hundred, we could send lifeboats and save them. But what can we do for millions? If they were within hearing and they understood our tongue, we could cry aloud and tell them which way to steer to find the safe harbor. But they are on the other side of the globe and they speak other tongues and our words would have no more meaning to them than the sea bird's cry or the wail of the storm.

So when we offer our prayer, in the distance, for the rescue of benighted millions from the bondage of ignorance and superstition, we are afraid to believe that it will ever be answered. When we give our money for the same object, we never expect to live the many days which must pass before it will come again with blessings on our head. Such is apt to be the home view of many who look out upon the great missionary field of the world and wait for some new revelation of power from on high to scatter the clouds of ignorance and superstition and fill the habitations of the heathen with light. Some even are so oppressed with the sad condition of millions of the human family, as seen from afar, that they feel obliged to resort to vague theories and blind conjectures to justify the ways of God to man in making such a world and keeping it alive so long. When appealed to for help in sending the light of truth into the dark places of the earth, they are inclined to answer, as did the devout king of Spain, whose subjects petitioned him for permission to unite two rivers by a canal, and who replied that if God almighty had ever designed those rivers to be connected he would have made the canal himself, and it would be presumptuous for man to interfere with the ways of divine providence.

But suppose we lay aside all our theories and conjectures and go out into the field itself and join hands, for a while, with the toilers in the heat of the day and the damp of the night. We set our shoulders to the burdens which they bear, and we come so near to them that we feel the beating of their hearts and catch the inspiration of the lives of toil and sacrifice which they lead. Then the darkness about us will at first seem deeper than it did when we stood afar off and looked on; the state of the heathen will appear more pitiable than we ever thought it to be; but when once in the field, keeping company with the reapers and trying to share a little in their work, we no longer look about us with vague curiosity or silent wonder or helpless despair. We find now that the great sea, which looked so dark in the distance, is studded here and there with islands of the blessed, from which go up songs of faith and hope, such as we sing in the home land. The howling wilderness of the shore has many gardens of God, watered from the fountains of life and shaded with palms of victory. The strange tongues of heathenism have been mastered and made to speak the words of eternal life and to sing the songs of triumph over death. The hidden places of darkness have been searched by the light of truth, and the habitations of cruelty have been consecrated with words of peace and deeds of kindness. Among the wreckage of immortal hopes which we thought were utter ruin, we find gems fit to shine in the crown of the King of kings.

All over the dark immensity of heathenism we see, on closer inspection, light bearers, heralds of hope and salvation. Some are out on the sea and some are lining the shore with beacons. Some are climbing wild mountains, some are crossing burning wastes, some are making their way through jungles and lowlands where the fever poison fills the air, some are in the narrow and filthy streets of crowded cities or in the mud cabins of scattered villages, some are ascending mighty rivers and exploring the desolations of many generations. All are intent upon one object, all are working in the manner and with the means that suit them best, with the one desire to fill the dark places of the earth with light. All are looking for wanderers to bring them home to their Father. On all the continents of the earth and all the great islands of the sea, in the midst of the swarming population of great cities and in the waste places of the wilderness, they are seeking to save men from the wretched life and the hopeless death into which heathenism has been weighing down the nations of the East for ages. Living, immortal men, by millions, are walking in darkness, not knowing at what they stumble, and we have sent out, here and there, a messenger to show them the path of life, to bring them home to habitations of peace, to the blessed land of rest and security forevermore.

In India the Brahmins say that the Christians have flung their net over the whole land from the northern mountains to the most southern cape. They compare their own traditions and customs to a tank from which the water is always running out and none is coming in. In Japan the people have awaked from the long sleep of ages and are groping about bewildered and half blinded by the sudden coming of the new day. In China, the darkest and most hopeless of all the great lands of the East, a thousand messengers are going to and fro, publishing glad tidings of liberty from long bondage, holding up the light to show the way of peace and salvation to three hundred millions who are blindly following the steps of their ancestors in wandering mazes lost. Our brethren have led thousands into the safe path, but there are millions more that have not seen the light or heard the call. Every breeze from the ocean comes to us freighted with the cry of our messengers, saying, "Come over and help us. The heathen are multiplying faster than we can save them. We must set a light on every hilltop, we must search the lanes and alleys of every city with lighted candles, we must plunge into the great currents of humanity which are flowing along all the coasts and up and down all the mighty rivers and over the vast plains of this great eastern world. We must cry aloud or we shall not be heard above the millions of voices which proclaim the blind gods of heathenism and promise the base indulgence of lust and passion."

It helps us very much in deciding how that call should be answered when we go over to the other side and spend a year with the good soldiers of Christ who are lifting up the standard of the cross in the hard places of the heathen field. The Christian traveler, on his journey of observation, traverses the great and populous lands of the East, everywhere meeting multitudes of people, multitudes without number. He crosses vast plains where a hundred villages are embraced in a single glance of the eye. He ascends mighty rivers that bear the food of millions in their waters. He passes over mountains that have separated hostile tribes and races for ages. He wonders at the invisible wall of caste which has built up a barrier of division between people of the same race as high as heaven and as deep as the grave. He makes his way through the crowded streets of great cities, everywhere looking into the faces of the poor, the ignorant, and the burdened, and feeling as if it would break his heart to think of their hard and hopeless lot in this world and the darker prospect before them for the world to come. Then he thinks of millions at ease in the home land, and more millions of money in their hands waiting to be put to good service in God's great field of the world. Then he feels that he must come back to his own country and lift up his voice in one continual cry in behalf of the millions that are wandering in the darkness of heathenism without a guide, and living without hope in the habitations of cruelty.

And what is the most important thing which such a returned traveler from the eastern lands can say to the Christians in his own country? What is the one thing which must needs be done in order to put the great missionary enterprise in its right place before the Church and before the world? What one thing done will cause all branches of the one universal Church of Christ to advance as an exceeding great army, a mighty and ever-victorious host, enrolled and commissioned by the living God for the conquest of the world?

The first thing needed is a full, honest, entire, universal acceptance by the Church of the divine commission to make disciples of all nations. As a new starting point there must be an open, hearty, and habitual declaration on the part of all Christians of every denomination that they, by virtue of their profession as Christians, are committed to the great enterprise, and are determined, at whatever cost of men and money, effort and sacrifice, to send recruits, to fill up the vacant ranks in the field, to sustain work already begun, and to press on with united front to the conquest of the world. The Church, as a whole, and all individual members must accept the charge which Christ gave his disciples as fully and personally as it is expected that missionaries in foreign lands will accept and act upon its high demands. It must become a thing settled, known, and accepted by the world at large, that the Church is God's host enlisted and enrolled for perpetual war against the powers of darkness, and that its great interest and plan of campaign must embrace all lands, all nations. The teaching, the efforts, the gifts, the daily life of Christians in this land should say continually to the world, "It is our special commission from Christ to make known his Gospel to the ends of the earth and to persuade all nations to acknowledge him as Saviour and King. We will not rest, we will not relax effort, we will not withhold gifts, we will not shrink from sacrifice so long as there is one people still to be evangelized, one remote corner of the earth to be visited with the gospel light." Every individual Christian coming into the Church by profession of faith in Christ must be made to understand, at the very outset, that he is enlisted in the ranks of an exceeding great army whose divine commission and supreme purpose can be accomplished only by the conquest of the whole world for Christ.

We have been saying something like that for a long time. We have sung it in our hymns, repeated it in our prayers, adopted it in resolutions, preached it in sermons, taught it in our Sabbath-schools, and commended it in our conferences; but the trouble, as the case now stands before the world, is this: the outside world does not fully believe in the sincerity of the Church, the strong, persistent, well-considered purpose of the Church to fulfill its divine commission at whatever cost of toil and men and money, and with the least possible delay. The world is not impressed with the fact that the Church is possessed and carried away with this sacred and divine ambition which can rest with nothing short of the spiritual conquest of all nations to Christ. The Church does not fully believe that, as Christ was sent into the world for the redemption of the nations, so all who follow him are called to take up his work and carry it on to the end, and that the evidence of sincere discipleship is the personal acceptance of that divine commission from the Master.

The Church, to be true to itself and to Him whose name it bears, must fling out that high and glorious proclamation in the morning light of every land, in the native speech of every people, ever saying by deed and word, "We are fully committed to this command of Christ, whom we follow as the Prince and Captain of salvation. We will never lay down the weapons of our spiritual warfare until the final victory is gained and the kingdoms of this world have become the kingdoms of our Lord and his Christ. We wish it to be understood that we stand committed to this proclamation, and wherever we set up the standard of the cross there we have come to stay and to conquer. We have provided no means of retreat, we have no armor for the defense of those whose face is turned from the foe; in all our hymns we have no song fit for the flying and the vanquished to sing. The march of God's host is onward, forever onward!"

The world must be made to hear on all occasions such high and clear proclamation of the mission of the Church, and the world must be impressed with the belief that the Church will make good every promise in the proclamation. The world must be made to know and to believe that Christians, by virtue of their profession as followers of Christ, are bound to go wherever he leads the way, and are fully in sympathy with all his plans and desires for the salvation of men. Whenever a band of Christians meet in conference to inquire, discuss, deliberate, the impression must be made outside that they are supremely interested in just one question: How shall men be recovered from the power of sin and death? How can the reign of righteousness and peace be established among all nations and over all the earth? How can the long, dark reign of ignorance and superstition and wrong give place to truth and purity and love? It must be made to appear on the face of all proceedings of Christian assemblies, in the tone and spirit of all preaching and prayer and exhortation, that all Christians are enlisted under Christ to do his bidding, go where he commands, fulfill his desire in all things. They are ready to do whatever he wants them to do, wherever their lot in life may be cast. That is their intelligent and well-considered estimate of all that is best worth living for. The best use they can find for money, time, labor, influence, is the use which best pleases their Lord and Master. That they esteem the highest aim and the chief glory of life. As Christ gave himself to death for the salvation of men, thus testifying his desire that all men may be saved, so his followers, actuated by his mind, moved by his spirit, will individually give themselves, their time, labor, thought, possessions, to the accomplishment of Christ's one desire in respect to all nations that they may be saved.

We have meetings of mission bands, missionary societies, mission conventions and conferences; grand resolutions are passed, eloquent addresses, earnest appeals are made, the loudest applause greets the most earnest and fervid speaker, reports of such meetings are sent out to all the churches, religious papers comment upon them with high approbation, and much good is thus accomplished. The people are slowly educated by such means into the knowledge of the work actually going on in heathen lands and are brought somewhat into sympathy with the laborers in the field. But the world outside does not understand such speeches, votes, and resolutions to mean that the Church is intelligently and thoroughly in earnest about fulfilling the divine commission to evangelize all nations at whatever cost and with the least possible delay. After such conventions the world does not say as a matter of course, Now we are to see a grand advance along the whole line of missionary forces; now the offer of men and money for the work will be made as fast as new fields of labor can be found and new calls for help shall come from beyond the sea.

I cannot call to remembrance any church or missionary convention which has produced the impression, beyond all question, upon the outside world that the attendants upon the meeting, and the framers of the resolutions, and the speakers upon the platform, and the approving and applauding audience that filled the house, thenceforth counted themselves wholly committed, body and soul and spirit, property and time and talent, to the fulfillment of Christ's command, wholly intent upon doing for all the heathen world what Christ desires most of all to have done. The world does not believe the Church to be intelligently, profoundly in earnest, simply because the world does not see, beyond all doubt or question, the evidences of entire devotion to the fulfillment of Christ's command, "Go ye and disciple all the nations."

Suppose the Church of God in this blessed land of America, Christians of all denominations, each in his own way, and yet all as one body, should rise up with united strength and resources, with intelligent and honest purpose, and take to heart the last great commission of Christ with the firm intent to fulfill its demands; suppose they should go on for one year devoting all their material and spiritual resources to that commission, as fully as a great people give themselves to meet the awful demands and sacrifices of war in time of invasion, the world would feel the greatness and the divine authority of the missionary enterprise as it has never yet done. Every secular newspaper in the land would be filled with reports of that mighty movement for the conquest of the world. It would be the subject of conversation and inquiry and debate in every house and shop and assembly of people. Every city and village would feel the throb of the millions of hearts beating with one sacred and mighty passion. All colleges, schools, institutions of learning, would confess the mighty power of Christian effort and consecration. The doubting, the indifferent, and the skeptical would be obliged to say, "This is indeed the finger of God. We never saw Christianity on this fashion, we never saw such divine power given unto men, before. These ten millions of American Christians have wealth and education and power enough to carry everything before them now that they are wholly intent upon fulfilling their Master's command."

All Christians admit the binding force of the command of Christ. All admit that the heathen nations are greatly in need of the gospel. All admit that the success thus far attending faithful efforts gives promise of greater success all around the world, when once the work is undertaken with set resolution to carry it through to a triumphant conclusion with the least possible delay. Now, the one thing wanting is the open, honest, outspoken committal of the Church to the evangelization of all nations. Let the committal be as clear and full and strong as words and deeds can make it. Let it be as unconditional as the enlistment of the soldier to fight for his country in the time of invasion. Let it be as complete as the committal of a capitalist when he has staked all his property upon the success of some worldly enterprise, and he will not allow himself to think of such a thing as failure. Let all differences, on unessential matters of doctrine, taste, feeling, form of worship and church organization, give place to the one great working article in all creeds that rest on Christ — personal devotion to him. Let old and young, rich and poor, business men and missionaries, at home and abroad, put themselves on the same level of duty and rise to the same height in living consecration to Christ. Let it be openly declared to the world, in this land of America, that ten millions of people are determined to fill the world with their doctrine : that any one of them, who is wanted to go into the uttermost parts of the earth in the name of the Master, is ready to go ; that any one who can do the best for the common cause by staying at home and working in the shop, the house, or the field, is ready to stay and work with equal devotion to the same cause ; that any one who has money can be relied upon to give, any one who has strength of body and mind to work will only ask where he is wanted most and report himself at once on the post of duty and ready for service.

Let all that, or anything like that, become a fact of daily history in the lives of ten millions of Christians in this land of America, and the world would feel the power of such consecration and unity of purpose and effort as it has never felt it before. The moral force, going forth from the lives of so many millions wholly devoted to the publication of the gospel through all the earth, would reach the uttermost parts of the great field; the strongholds of heathenism would totter to their foundation at the bare rumor of the coming of such a mighty host for the deliverance of its enslaved millions from bondage and darkness. The skeptics and the scoffers, who now talk flippantly of the Bible and deny the divine reality of Christian living, would not receive a moment's attention when ten millions of Christians are going forth, with tongues of fire and hearts of love, to fill the world with the knowledge of Jesus Christ and the way of salvation by faith in him.

The number of professed Christians in America is great enough; they have wealth enough at their command to fill all the waste places of heathenism with laborers to sow the seed and reapers to gather the harvests of eternal life. And this open, honest, hearty assumption on the part of the Church of the evangelization of the world is both reasonable and practicable. The work can be done without exhausting the riches or impairing the prosperity of the people. The culture, the conversion, the civilization of all other nations will bring back to America twofold more wealth than is expended in preaching the gospel wherever the heralds of salvation have not yet been heard. It is said that for every dollar expended by England on foreign missions ten come back as the profit of trade with peoples whose wants have been created by the diffusion of civilization and Christianity by the hands of missionaries. That may not be quite true yet of America. But the time is fast coming when it will be. Fill all the dark continent of Africa with gospel light, make every valley and river and plain a highway for the ransomed of the Lord, make every hilltop blaze with beacons to show the path of life to wanderers, and our own land will catch the radiance from afar, and the ships of commerce which pass between the continents will carry exchanges of mutual profit and congratulations of mutual joy. Raise up the swarming millions of India and China and Japan from the ignorance and superstition and poverty and degradation which heathenism has put upon them for ages, let all the people be clothed and educated, let them be gathered in bright homes and inspired with great hopes, let them be started upon a new millennium of power and riches and prosperity, such as the gospel brings to people wherever it goes, and then they will send back to Christian lands tenfold more then they have received, and the whole round world will be blessed when the dark cloud of heathenism has melted into day.

The gospel increases the wants of every people to whom it comes with its message of light and liberty; but it enriches them at the same time by increasing the supply and stimulating the minds of all into new activity and invention and new discoveries of riches that before were not known to exist. So the gospel makes new demands for effort and gifts and sacrifices. But it brings back to the heart and home of every giver and doer ten times as much as it takes away. When the Zulus lived in kraals and bought and sold their women for cattle, they were worth nothing to themselves or the rest of the world. But when they became Christians, they wanted houses to live in, clothes to wear, tools to work with, books to read, schools for the education of their children. The quickening power of the gospel made them feel the need of a thousand things which they never thought of before. The necessity to labor for the satisfaction of new wants made them new men, and brought them out into the great commonwealth of nations, and made them givers as well as receivers for the increase of the wealth of the world. Let the Church expend upon the propagation of peace and good will among men as freely as goverments expend upon war, let Christian people pour out wealth for the diffusion of the water of life as freely as drinkers expend upon the liquor which poisons and destroys, and there will be money enough to answer every call and men enough to fill every post. And the life of consecration to Christ, which goes out in such gifts and sacrifices for the good of men, is strong, reasonable, and happy. It secures the highest enjoyment of everything the world has to give, and it uplifts and glorifies all earthly conditions by the powers of the world to come.

Christ himself makes a full, personal acceptance of his commission to convert all nations the condition and qualification for good standing in his Church. The moment one is voluntarily enrolled as a disciple of Jesus, he is committed, in all honor and truth and good conscience, to bear a part in the fulfillment of Christ's great commission. Every new candidate is received only on condition of pledging himself to do whatever Christ commands. And Christ explicitly commands his followers to go and disciple all nations. The only reliable evidence of true discipleship is the full and hearty acceptance of the work which Christ came to begin and which he has passed over into the hands of his Church to complete. He says that he has sent them into the world to take up his work and carry it on unto the end. Just as truly as the Father sent him into the world to do a specific work, he sends his disciples to follow in his footsteps and finish well what he began. That will be only when all the nations and all the ends of the earth shall see the salvation of our God.

Christ did not come to enter upon any of the common fields of human ambition or to put himself forward as a competitor for any of the riches or pleasures or glories of the earth. He came only to seek and to save the lost. He came to destroy the kingdom of darkness and to set up the kingdom of God for the protection and enjoyment of all mankind. He says that, just as truly as he was sent of the Father for that purpose, he has sent his followers into the world to do the same thing. It is on condition that they accept his commission that he promises to be with them alway, even unto the end. The only satisfactory evidence that we are his disciples and belong to him, and so can claim the fulfillment of his promise, is the fact that we keep his commandments, we fulfill his commission, we enter heartily into his plan and desire for the salvation of all mankind. The only true church, the only holy, undivided, orthodox, apostolic church in the world, is the church which puts first and foremost in creed and practice, in spirit and letter, the chosen and divine work of Christ in seeking and saving the lost.

This great Christian enterprise, the conversion of the whole world to one faith, one law of right living, one brotherhood of duty and of love, is the greatest, the most inspiring, the most sublime, the most godlike, that can call forth the efforts or move the hearts of men. It should stand out, clear and commanding, in all preaching of the gospel, in all plans for church work, in all training of young Christians, in all Sabbath-school teaching, in all home and household religion, in all public appeals for the support of Christian institutions at home and the prosecution of missionary work among the heathen. Never, never must the Church forget the Master's word, "The gospel must first be published among all nations." That is the first duty which he charges upon his followers, and they should give themselves no rest until it is done. When the word of the Lord came to the prophet in the old time, and he withheld the message from the people, it was in his heart as a burning fire shut up in his bones and he was weary with forbearing and he could not stay, and he said, " Woe is me if I deliver not this word of the Lord to those for whom it is sent." That word of the Lord is now given unto the whole Church to make known unto the nations. To all that hesitate and delay, the command comes from the Master, as it came to the recreant prophet in old time, saying, " Go into all the earth and preach unto all the nations the preaching that I bid thee."

No church can live and grow in grace and power, in love and unity, while standing aloof from the special work which Christ has given his Church to do. No individual Christian can come into the full enjoyment of life and liberty in

Christ unless he takes an open and honorable part in the fulfillment of the divine commission to disciple all nations. Sir William Hunter, speaking simply as a master in statistics and an intelligent observer of the world's progress, says that he should consider any abatement of interest in the great missionary work on the part of English Christians as a sure sign of national decline. In his opinion, if England does not employ her wealth, her education, and her faith in Christianizing the millions of the heathen in India, the sources of her power and prosperity will dry up at home. And it is just as true that the spiritual life of the home churches in our own land will decline and die, if they do not sustain missionaries on the ground and send them more men and money to advance to new fields and greater conquests for the Master.

The only effectual safeguard against deadness and indifference, against worldliness and materialism, against vain speculation and false doctrine, against positive unbelief and renunciation of all faith, is to be found in keeping the divine commission to disciple the nations ever before the Church and the world. Give that its due place in all doctrine and duty, in all preaching and praise and prayer, in all plans and organizations for church work, in all training of the young, and in all collections for the treasury of the Lord, and then there will be little danger of letting down the standard of Christian living and consecration, little danger that many will cease to hold fast the form of sound words or drift away from the firm anchorage of faith.

It is especially important that the young shall be impressed early and intelligently with the greatness and the divine authority of the commission to disciple the nations. They must be taught to feel and believe that the object for which we send missionaries to India and China and Japan is the greatest, the most urgent, the most sacred that ever can enlist the efforts or inspire the hearts of living men. The conquests of Alexander and Cæsar and Napoleon, the framing of constitutions and the founding of states and empires, the building of the Pyramids, the Parthenon, and the Coliseum, the opening of new highways for commerce, the invention of new arts, new discoveries in science and new mastery over the hidden powers of nature, are great and inspiring themes for the study of the youthful mind. But they all sink into insignificance when compared with the divine commission to disciple all nations: to change the character, the faith, and the eternal destiny of immortal millions; to scatter the cloud of ignorance and superstition which has brooded over the homes and darkened the hearts and defeated the hopes of nations for ages; to put an end to the waste and the wickedness of war, the misery of want, the prevalence of crime, and the power of falsehood and wrong in every land; to begin and build up a redeemed and immortal brotherhood of the whole human race; to make the law and the life of earth and heaven one; and so to establish among men a kingdom that shall be blessed in experience and universal in authority and endless in duration.

All that is included in the divine charge to go and disciple all nations, and all that will be done when the requirements of the commission are fulfilled. All arts, sciences, inventions, improvements needed for the highest development of the human family will follow as a natural and inevitable consequence when the religion of Christ has become the law of duty and the guide of conduct in all nations. Let children grow into the knowledge of these great facts of life and duty as fast as they grow into the knowledge of the world, and as soon as they begin to look about them and ask what is best worth living for, what needs to be done to make things all right in the world where so many things for ages have been wrong. Stimulate their minds, inspire their hopes, draw out their affections, direct their choice of study and occupation by setting before them continually the demands of this great enterprise, this mighty revolution which contemplates the uplifting and the emancipation of all nations. In that way they will best learn how to be brave and patient and generous, how to be kind and gentle and strong, how to be cheerful and magnanimous and victorious in the great battle of life. Teach the child early to come out of himself and take the whole world to his heart in love and sympathy and to seek his own happiness in effort and desire to make others happy. Teach the little children that they are especially blessed of Christ and called by him to take their place in the kingdom of heaven. Help them in every possible way to grow up into the feeling and the belief that the privilege, the duty, and the joy of living are to take the words of Christ from his own lips and send them out to the ends of the earth to bless other children whose homes are the habitations of darkness and cruelty.

Teach children from the earliest years, by precept and by example, that Christian service ennobles and beautifies character, Christian giving enriches and rejoices the heart,

Christian living is the only right and true and happy living. Let the discipline and the daily conversation of the Christian family impress the children with the feeling that the beauty, the attractiveness, and the high authority of the Christian life surpass all worldly promises of good, all possessions and pleasures which begin and end in selfish gratification. Let every Sunday-school lesson be so taught that the classes shall be impressed with the universality of the truths set before us in the gospel and their fitness to carry light and peace to all races of men, to all lands and for all time. Let the tone and spirit of everything said in meetings for prayer and exhortation lead observers from the outside to say, " These people are in earnest and they mean to put their religion through the world. Whenever they get together, they are always talking and planning and praying about the coming of the kingdom of God, and, judging from the way they talk, it would seem as if they thought the kingdom to be close at hand." Let the habitual conversation, judgments, opinions, and conduct of Christians wherever they go, wherever they are, assume that the one thing most needed by all the nations is the gospel of Christ, and that the highest honor, the most complete success in life is gained by him who does most to hasten the coming of a reign of righteousness and peace in all the earth.

Let every minister preach on the Sabbath and carry himself before his people on all occasions in such manner that they will see in him a man who has a message from God, and who is all intent upon delivering that message as God has bidden him do. Let him so act and speak in the fulfillment of his high commission that all who hear his words and observe his conduct will take it for granted that Christian profession means obedience to Christ's commands, devotion to the work which Christ has given his followers to do, full acceptance of the charge to proclaim his truth to all nations. Let these greatest, simplest principles of Christian service be fully accepted and honestly acted upon by ten millions of Christians in America, and every heathen nation would feel the touch of that new life in a single year; every missionary station would celebrate the event with hymns of thanksgiving and praise; every objection which skeptics bring against practical Christianity would be answered; every honest doubter would be led to see the foundation of faith, and every scoffer would be compelled to shut his mouth in silence and shame.

XX.

ONE LAW OF DUTY FOR ALL.

THE standard of duty and of individual consecration is the same to all Christians, whether serving as missionaries in the foreign field, or enjoying the advantages of Christian culture, refined society, and domestic peace in the home land. Indebtedness to Christ for the forgiveness of sin and the hope of salvation is the same to all. Christ gave himself as freely and as fully for one as for another. He lays equally upon all who receive his word the command to carry it to the ends of the earth and cause all nations to receive it as the message of life and salvation. He gives to all alike the privilege and the honor of bearing a part in the greatest commission ever given to man, the mightiest work which God himself undertakes to do in this world. No one can make a greater mistake in his plans for life than to stand aside and let God's work go on without help from him. No one can make a sadder misuse of time and talent and property than to keep all for himself and leave the sacrifices of duty for others to make and the rewards of duty for others to enjoy.

It will be a new and glorious era in Christian work when all Christians in the home land openly accept and faithfully act upon the same principles of duty which are enjoined upon missionaries and converts in the foreign field. Let ten millions of Christians in America adopt the same plans for individual effort for the conversion of men, and let them manifest the same degree of personal consecration to Christ, which we all expect as a matter of course in men who go to the far-off lands of the East to preach the gospel, and the change for the better in our own country will be as strongly marked as that which we pray for among the heathen.

Christians at home are quite ready and agreed to see that the foreign missionary gives his whole time and strength and resources to the work of seeking the salvation of the heathen to whom he is sent. We criticize his plans and principles of working and preaching solely with a view to decide whether they are the best to secure the acceptance of the gospel and the beginnings of the true life in the hearts of individual men. Whatever else he may do, and however well he does it, we are not satisfied with his labor unless we see the result, or at least the one thing aimed at, in the actual conversion of men. If in any case it should be reported that the missionary is not diligent, devoted, and self-denying for the souls of the ignorant and degraded people about him, there would be a great cry of surprise and indignation at home. Many who give themselves very little trouble or self-denial for the conversion of men at home would be ready to say, "What right has he to call himself a missionary of Christ if he is not wholly devoted to the work which Christ sends him to do? For what purpose do we give money to support him in the foreign field if not that he may give his whole time and strength to the work of bringing the heathen to the acceptance of Christ by living faith and personal devotion to him?" All that would be said of the missionary, if he should give himself to the work of secular education and social improvement among the heathen, and not put their conversion first and foremost as the object of his mission. And all that would be said by men who give little to foreign missions and who manifest little interest in the progress of the work.

But who shall say that the foreign missionary is under greater obligation to give himself wholly to Christ than any professed Christian at home? Has Christ done any more for him than for those who are surrounded by all the comforts and advantages of Christian civilization in the home land? Was the apostle speaking only to one Christian in a million, or to the whole Church, when he said, "Ye are not your own, ye are bought with a price"? It is quite time that the Church should learn to look at this matter of Christian consecration in its true light. The law of duty is the same to all. The least and the lowest qualification for good standing in the family of Christ is obedience to him. No one has the right to count himself a Christian until he makes a full surrender of himself and all he has to the service of his new Master. That service of submission and consecration is required equally of all, whatever may be the occupation that any one pursues or the position which he holds in society. Rich or poor, learned or ignorant, his first word of faith must say to Christ, "Lord, I give myself to do whatsoever thou wilt."

We cannot be Christ's disciples at all unless we give up all we have and are to him, even as he gave himself freely and fully for us all. His own devotion to his chosen work in seeking and saving the lost is the only safe rule by which we must judge our devotion to him. No one who reads the gospel thoughtfully can fail to see that Christ gave himself wholly to the work which he had received of the Father to do. He came into the world to save sinners, and he gave his time and strength and heart to the fulfillment of that mission to the end. We are all to follow him, imitate him, imbibe his spirit, believe his word, count our lives successful only so far as we enter into his work, obey his commands, finish the work he has given us to do.

We expect all this of the missionary who goes to spend his life in India, China, or Japan. We think we have the right to expect it of him. But has he not the same right to expect that we in the home land shall be just as much devoted to Christ, just as much in earnest to use our time and efforts and possessions for the advance of the kingdom of God among men? He severs the ties that bind him to home and friends, he makes himself an exile from his beloved country, he goes to live with men of strange tongues and rude manners and dissolute habits. He submits every day and through all the year to the sight and sound and smell of abominable things. He labors under sore discouragement and in the face of blind opposition, and he does all that because the love of Christ constrains him to yield the service with a glad heart, and because he feels that his fellow-men have a claim upon him for his best service in the name of our common humanity as well as in the name of our common Lord and Saviour. Has not the missionary the right to expect that those Christians who are in the full enjoyment of all the comforts and advantages of the home land will be glad to show their gratitude for all that Christ has done for them by doing their best for those who live in the dark places of the earth?

The Church must look into this matter seriously, earnestly, dispassionately; not in the spirit of fanaticism, not from the impulse of some sudden flame of zeal which burns only while it is blown upon by the hot breath of excitement or kept alive by persistent and personal appeal. There are principles of doctrine and of duty to be weighed, facts to be ascertained, histories to be studied, arguments and evidences to be examined, and conclusions to be drawn, in the most calm, deliberate, and rational spirit. And we are to act in view of the demands that come from the highest authority and in answer to claims which are sustained by clear and unquestionable truths. If we do that, we shall be obliged to adopt the same standard of duty and personal consecration to Christ for ourselves which we apply to the work and responsibility of the missionary in the foreign field.

If we count ourselves Christians, followers of Christ, it should be all a matter of course that we make his work our own, our interest in the great human family the same as his, and give our time and strength and heart to the completion of the one great enterprise for which he came to our world to labor, to suffer, and to die. So we all expect the missionary to do. Why not we at home, as well as he in the foreign field? We are all indebted to Christ as much as he; the gospel has conferred as great blessings on us as on him. He has given up the enjoyment of the countless and priceless blessings which come to us all from living in this favored country, and he has gone to people who live in the dark places of the earth that he may teach them how to make their land as good as ours. Seeing that he has denied himself so greatly for the good of others by voluntary exile from his native land, and we are here to enjoy all that he has left behind, there is even more reason why we should devote our time and influence and property to the advance of Christ's kingdom on earth. If we do not go in person to live and die among the heathen for their salvation, we should at least sustain those who do go with our confidence and our contributions, with our believing prayer and our warmest sympathy.

When young converts come into the Church and enroll their names as followers of Christ, they should be taught in the very outset of their profession the great principle of unreserved, undivided devotion to Christ. They are to take that consecration on themselves, not as a bondage, but as the highest liberty which man can attain; the freest, fullest, happiest use and enjoyment of every faculty and possession. They are to give themselves to the greatest work, the most honorable and glorious career that is open for man in this world, a work that will demand toils and sacrifices all the way, but which will be to them its own exceeding great reward.

Let nobody take time and argument to make the conditions of following Christ easy. The young convert need not be told how little he has to do, or to be, in order to be accepted of Christ as a good and faithful servant of his. When Paul was started upon his career as the apostle to bear the name of Jesus before the nations and kings of the earth, he was shown how great things he must suffer in the fulfillment of his divine commission; and the revelation of the greatness of the work which he was called to do for his Master girt him with strength and courage to do it well. So let every young Christian be taught in the very outset of his profession how complete is the consecration which Christ demands, how great is the work which Christ gives the humblest of his followers to do, how glorious is the reward which awaits all who are faithful unto death. Such teaching will lift him above all fear and complaint and discouragement; it will give him joy in every trial and triumph over every temptation; it will fire his soul with the fervor of love and the strength of faith which made the apostle to the Gentiles the greatest man of his time. With such a membership trained up from the beginning of Christian profession to follow Christ in all things, any church will be strong, prosperous, united, and happy. With them, work, gifts, prayer, effort, will always bring enlargement of heart, enlightenment of mind, steadiness and constancy in character, such as no worldly plans or policies can give. They will lead the advance of the age towards a greater and better life than has been seen on the earth in all the past.

Possibly it may be said or thought by some that the necessary industries of life could not be carried on successfully in Christian lands if all, equally with the foreign missionary, were devoted to the work of publishing the gospel to all the nations. It has actually been said in public address by some who claim to lead the advance of the age, that the human family would be reduced to a state of barbarism if all should attempt to live by the rules of life laid down by Christ himself in the Sermon on the Mount. All such speakers lose sight of the fact, attested by eighteen hundred years of Christian history, that Christianity, in the most enlightened and liberal acceptance of its doctrines and requirements, promotes the highest welfare of men in this world, while its chief aim is to prepare them for the endless life to come. It teaches every man to work, each in his own order, with the best use of his own faculties, in some one of the necessary and profitable industries of life, and all with the same degree of devotion to Christ and his kingdom on the earth. Christianity brings men into harmony with all the laws and forces which are in operation in the physical world, and at the same time it also brings them into everlasting harmony with the higher laws of our spiritual and immortal being.

The original act of creation set man over all things in the earth and put all material forces and irrational creatures under his feet to serve him. By ignorance and dissipation and disobedience, men have lost a large part of the dominion over the powers and resources of nature which belonged to them by gift of the first creation. Christianity comes to restore the lost estate to those who have recklessly thrown it away and have been mourning and complaining over their poverty for ages. Slowly as it advances, it gives sight to the blind and hearing to the deaf and power to the palsied and freedom to the enslaved. In this nineteenth century of Christian progress, men are just beginning to find out the greatness of the powers and possessions given them of God, and which, in their ignorance and perversity, they never saw, never suspected, until they recovered their lost "vision and faculty divine," by faith in the Son of God. Now, everything about us seems to be endowed with new life and power, just because we begin to see things as God made them and meant us to see and use them when he put man into the world with the command to subdue and possess the wide domain of earth, air, and sea.

New arts and inventions are constantly coming into use, new mines of wealth are opened, new applications of the original forces of nature are devised every year, as time moves on, just because men are beginning to know God better and are coming to live more in accordance with the laws of life and well-being established in the original creation. When all the people praise God, both in practical service and in grateful song, the earth will yield her increase in such abundance as never before. All arts and inventions which increase the wealth and the resources of the human family are best known and used in lands where the gospel of Christ is most fully accepted and believed and obeyed as the true law of life and duty for all men. Let the merchants, the mechanics, the manufacturers, the farmers, all classes and conditions of men in America, pursue their chosen occupations with just as clear and firm a purpose to use all their influence and possessions for the establishment of the kingdom of God on earth, as all expect the missionary to do, and the homes of our own dear land would be filled with peace and plenty to such a degree as never before, and there would be millions to spare every year for the evangelization of the heathen.

The most Christian nations are already the richest, and they are accumulating wealth more rapidly than any other people in the world. And their religion is the source of their power and their prosperity. The heathen of Japan to-day would vote themselves Christians, if by so doing they could secure the wealth, the arts, the inventions, the science, the progress, the hope which the gospel has given to Christian nations. They can see that the religion of the Bible, believed and obeyed, brings people into harmony with the great powers about them in the physical world and gives them the most complete command over the riches and resources of the earth. And they are right in supposing that the religion of the western nations has given them their superiority to the nations of the ancient and decaying East. Let Christianity have full course and command in any country, and the wastes of war and intemperance and vice and ignorance and idleness will be stopped at once. There would be hundreds of millions to spare every year for the diffusion of the same light and liberty among all nations, until all lands were enlightened and all people were free. Let the degraded millions of Africa and Asia learn to live by the law of the gospel, and the wealth of the world will be increased a hundredfold. Everywhere there will be skill and labor and capital and tools and machinery to construct all manner of needed public works, to establish all useful institutions, to provide everything for the universal good of all the people of all the earth.

The want of men and money to carry the gospel to the ends of the earth within the present generation comes only from the fact that people in Christian nations have not yet fully come up to the gospel standard of right and happy living. Let ten millions of Christians in America adopt that standard and carry it out in all the social and business relations of life, and their example would bring twice as many millions more to join in the great crusade for the world's redemption. Such an exceeding great army, marching to battle against the powers of darkness, under the leadership of the Prince of peace, would be mightier than all the armies of the nations. They could cause wars to cease upon the face of the whole earth. They could close up the recruiting places of vice and infamy in all the great cities of the world. They could save for education and humanity millions which are now worse than wasted upon wickedness and dissipation. They could compel all kings of the earth and all rulers of the people to respect their will and help them in their beneficent designs for the common good of all mankind. They could supply a preacher of the gospel for every five hundred of the heathen world. They could lift education and social culture to so high a standard all round the earth that books and engines and furniture and tools and all manner of instrumentalities of refinement and civilization would be in use and demand in all places where now men live in hovels of mud, and women carry burdens like the pack horse, and children have no homes but the habitations of cruelty.

In order that Christianity may show its full power to uplift and enrich the whole human family, it is only necessary that those now professing faith in Christ should accept, with the whole heart, his new commandment of love and his one Great Commission to disciple all the nations. Let the Church become a living body of enrolled followers of Christ who stand ready to do his will in all that he commands, let them devote time and strength and ability and possessions wholly and cheerfully to the work which Christ has given them to do, and soon all the riches and powers of the earth would come into their possession and the possession of those who join with them in the endeavor to establish the kingdom of God among all nations. Then would come the time when a handful of corn on the mountains would bring forth a harvest waving like Lebanon. The least labor would bring the greatest reward. All questions of work and wages would be peacefully settled in accordance with the supreme law of right, and all the children of want would be blessed. The waste places of the desert and the wilderness would become like the garden of Paradise in beauty and fertility; the bitter cry of starving children would cease to be heard in the crowded cities; the residents in scattered villages would become like members of the same family, living together in happiness and peace.

XXI.

THE CONSECRATION OF WEALTH.

ONE prime condition of advance in the great missionary enterprise all over the world is the consecration of the great and growing wealth of Christians in America and in all Christian lands to the establishment of the kingdom of God in all the earth. The most Christian nations are the richest, and wealth is accumulating in their hands more rapidly than in the hands of any other people. It must necessarily be so. Among them, mind is most active and inventive; the great and exhaustless resources of nature are best understood and mastered; there is less waste in war and ignorance and vice and idleness; life is longer, and effort is more wisely applied, and the fruits of labor are more securely held; there is greater freedom of action and a higher inspiration of hope and reward.

In all heathen and Mohammedan countries there is always great wastefulness, loss of time and labor and resources and power. The traditions and observances of caste and custom check all progress, discourage all effort, and destroy all hope. The government taxes and oppresses and plunders. The rich acquire and keep their property by bribery and fraud and falsehood, and the poor have no helper, the suffering no pity, and multitudes think it better to die than to live. In such nations there is no honorable way open to all for the acquisition of wealth; there is no way in which it can be safely kept or profitably used if gained; injustice and fraud, crime and cruelty, are the qualifications for success, and a dark shadow of hopelessness rests on the people.

But in Christian lands there are law and order, protection to life and liberty, the highest stimulus to effort, and the surest prospect of enjoying the reward of labor. Far-reaching plans are made; vast resources from the treasure-house of nature are developed; study and experiment and invention are ever going on; the discoveries and accumulations of one generation are passed safely on to the next to be continued and increased; roads, travel, means of intercourse, distribute the results of industry all round the globe and gather in the riches and productions of all lands. The laws, the education, the freedom of Christian lands alone make such material prosperity possible. And far the larger part of the wealth in the hands of men in Christian lands has come to them through the enlightening, uplifting, and humanizing influence of the gospel. And still more, the liberty to possess, to use, and to enjoy their great wealth has come to them through the just laws, the social order, good education, improvement in the practical arts, multiplicity of inventions growing out of the mental and moral activity infused into the minds of men by the teaching and the spiritual impulse of Christianity.

It is only a fitting expression of gratitude to the Giver of all their prosperity that Christians in America should use their wealth in promoting a wider diffusion of the knowledge, the power, the truth from which their material and intellectual prosperity comes. The best, the most effectual way of getting the highest good of the wealth which the gospel brings to nations is to use it, as the gospel enjoins, in promoting the highest welfare of the whole human family. The vast accumulation of the means of luxurious living and the strong temptation to live in ease and pride and sensuality will certainly bring corruption, weakness, decay, if wealth be not used in lifting up the tone of national purity, promoting enlarged views of Christian beneficence, bringing the whole family of man to share in the glorious light and liberty of the gospel. No nation on earth can long withstand the terrible temptations of great wealth and great facilities for luxurious living, unless ever-accumulating riches be used generously and persistently in the service of humanity, in the promotion of the kingdom of God. Wealth without principle, conscience, Christian consecration, brings pride, selfishness, sensuality, enervation of character, all manner of vicious indulgence, all social disgrace and disaster, want of patriotism, want of courage, endurance, faith, conscience, justice, purity. Wealth without the will to use it rightly corrupts and debases manhood, undermines the foundations of society, takes away all stimulus to healthful exertion and self-denial, makes a nation mean and sensual and contemptible

Such was the effect in Rome when her nobles were enriched with the spoils of conquered nations, and her populace gave themselves up to the debasing pleasures of the bath and the brothel, the race course and the amphitheater. Never in all history has there been a more revolting exhibition of meanness and cowardice and sensuality than there was in the great Imperial City when the products of all lands flowed into her markets and the wealth of all nations enriched her treasuries. So was it with Venice, when her senators were robed in purple, and " her daughters had their dowers from spoils of nations," and her marble palaces rose " from out the wave as from the stroke of an enchanter's wand." Meanness and treachery and every excess of profligacy reigned in her homes and streets and made the once brave and beautiful city a Sodom of the sea. All this was the natural and inevitable consequence of great wealth coming into the hands of proud and prosperous men, who became false and effeminate and licentious just because they lost all regard for the public good and learned to live only for themselves.

Such will be the effect of the vast and rapid accumulation of wealth in the hands of the Christian people of America unless it finds the healthful and happy outlet of Christian beneficence, Christian enlargement of effort, sacrifice, and enterprise, in all manner of Christian work. Christian parents who lay up wealth for their children without teaching them to use it in the service of God miss the main condition of promoting their children's welfare. If the children are trained up to bear an honorable part in the great work of enlightening and redeeming all nations, they will have the highest enjoyment life can give, whether rich or poor. They will not be pensioners upon the legacies of their parents, nor will they depend for support and happiness upon the work which somebody else has done for them.

Successful business men who have accumulated large property in consequence of the great opportunities afforded in a Christian country will never get the full value of their acquisitions unless they learn to use them in the endeavor to bring the greatest possible number of others to enjoy the same privilege, secure the same prosperity. They cannot help knowing that the great mass of the people in all heathen countries are poor, very poor. They live in wretched homes; they wear the scantiest and the meanest clothing; they suffer daily for the want of sufficient and suitable food; multitudes of their children, millions and millions, wear no clothing at all. They have no books or pictures or furniture to brighten their lowly dwellings; mud walls and earth floors and moldering thatch of reeds or straw make up all the beauty and comfort which they associate with the name of home. They are taxed and oppressed, if they live under heathen governments; they are worse taxed and oppressed by traditions, superstitions, and social distinctions that have come down to them from their fathers. They see no way in which it may be possible for them to rise above the wretched condition into which they have been born, and in which they must live from birth to death. The whole world about them is peopled with imaginary beings that are ever lying in wait to do them harm. They resort to all manner of spells and enchantments and sacrifices to guard against unreal dangers. So they spend their whole life in fear and dread of beings that have no existence and of dangers that never come. They are tantalized with hopes that are never fulfilled; they pray for blessings that are never given.

Such is the life of millions of the great human family. They are not so far off but that we can go to them: we can understand much of their troubles and fears and sorrows. Facilities for travel and for the transmission of information growing out of Christian civilization have brought the heathen in the remote parts of the earth to our very doors. We can know as much about them as we can about some parts of our own country. Friends, neighbors, intelligent, conscientious observers are constantly going round the world and coming home to tell what they saw and learned on the journey. The heathen of India and Japan are now as near to us as were the settlers on the banks of the Ohio and the Mississippi a century ago to the people of New England. Christians in America hear and see and know all this; and therefore they are called upon in Christ's name to do all in their power to lift the cloud of ignorance and superstition which overhangs the heathen world. If they look on and send no help out of their abundance, then they will grow hard and selfish and faithless, and they will get very little comfort or satisfaction out of their wealth because they are doing nothing to make other lands as rich and prosperous as their own. It were better and safer to be poor and have a heart to sympathize with the suffering than to be rich and do nothing to help the needy.

The gospel truth is intrusted to us, not to keep for our own personal advantage alone, but to send it forth upon its message of mercy to lift the burdens from the shoulders of the weary, scatter light upon the path of the darkened, give songs of gladness for the sighing and the sorrows of the millions who walk in the region of the shadow of death. The gospel has made the American people rich and free and strong. Our ancestors were more degraded and brutal in their superstitions than the Hindus or the Chinese of to-day. The light of Christian truth alone has brought us our great liberty and power and prosperity. And we shall be hardened in selfishness and enervated in sensuality, as a people, if we have the source of all our blessings to give to millions who need it as much as our fathers did, and we give it not.

Trade and travel have brought the heathen to our very doors. It is almost as if we could look out of our windows upon their wretchedness, and the voices of gladness in our homes were mingled with the cries of their misery. Every morning paper brings intelligence from the ends of the earth. The word foreigner is fast losing its meaning and the lines of neighborhood encompass the globe. If the intelligent and prosperous people of America, the richest and the freest people in the world, sit in their pleasant parlors and ride in their palace cars, and look on their pleasant pictures and bright landscapes, and give no help to millions of the poor and the ignorant in India and China and Japan, then they will grow hard and selfish and cold-hearted, incapable of enjoyment, dissatisfied with themselves and with everything about them. They will begin to lose faith in the truths which they have believed; they will become ungrateful for the blessings which they have received; they will have little peace of mind and heart under the inevitable trials of life, and they will have less hope for anything better to come when life is done. So the great advantages which they possess will prove a curse rather than a blessing because they fail to use them in the service of God and for the good of their fellow-men. And so the great inheritance of freedom and knowledge and salvation will be taken from them and given unto a people who will bring forth the fruits of faith and humanity, gratitude and love.

At the present time in America there is a vast accumulation of wealth in the hands of a few individuals. It is said that twenty-five hundred persons own one half of the property in the whole country. And yet many of them seem not to know how to get the highest good from their great wealth. They build palaces; they put money enough into a steam yacht to endow a college; they give a head cook twice as much as the salary of the president of a university; they expend millions in pictures and jewelry and furniture. They drive fast horses, and their splendid equipages are attended by liveried servants and lackeys. They give great dinners and midnight dances, and there is music and wine in their feasts. Yet they get tired of their riches and their pleasures, and they are apt to say that neither are worth having. They are surprised and mortified that they can get so little out of their great wealth. They are apt to suspect that the world is all against them and that there is a general conspiracy to rob them of their riches.

They need to catch the inspiration of Christian benevolence from those who find the highest joy of life in giving and working for the kingdom of God on earth. They need to be surrounded by people who are rich in faith and happy in self-denial and full of all joy and peace in believing that God's kingdom is coming and that it is a great privilege to have a part in promoting its advance. Let there be ten millions of Christians in this land of ours, united in heart and soul in the work of establishing the religion of Jesus Christ among all nations; let the great millionaires have to do every day with earnest, intelligent, strong men who are wholly committed to the Great Commission to disciple all nations and in the shortest possible time ; let rich men see that Christians find great joy in that work, and that they themselves become noble, manly, magnanimous, day by day, because they are devoted to the interests of so great a kingdom, and they are working in harmony with the one infinite and eternal Mind ; let all the professed followers of Christ in America stand out before the world as wholly devoted to the one cause for which Christ gave himself to the cross, — and their spirit will affect the public mind, correct popular opinion, enlarge the range of human sympathy and charity, until millionaires feel its power and begin to look for new and higher uses for their great wealth. So, in the end, the very constraint of usage, the infectious influence of Christian example, the controlling power of a purified public opinion, shall lead rich men to find the true use of riches in the joy of giving for the kingdom of Christ ; and so shall come to pass the saying of the prophet that in the good time of the Messiah's reign kings shall minister unto him and the ships of merchants shall bring gold and silver from afar, and all beautiful things shall be devised and given to make the place of his presence glorious, and all people shall be blessed in him.

XXII.

THE HIGHER EDUCATION.

IN all Christian lands there should be especial institutions and courses of study established for the purpose of preparing young men for the work of world-wide evangelization. The one aim should be ever kept in view, and the students should be animated by the conviction that they are to prepare themselves to take up the highest profession ever pursued by man in this world. The work to be done is the greatest, the most difficult, the most complex, the most far-reaching in its consequences, of any ever given men to do. It undertakes to accomplish a greater revolution than any recorded in all the history of the past. It would change radically and permanently the faith, the character, the life, and the hope of uncounted millions. It must overcome the strongest appetites and passions, the most inveterate prejudices and superstitions, the traditions and customs deemed the most sacred: it must enter the sanctuary of every household and the secret place of every soul.

The laborers who undertake this work must needs be wise and considerate, patient and courageous, cheerful and hopeful in the face of every difficulty, unyielding, unconquerable in the face of all opposition. They must go out into the uttermost parts of the earth, and they must learn to live with people of strange tongues and rude manners and dissolute lives. They must master hard languages and accustom themselves to hard modes of travel and means of living. They must understand the best means of preserving life and strength and vitality in depressing climates and under all the hindrances and discouragements which attend their labor. They must be so thoroughly grounded in the doctrines which they teach that nothing can shake their faith. They must be so fully inspired with the loftiest motives that nothing can turn them aside from their sacred work. They must be so firm in purpose, so fearless in heart, that nothing can daunt their courage or weaken their resolution or quench their zeal. They must be so well versed in science and history and the general literature of the world, and also in the theories and speculations of critics and skeptics and philosophers, that they can hold their ground with reason and constancy in contact with all classes of men, and carry themselves with dignity and propriety in all ranks of society.

To take such a stand before the world and to be leaders in the greatest work of the age and of all ages, missionaries must needs have all the help which the most diligent study and the most careful preparation can give. They must be trained and educated with the distinct understanding that theirs is to be the most sacred, the most difficult, and the most important profession which any man can undertake in this world. They should be put under the instruction of teachers whose whole mind and heart are set upon carrying forward the grandest enterprise ever intrusted to the hands of men — the establishment of the kingdom of God among men of every race and nation under heaven. Our highest institutions of education have professorships in every department of literature and science and art. The most brilliant men spend long and laborious years in preparing themselves to occupy the chair of the professor in teaching some branch of human learning which is only incidental to a polite education. Why not have professorships of the one grand science which has for its aim and purpose the highest possible improvement of every class and condition of men on the face of the earth? Why not set the most learned, the most inspiring, the most enthusiastic men that can be found in the whole land to teach the divine art of saving men from the delusions of superstition, the bondage of error, and the dark ways of death?

Political economy proposes to increase the nation's wealth by teaching the laws of growth and decay, of supply and demand, of production and consumption, of possession and exchange, of invention and application of all materials and forces in the earth to the improvement of man's condition in this world. It claims high rank among the most practical sciences because its whole aim is to advance the material interests of the individual man and society at large. It assumes that a young man is not well educated for practical life unless he has made a study of the modes and means by which people can be better clothed, housed, and supplied with all the comforts of physical well-being in this present world. Why not say that a young man is not well educated unless he has made a distinct and devout study of the higher laws of faith, duty, benevolence, happiness, by obedience to which the nations can be raised to the highest possible condition of wealth and prosperity in this world, and at the same time shall be made heirs of infinite riches and endless life in the world to come? Why not say that the young man is best educated who is best prepared to go out into the waste places of the earth and set up the reign of righteousness and peace where cruel superstitions and wasteful wars have prevailed over all the people for ages? Why not call him the best educated man who best knows how to deliver his fellow-men from bondage to wasteful appetites and passions, and bring them forth into the glorious light and liberty which the gospel of Christ gives to nations?

We have learned men to teach dead languages, dead literatures, dead antiquities — things that once had great power on the earth and are now passed away forever. We have learned and enthusiastic men who spend large sums of money and expose themselves to danger and weariness and toil and sickness and death, to dig up the foundations of buried cities and gather up relics of an age long gone by. Why not have equally learned and enthusiastic men to teach the living and immortal interests of all nations, the personal duties and responsibilities of all classes and conditions of men, the endless destinies which are to be decided by the character and conduct of men in time? Why not have special schools and colleges whose sole aim shall be to prepare young men to go out to the waste places of the old world, not in search of dead antiquities to be brought home and cased up in museums and cabinets, but to find living men, and train them up to a new and glorious life, surpassing the highest attainments of the men who waged war and overthrew cities and gained great earthly fame in ancient time? Why not train our young students, by special courses of study, to understand that the present is the great age of the world; that living men of to-day, however depressed their condition, are of more consequence than all the dead relics of the past? One Greek shepherd, watching his flock in the Troad, or climbing the rocks about Delphi, or lurking among the fallen columns about Corinth or Argos or Mycenæ, is worth more to the living world and the hopes of humanity than all the images of dead gods and all the rusted shields, swords, and helmets ever dug up from the ruins of buried cities or ever stored in all the antiquarian museums of all the world. The traveler who gazes upon the Taj of Agra by sunlight or by moonlight is expected to go into raptures of admiration over the wondrous beauty of the dome and the elaborate finish of the walls and the matchless symmetry of the whole structure. But it is all dead, cold stone: it commemorates an age of oppression and cruelty: it perpetuates a story of passion and profligacy which it were better for the world if it had never been told.

One poor pariah watering the Taj gardens is worth more to the world and to the universe of immortal beings than the gorgeous tomb which cost twenty millions of money and wasted the strength and labor of twenty thousand lives. The poor pariah may be enlightened and raised up to a life that shall grow greater and mightier and more blessed when the Taj has become as the dust of the whirlwind or the withered leaves which are swept before the storm. If men are saved from ignorance and vice and superstition, there will be no want of works of art surpassing all the highest achievements of the ancients, and the age of the future will become so glorious that the past will be remembered only with wonder at its folly and regret for its wickedness. And our young men who go out from our colleges into the world armed with all the resources which education can give them should go to save living men, not to gather up the relics of the dead past, not to study and admire works that might better never have been done.

No study can do more to enlarge, to liberalize, to purify, and to cultivate the minds of young men than the divine science of saving the lost talents, the wasted resources, and the fruitless labors of men of all races in all lands. No study can do more to train up a new generation of brave, strong, progressive leaders than the great, the divine science of world-embracing beneficence, philanthropy, charity, which has for its aim the highest good of all, the fullest enlightenment of all, the everlasting salvation of the whole human race. Teach the young men at the very outset of their education and all the way on that there is ever before them one supreme interest, so urgent, so important, that all others sink into insignificance in comparison with its demands. Kindle their highest ambition to do their best in their brief day and generation to make the world remember them gratefully when they are gone. But show them that the way to be held in everlasting remembrance is to work with God and join hands with all of God's servants in the endeavor to fill the earth with righteousness and peace.

The world has had great statesmen, commanders, poets, orators, merchants, millionaires. They have done their best in their line of work. They have done much to quicken mind, inspire lofty thought, incite to great enterprise and heroic daring, even sometimes in behalf of a failing cause:

but the world is not yet instructed, emancipated, saved. The old wastes of the past are still going on. Millions are toiling all their life long and getting no adequate reward for their labor. Millions are walking in darkness through the whole length of life's journey and never finding the light. The homes of millions are hovels scarcely fit for cattle. Millions live and die in the habitations of ignorance, cruelty, and superstition. They have nothing to comfort them in their great sorrows, no helping hand put forth to lighten their burdens, no star of hope shining with clear light to guide their steps to a home of rest and peace.

What the world wants now is men who have been trained and fitted for a higher mission than princes and philosophers ever bore; men who go forth by divine appointment through all the earth to save the lost, to reclaim the wandering, to redeem the enslaved. They are to make it the study of their lives to master the divine art of doing good. They want just so much of science, history, literature, philosophy, as will help them in the endeavor to make the long, dark reign of error and wickedness and superstition in the earth give place to universal light, peace, prosperity, righteousness. They must be put under the instruction and personal influence of teachers whose one supreme object is to fit them to take the religion of Jesus Christ with them into all the dark places of the earth and set its holy light to shine in every human habitation.

The medical school is instituted for the sole purpose of making physicians, the law school for making lawyers, the industrial school for making mechanics and artisans of every kind. So we want schools of the highest order, manned by the best men that can be found in the whole land, and concentrating all their efforts and abilities upon the one purpose of preparing men to preach the good news of God to all the nations. The pupils in such institutions must be fired with the most sacred and lofty ambition to conquer the whole world for Christ. All their courses of study are to be chosen with one object — to fit them for the great work of world-wide evangelization. Mere professional students, cloistered scholars, ingenious theorists, daring speculators in philosophy and theology, should have no place in the corps of instruction in seminaries for training men to be leaders in God's host and to be foremost in delivering the divine message unto the nations. Earnest, devout, practical men, who keep themselves in daily contact with the living world, are needed to train students for the world's most urgent work in the coming age. They should even be men whom the world will look upon as beside themselves with the one absorbing passion for the world's conversion to Christ. We have schools and colleges enough already for general education. What we want now is institutions for the special training of men to carry the gospel through the world and put an end to the long and wasteful reign of ignorance and vice and wrong.

We want — we must have — a generation of Christian students growing up into strong manhood with the full, practical conviction that the greatest question now before the world is how most speedily to bring all nations to the acceptance of Christianity as the one only divine, universal religion, equally adapted to all lands, all time, all races of men. Whoever is wisely, laboriously preparing himself for an honorable share in that great work is seeking the highest education, is preparing for the most glorious career open for man in this most enlightened and progressive age. Whoever fills earnestly and faithfully any post of duty which has been assigned him by the Prince and Captain of salvation, whoever keeps even step in the march of God's host for the conquest of the world for Christ, is sure to make his life a joyous and glorious success.

The highest Christian education will not neglect or ignore any branch of useful knowledge ; but it will strive first of all to know Him in whom are hidden all the treasures of infinite wisdom and knowledge and from whom cometh forth the light which lighteth our feet into the way of peace. It will teach all that can be known about God's great work in the world and all that can be known about the deeper mysteries of mind, spirit, soul. But it will make all attainments in art, science, literature, language, history, instrumental in gaining the most perfect knowledge of Jesus Christ, in whom are infinite riches of wisdom and power and love. The highest Christian education would put first and foremost in all its courses of study the knowledge of the truth as it is in Jesus, the way of life and salvation open to all men through faith in him.

In this enlightened and Christian land it is a surprise and a shame that young men are so seldom taught to put Christianity first and foremost in all the courses of study that discipline the mind and arm the student for the great conflict of life. They should be made to see at the very outset of their course, and all the way on, that Christianity has given the stimulus, the activity, the progress, the new life and force to this nineteenth century. Christianity alone gives us the hope that the ages of the future will be better than the dark and evil ages of the past. Christianity, by right of divine inspiration and by right of long-tried and proved efficiency, should stand before all sciences and civilizations as the leader in the march of the nations to a truer life and a better age. Our American students will miss their calling, lose their great opportunity, if they do not stand forth, full armed and fired with faith and love, to carry the religion of Christ to all the nations. It will be to little purpose that they learn science and philosophy and literature and art and antiquities and dead languages and criticism, if they do not learn how to bring men to the acceptance of the greatest gift heaven has to give to earth. Of all young men in the world American youth are most sacredly bound to carry Christianity to all the nations, because the American youth have received the greatest advantages from the gospel themselves.

XXIII.

THE CHRISTIAN PRESS.

THE great enterprise of world-wide evangelization should always have a most efficient ally in the Christian press. We have a few special missionary magazines; they speak mostly for one board or society, and their circulation is limited to the constituency of the organization by which they are published. To a very great degree they are understood to be begging circulars whose main object is to get money, and the cost of which must be met by drawing upon funds given for the general cause. Such magazines always labor under great disadvantage, because every monthly issue must carry the appeal for more money. They cannot have space for lengthened argument and illustration and appeal in behalf of the one great, world-embracing commission to disciple all nations. For the most part they are obliged to take it for granted that their readers will seek general information in regard to the condition of the heathen world from other sources. They must report the labors of their own missionaries and keep them ever before the eyes of their readers so that to some it may seem that there is no other force in the field.

What is wanted is an open avowal on the part of all Christian magazines, reviews, newspapers, periodicals, made constantly in every variety of form, that the one great mission of the Church in all its branches and denominations is the evangelization of all nations. Every Christian newspaper should be a mission advocate, a loud and earnest pleader for the oppressed, the poor, the ignorant, the lost, of every land and language. It should stand out on every page of the Christian periodical that it is enlisted in the world-wide campaign for the recovery of all nations from the dominion of the powers of darkness.

We have political newspapers devoted to the interest of some particular party or policy in the management of the affairs of government. We cannot read a page or a column without seeing at once to which party the paper is devoted. Through all the year it carries the flag of its party; it attacks every opposing party with leaded lines and lengthened columns. Day after day, week after week, year in and year out, the whole staff of editors, reporters, contributors, correspondents, is gathering up arguments and evidences, facts and testimonies, theories and speculations, to sustain their policy, to elect their candidates, to lead the public mind, and to rule the whole land. Millions of money and the time and labor of thousands of the most active and brilliant men are expended upon such papers every year, and to support measures which are so little essential to the prosperity of the country that good and wise men are often found taking opposite sides, and the country goes right on in the even course of growth and prosperity whichever party prevails. It is very seldom that any great political party is animated and controlled by some one great, underlying principle of truth and justice and humanity — one which is equally true and important in all lands and for all time. Principles and parties change, but the contention goes on; and the best talent is given to the support of measures that affect only a small portion of the people of a single country and will last only for a little time.

But the divine commission to disciple all the nations is infinitely more important than the issues of the most hotly contested political campaign. It takes in the most sacred, the most widely extended, the most lasting interests of humanity; it is inspired by the loftiest and the purest motives; it depends for its success upon the eternal principles of truth, justice, and love; it is not confined to any one country or age or race; it aims to secure the highest welfare of all people, all races, all ranks in human society, through the whole of this present life and forever in the life to come. If it be reasonable that a thousand secular journals shall be pleading every day in the year for a local and temporary and questionable policy in government affairs, it surely is not fanatical for a hundred Christian newspapers to plead with equal earnestness and constancy for an enterprise which aims at the removal of all sin and misery from the face of the earth, and which will be complete only when the wars and the desolations of the past give place to peace and prosperity among all nations. It is not bigoted or narrow-minded or irrational that we should crowd the columns of religious newspapers all the year through with facts and testimonies and arguments and appeals to stir up Christians of every name to be true to the demands of their Great Commission and carry the gospel of their Master through the world. They should always assume that their cause has the right to take precedence of all political issues, all party policies, all questions of local and temporary interest to individuals and nations. They should make it the great aim of all their appeals to the Christian mind of the people to educate them into a right understanding and full acceptance of the command of Christ to maintain unceasing warfare against the principalities and the powers of darkness until light and liberty become the inheritance of all nations. Every Christian newspaper should put itself before the world as an advocate of that one great movement, just as fully and constantly as any political newspaper puts itself forth as the advocate of the principles and the measures of its party.

The growth, the power, the unity, the orthodoxy, the sanctification of the Church at home can be best promoted by drawing out all the resources and activities of Christians in labor to publish the gospel to all the world and secure the conversion of all nations. The Christian publication, which comes into the family or finds its way into the hands of the individual Christian every week, should always be a gracious and instructive messenger, making the visit on purpose to keep the word of the Master ever in mind and set his claim before all others. It is not true to its name as a Christian messenger unless every number does something to quicken its readers in faith and effort for the entire conquest of the world for Christ. It should strive to make its readers better acquainted with their duty, their privilege, and their ability to bear an honorable part in the greatest revolution of all the ages, the most glorious triumph that shall ever be sung or celebrated on earth or in heaven. The Christian newspaper should encourage and stimulate its readers every week to give, speak, influence, pray with ever-increasing faith and fervor for the speedy accomplishment of all that Christ desires to have done on earth, all that must needs be done before God's kingdom will fully come and the rule and the practice of obedience to God shall be the same on earth and in heaven. So its whole influence shall be to animate its readers with the most glorious hope and to raise them above all meanness and littleness of spirit, by keeping their minds and hearts fixed upon the greatest enterprise of all the ages.

Millions of people in the most Christian lands do not understand, and because they do not understand they do not believe in the possibility and promise of a reign of righteousness and peace among all nations. They are not fully possessed with the conviction that it is the main business, the divine commission, of the Church to prepare the way for the coming of the King, and to bring in the glorious day of his appearing, in power and spirit, for the redemption of all nations from ignorance and superstition, from sin and death.

The sentiment of loyalty to the King must be cultivated: it must be deepened and purified by self-denial and sacrifice; it must be commended to the young by precept and by example. The devotion of the ancient Hebrew to the Holy Hill of Zion must be reproduced and enlarged in all Christians until each follower of Christ feels that it were better that his tongue should be dumb and his right hand withered than that he should forget his allegiance to Christ or become indifferent to the advance of Christ's kingdom on the earth. All Christians must be trained up to the feeling that the Church, the kingdom of Christ, is their own dear country, their beloved and blessed home, and that they can give and labor and suffer and die for it with greater willingness and devotion than the patriot suffers and dies for his country. The Christian's country is the whole world, and it is but one province of a universal and an everlasting kingdom. To give and labor and suffer for that is to bear a part in the work which the infinite God is carrying on throughout all worlds and through endless ages. When Christians are fully educated into that great mission, their own lives will be great and blessed, and when the prince of this world comes to them, as he came to Christ, he will find nothing of his own in them, as he found nothing in their Master.

This is not a fanatical or an impracticable sentiment which I am urging. The kingdom of Christ in the world is a reality, not a fancy or a fiction, and it is a much greater reality than the kingdom of Britain or the empire of Russia or the republic of America. Devotion to the kingdom of Christ is just as rational as devotion to our own dear country, and it is a sentiment as much loftier than patriotism as the welfare and freedom of all nations are more important than the prosperity of one people, the reign of universal and everlasting righteousness and peace is more important than the success of a party in a political campaign.

Men of the greatest intellect, the highest culture, and the most extended resources of influence and property, give themselves night and day with quenchless zeal and fiery devotion to the support of a party platform in political strife. Why should not men of equal culture and power and resources give themselves with a superior and more lasting devotion to the establishment of a spiritual commonwealth which shall bring all nations into one harmonious and happy brotherhood and fill every land with the abundance of peace? Why should not eloquence lift up its mightiest voice and poetry sing its loftiest song and science offer the fruit of all its researches and wealth open all its treasuries and art build its grandest works and millions of people unite in earnest and enthusiastic effort to break the chains of the enslaved of all nations, to hasten the coming of the great era of light and liberty, when the earth shall bring forth abundance for the supply of every want and the wastes of war and wickedness shall be known no more?

The editor of a religious newspaper or magazine stands at the head, the receiving office of all needed information concerning the condition of the world and the advance of the kingdom of God. He has intelligence constantly coming to him from all quarters of the earth and all branches of the great human family. He stands upon his high post of observation to take up the word which God's providence is speaking among the nations and to pass it on to his readers with increasing clearness and power from his own mind. He is called to his responsible position that he may use it simply and solely for that one great purpose: the enlightenment of the Christian public upon the one subject which is of more importance than all others in this most enlightened age, the full and speedy evangelization of all nations. He is at his post as a watchman on the walls of a besieged city, to hear the sounds and descry the signs of coming danger. And his is the still more grateful task of announcing the approach of the King, who comes in triumph for the deliverance of the nations from the long bondage of ignorance and oppression, of sin and death. Let him withdraw attention from all other sights when he sees the hosts of the living God on the march, and he hears songs of gladness rising from myriads of voices that have long been accustomed to the cry of sorrow and the wail of despair. Let him continually do his best to fire the hearts of his thousands of readers with a sacred and divine enthusiasm for the advance of the one cause on which rests all our hope of the coming of a better day than the past has ever seen.

We have papers and periodicals in abundance to tell us of wars and rumors of wars, of famines and plagues and earthquakes in divers places. Political and commercial and social events are sure to be reported in long array for all to read. The doings of congress and parliament and conventions and caucuses crowd the columns of morning and evening journals. The progress of industry and inventions and arts, letters of travelers from all parts of the earth, reports of lectures on all subjects of popular interest, accounts of social doings, amusements, matches, and theatrical representations, concerts, excursions, and assemblies all over the land, keep a thousand printing presses running night and day. The poorest buy; the richest stop in the pressure of business to read; everybody is expected to know what the papers say; nobody thinks an intelligent and progressive people could hold their own, much less make advances in wealth and power, without constant reading.

All that is well so long as things limited, incidental, and

temporary are kept in their proper place. But in the face of all such conflicting and diversified interests the religious press should come forward as the advocate of interests surpassing all others in importance, in extent, and in authority. It should stand forth always and everywhere as the fervid, untiring, and unyielding promoter of a revolution, the greatest, the mightiest in all the ages of human history, in all the lands of the earth — the deliverance of immortal millions from the dominion of darkness and their triumphant entrance into the kingdom of light. The religious press should continually bring before the world in every variety of form the growing evidences that the kingdom of light is advancing, the proclamation of everlasting liberty is going forth in every language unto the ends of the earth, peace is showing itself mightier than war, truth is beating down the hoary forms of error, and righteousness is exalting itself above the thrones of iniquity in the old lands of the East as well as in the new world of the West. Every week the Christian editor should press upon his readers the unrivaled claims of the kingdom of God over all human policies, over all earthly interests. All leading articles, editorials, and communications in the Christian newspaper should constantly maintain that Christ has the first and highest claim upon property and time and labor, and that human effort and possessions will never bring so great a reward as when they are employed most earnestly in his service.

No Christian newspaper should apologize for the prominence which it gives to the claims of the kingdom of God in every issue and in all its columns. The political editor does not apologize for the prominence which he gives to the plans and principles of his party every day in the year. Why should the Christian editor make excuses for pressing upon his readers the demands of the greatest, the most sacred enterprise which can ever engage the attention of men in all the ages? As soon apologize for the presence of the sunlight at noonday, or for the falling of the snow in winter, or for the springing of the grass in the opening year, as for the light of the Sun of righteousness beaming upon the darkened nations.

Christian ministers, Christian men, Christian newspapers, should always take it for granted that God's kingdom must stand first in all public and private appeals for money and effort and time and consecration. Fidelity in the service, devotion to the interests of his cause in the earth is so great, ennobling, and true in its influence upon character that it must ensure fidelity and devotion in all the relations of life. Generosity, justice, humanity, in all the transactions of business and in all the intercourse of society, must be the natural consequence of yielding all to the one claim which is infinite in authority and promotive of infinite good. Let the Christian newspaper be considerate and helpful towards all enterprises which have for their aim the lightening of human burdens, the healing of human sorrows, the rewarding of human labor. But always let it be seen on every page of its numbers that the full coming of the kingdom of righteousness and peace in all the earth is the one grand consummation which it seeks.

What has been said in this chapter should not be understood as an attempt to throw discredit upon the many and excellent religious papers and periodicals which we have already in the field. They give a vast amount of information and instruction with every issue from the press. It would be impossible to keep up the tone of religious intelligence and activity without them. They are all laboring directly or indirectly for the advance of the kingdom of Christ among the nations. I am amazed at the amount of knowledge, experience, sagacity, and hard, plodding toil which the managers of such publications put into their columns week after week. What I would have them do in addition to all their present good work is simply this: I would have them stand more explicitly for the Church before the world, as a campaign paper stands for a political party in the year of a national election. I would have them proclaim in every variety of form and with constant repetition that the divine mission of the Church is to establish the religion of Christ over all the earth and cause it to be accepted, believed, and obeyed among all nations. The most careless reader should be made to see on every page of our Christian periodicals that they are devoted to that one object, they are campaign papers, and the election which they advocate is the voluntary choice of Christ as the Lord of all the nations. I would have our religious papers bring all leading articles, correspondence, and communications, to bear upon that one theme, the conversion of the world to Christ. If they did so, I suppose the outside world would call it fanaticism, bigotry, narrow-mindedness, illiberality, and all that. It will be a good sign when the world begins to talk in that way of all Christian work and faith and character. There can be no greater fairness, liberality, magnanimity, nobleness, than to speak, write, labor, give for the highest interest, the supreme welfare of all nations, all races of men that dwell on the face of all the earth. Let all who speak for the Church through the printed page proclaim it openly that the followers of Christ stand committed to the fulfillment of the divine commission to disciple all nations, and that they are determined not to fail in securing the election of their Lord and Master by the free, voluntary choice of all mankind. The more openly and persistently that proclamation is made, the better it will be for both the Church and the world, and the sooner will come the grand consummation for which the faithful have prayed for eighteen centuries and have finished their course in full faith that it would surely come, and yet have not been permitted to see the longed-for day.

XXIV.

THE LAST CRUSADE.

THE main facts concerning the command of Christ to disciple all nations, the dark and hopeless state of the heathen world, and the power of the gospel to scatter the darkness and bring the divine day are well known by us all. What is wanted is some most effective agency to arouse the millions of Christians of our country to new activity, and prevail on them to concentrate their efforts and their resources upon the great work of publishing the gospel in all languages and to the ends of the earth. The divine commission to disciple all the nations must be brought before the churches with such constancy and urgency that no follower of Christ can fail to feel the force of the appeal. It must be preached with such earnestness and tenderness and fervor to Christians as we expect the gospel of repentance and faith to be preached to sinners for their salvation. The most thoroughly tried, efficient, and consecrated men should be employed to go constantly to and fro through all the churches, preaching and proclaiming the last great, divine crusade for the deliverance of all nations from the thraldom of sin and superstition, and for the establishment of the kingdom of Christ among men.

Centuries ago, one enthusiastic but ill-informed man aroused all Christendom to go forth in battle array, by the hundred thousand, for the deliverance of the one little city of Jerusalem from the dominion of the Moslems. How much more should trained, enlightened, eloquent, and devoted men in our day stir the hearts of Christians of every name and denomination with appeals for the enslaved and degraded of every land and nation, for the deliverance of hundreds of millions from the bondage of sin and death! The fiery and impassioned pleading of Peter the Hermit was answered by shouts from countless voices — "God wills it, God wills it!" Surely with much more truth can it be said now that God wills the publication of the gospel unto every kindred and tribe on the face of the earth. He has given distinct and positive command that his Word shall be carried to all nations. This divine commission is the one sacred charge which has been laid upon the Church of Christ these eighteen hundred years, and it has never yet been fulfilled. The marching orders of the militant host have never been recalled, and they never were more fully in force than in our time. The evidence that the gospel is of God and is fitted to answer the deepest necessities of individuals and of society has been increasing from century to century; it never was so complete and satisfying as it is now, in the full blaze of the nineteenth century light. Three thousand were added to the Church on the day of Pentecost, and that was thought to be a sufficient demonstration of the fitness of the gospel for all nations. But in this single land of ours three thousand are added to the Church every day in the year, and the Bible has been translated into twenty times as many languages as were spoken in Jerusalem when the inspired company of the apostles told the wonderful works of God in the native tongue of all that heard.

The power which goes forth with the missionary to give success to his effort in lifting up the most degraded races of men is proved, ten thousand times over, to be the mightiest on earth. It is doing, in our day and within reach of our personal observation, greater works than were ever done by armies or legislators or philosophers. It takes whole libraries of Christian literature to tell how great things the gospel has done and is still doing among the nations to bring the reign of righteousness and peace in all the earth.

But the churches in the most Christian lands do not know these facts, or, knowing them in some degree, they do not grasp the fullness of their meaning, they do not feel their power. To rouse their slumbering zeal and strengthen their feeble faith and bring into the field their reserves of power in men and money, the divine command must be taken up and preached by the most eloquent and devoted in every Christian land. Let diligent search be made for the best men to enforce the claims of the divine commission, and, when they are found, let them have every facility to prepare themselves by study and travel and observation to preach the last great and divine crusade for the deliverance of all nations from bondage to man's great foe. Let them be assured that the churches are ready to stand by them in their work as they go forth throughout all the country, visiting cities and villages and private homes, arousing the indifferent, directing the zeal of the awakened, encouraging the faint-hearted, and always and everywhere, by instruction, by argument, by persuasion, and by testimony, endeavoring to fill the minds of all Christians with one desire and purpose to bring all nations to the acceptance of the truth as it is in Jesus.

When a great political party lays its plans to carry a national election, it selects the best, the most persuasive and eloquent speakers, it sends them out all over the land to explain its principles, to inform the people in regard to the issues at stake, and to commend its candidates to the suffrages of all. The whole country is flooded with printed documents and popular appeals; vast sums of money are raised and freely expended; agents and committees and orators and private citizens labor and endure fatigue and watching night and day. The election is the subject of conversation in the house, the shop, and the field, every day of the week and in every place where two or three are gathered together. It may indeed make very little perceptible difference with the country at large how the election goes; and yet each party is ready to move heaven and earth to secure the choice of its own candidate.

But the Christian commission sets before us a campaign which is to embrace all nations, which will affect the deepest interests of every individual; and it will be completed only by the establishment of a perfect law of right and liberty and the bringing in of a new era of abundance and prosperity over all the earth. The principles at stake, the destinies to be decided, are the greatest, deepest, widest that can ever influence the human mind or control human conduct. The welfare of uncounted millions on the earth and the condition of immortal millions in the endless future must be determined by the success or the failure of the great campaign against the principalities and powers of darkness. Everything which needs to be said in carrying forward this great, world-wide contest, everything fit to be done, everything required to be given, is noble, truthful, profitable, and glorious to the utmost degree. Whoever undertakes to preach the great crusade for the conversion of the world only needs to put forth, in truthful and fitting words, arguments that are built upon the foundation of eternal facts, principles, doctrines, consequences. Whatever he says now, in earnest and solemn appeal to the hearts of men, to enlist their interest in the great crusade, will be regarded only as more urgent, truthful, and important the more thoroughly it is weighed in the balances of a good understanding, the more it is subjected to the light of clearer knowledge and larger experience in the growing faith and better life of the future.

Now let the Church find out its strongest, best informed, most enthusiastic, most devoted men, and let them be specially commissioned to preach a nineteenth century crusade for the deliverance of all nations from the bondage of sin and superstition. Let them make it a study to understand the high calling to evangelize the whole world. Let them lay their hearts open to the divine power of the Great Commission and the divine promise of almighty help to fulfill its demands. Then let them go and pour out all the fervor of their hearts and all the eloquence of inspired lips in the enforcement of the theme. Let them compass the whole land, east, west, north, south, holding conventions, preaching in churches, addressing schools, colleges, seminaries, everywhere unfolding to the full extent of their power and resources the claim of Christ's cause and kingdom above every other claim. Let them not be confined to any one denomination or connection of Christians. Let it be enough to secure them a welcome that they have taken it upon themselves to arouse all Christians to the one great duty of publishing the gospel to the ends of the earth. Let the churches be free as ever to conduct worship, carry on missionary work in accordance with their own preferences and established usages, but let all churches alike be open to welcome the preachers of the crusade against the powers of darkness that have long held the nations in captivity. Let all alike receive the great command of Christ as the marching orders of the Prince and Captain of salvation. Let them act and organize, each in its own way, and go forth under his banner to find the portion of the field which is most in need of recruits and is most hardly pressed by the common foe. Let it be counted as essential to good and reputable standing in any church that one shall give, labor, pray for the evangelization of the whole world. Let the preachers of the great crusade fill the hearts of young and old with fiery zeal for the great and final campaign, until the old crusading cry, "God wills it!" shall rise like the shout of nations in every Christian land.

It seems to me that the great missionary enterprise will never be put in its right place before the Church and the world until the best and fittest men we have among us take it upon themselves to preach a new and universal crusade against Satan's dominion in heathen lands. They must give themselves to such preaching as fully as evangelists give themselves to preaching for revivals and for the conversion of men in the home land. No one can have, or desire to have, a mightier or a more inspiring theme. It gives ample scope for the clearest reasoning, the largest learning, the most commanding eloquence, and the most tender and impassioned appeals. To conquer the world by force of arms, as Alexander fancied he had done, were nothing to be thought of in comparison with the establishment of the reign of righteousness and peace, prosperity and happiness, among all the peoples of the earth. If the destruction of thousands of lives in war confers the title of "Great" upon the destroyer, much more is that distinction deserved by him who brings the gift of life to uncounted millions and teaches them to live and rejoice in the gift forever.

The kingdom of the mightiest conqueror lasts but a little time; it begins with violence and wrong, it is supported by force and falsehood, it ends in disaster and dishonor. The kingdom of Christ shall stand when all earthly thrones are cast down and all the structures of human pride are brought to desolation. Its first message is peace, its mightiest weapon is love, it is sustained by truth and righteousness, it gives life and liberty to all who submit to its sway. For such a kingdom the most eloquent can plead, the most learned can reason, the most devout can pray. The poet and the historian, the orator and the philosopher will seek in vain for a loftier theme than that which inspired the angel song of Bethlehem and which was confirmed and consecrated in the command of Christ to carry the glad tidings of the heavenly messengers to every nation.

It costs the lives of millions of men, more millions of money, years and ages of toil and suffering and sacrifice, to create and sustain one of the great kingdoms of the earth. Yet all the way through its history are deeds of violence and blood. Sometimes its greatest glory comes from the greatest crime. The poor are trodden down under the iron heel of war, the wages of the laborer go to enrich the idle and the oppressor, all departments of human industry are taxed that a few may live in luxury and dissipation. Christ comes to save life, not to kill. Wherever his word is most fully received, riches accumulate, fields bring forth most abundantly, life is prolonged, home is sacred; its greatest glory comes from doing good to all. Surely for the establishment of such a kingdom the mightiest voices should plead, the greatest gifts should be willingly given, afflictions and losses and martyrdoms should be bravely and cheerfully borne. To put its high demands and its exceeding great and precious promises fitly before the world, we want the most eloquent to speak, the strongest to toil, the bravest to endure, and the truest to hope. The orator, who can fire the hearts of his hearers with lofty enthusiasm when describing the struggles and sacrifices of a single people in asserting their independence against a foreign power, should be still more eloquent when urging the claims of a kingdom under which all the nations shall dwell together in peace as one family, and the wastes of war shall be known no more. The merchant or the millionaire, who gives his thousands to found a library or build a college or a monument, should give much more freely to send out messengers who shall fill all the habitations of men with light, and drive the demons of ignorance and superstition to the covert of darkness. The philanthropist, who would relieve all human suffering, should support a commission which is sent out into all the earth to comfort all that mourn, to bind up the broken-hearted, and to proclaim liberty to the captives of every tribe and nation.

XXV.

RECRUITING OFFICES.

EVERY Christian church should be a recruiting office to engage volunteers for world-wide and lifelong service in the great missionary campaign; every church should hold itself responsible to contribute its quota to fill up the ranks and enlarge the host already in the field contending with the powers of darkness. In every church there should be a constant, earnest, and businesslike presentation of the divine call to disciple all the nations. There should be, not simply once or twice a year, a fervid exhortation, an impassioned appeal, from an agent or a returned missionary. The Church as a body should take up the business of gathering recruits out of its own ranks and training them for the Master's service in whatever portion of the world field they are most needed and can do most to urge forward the one great campaign. The preaching and the prayer, the conferences and the contributions, the Sunday-school and the social gatherings of old and young, should all aim to bring out the influence, the property, and the vital force of the church most effectively for the advancement of the one great cause. Let each church choose the means and the methods best adapted to the place, the people, and the usage of the denomination to which it belongs, and then make every measure and effort tell in favor of the one desired result: the active and full committal of all its membership to the demands of the worldwide compaign.

The Church itself, with all its societies, bands, brotherhoods, Sunday-schools, and committees, should be a united and strong organization, whose constant aim and effort is to awaken interest, to collect and diffuse information, to raise money, to educate the young, and to train up candidates for the mission field or for home service in support of those at the front. All followers of Christ should help each other by precept and by example into the assured and settled belief that the highest and best use of any property, business, or profession is to accomplish what Christ would have done. The most successful man, the man who goes out in the world with the strongest assurance that he has gained the truest and highest purpose of living, is the man who has given himself most fully to the advancement of the kingdom of God among men.

Faith in that one great practical fact of life and duty is not apt to come all at once, nor by one act of will. In some cases it may even cost one a lifelong discipline and education to get it. It is apt to come hard when it is not begun early. Therefore it should be inculcated in the minds of the young when they are most susceptible to impressions of any kind. In the Christian family and in the Sunday-school the true idea of Christian living and what constitutes success in life should be nursed tenderly, lovingly, patiently, by teachers and parents, in order that it may become a steady, natural, and strong growth, so thoroughly incorporated with the feelings and the faith of the full-grown man that it shall cost him no struggle; he will need no fervid appeal to prevail on him to give his time and labor and heart to the advancement of the kingdom of Christ on earth. He accepts it as his mission as easily as the bird takes to the air with its wings and the fish finds its congenial home in the water. Such should be the prevailing spirit in every Christian church. Such should be its main safeguard against all false doctrine, all falling away to the world; its full and hearty acceptance of the command of Christ to disciple all nations. When that command is ignored or little thought of, the church may have a name to live, but it has lost the life of Him who came to give, and to give most abundantly.

In time of war, when the very existence of the nation is imperiled, recruiting offices are opened everywhere; meetings are held at all hours; individuals of all ages are expected to declare themselves ready to give and to do whatever they can for the common cause; women and children join with strong men in singing songs of devotion to country; the flag is hung out from towers and steeples and chimney tops; sermons are preached, lectures are given, entertainments are set forth, fairs are held, morning and evening newspapers are crowded with communications every day, and all bearing upon the peril of the country and the call upon every citizen to come to its defense in whatever way he can. All that is done to ward off the danger which comes upon one people, to deliver one nation from loss and dishonor.

But we are summoned by the Prince and Captain of salvation to take part in a contest which involves the dearest and the most sacred rights and hopes and privileges of all nations. The Church is enlisted in a campaign which will be complete only when the kingdoms of the whole world are brought into harmony with the kingdom of righteousness and peace. We are summoned to a warfare which is waged against wickedness, ignorance, superstition, bondage, degradation of humanity of every kind in every land. By virtue of our profession as Christians we have taken on ourselves a solemn covenant never to cease from our efforts, never to lay down the weapons of our warfare, until Christ is accepted as the rightful and the universal King. It should follow as a matter of course that we resort to the most appropriate and effective plans and expedients for drawing all classes, young and old, rich and poor, into the support of the one great cause — the divine and heaven-directed enterprise of rescuing all nations from the bondage of sin and superstition. Children in families and Sunday-schools should be taught early and constantly that the gospel of Christ is the only effective remedy that has ever been found for all the evils that are in the world, and that they can all do something, many of them can do much, to bring the gospel within the reach of the whole human family. In doing their best for that one great object, they are undertaking the greatest, the most honorable, and the most needed work that they can ever set hands to, they can ever fix their hearts upon. They are coöperating with God, with all the excellent of the earth and with all the highest powers in the universe, in establishing a righteous and an everlasting kingdom on the earth. The highest ambition, the most fervent hopes, the most sacred aspirations of the young should be fixed earnestly and constantly on this, the highest work which the infinite God can give them to do in their lifetime — the only work which will give them joy and honor when they look back from the other life upon the toils and conflicts of this world.

If we accept the Bible as a revelation from God, then the one only great event of the future which we can be sure of is the fact that the whole world is to become subject to Christ, and his will is to become the accepted law of nations. That being so, our young people should be trained up to make all their plans and choices for occupation in life in view of that fact. They must learn to put forth their efforts and to cherish their hopes and to train their minds so as to be in sympathy with the divine tendency of events and so as to be prepared to take part in the great age of the future as fast as it comes on in their day. It is a sad thing to be behind the times, or to be left out, as if of no consequence, when God is leading the times on to one great consummation which shall fill the whole earth with light and peace. And of all others, children should be trained to join the march of the ages and nations towards a higher and a better life. If they are taught in the schools to master the whole circle of the sciences and to take in the whole range of literature and art and history, still they will be limited and contracted in their views and unused to the freest and highest thought unless they have learned to set the kingdom of God first in authority, in promise, and duration.

Often the most persuasive argument to induce young and old to begin the Christian life themselves is the call to help others into the true path. The attempt to teach others the great and sacred truths of divine revelation is often the means by which the teacher himself learns his need to be taught of God. The opportunity to give and labor to sustain the great missionary cause in the ends of the earth leads many to entertain a higher and truer estimate of the value of Christian institutions and instructions in the home land. The best missionaries to preach the gospel among the heathen are those who have grown up from childhood into the full and intelligent conviction that the command of the Master is their divine commission and that they are to go to their work as directly under his guidance and protection as the apostles went preaching the Word in their day.

In all churches the young people should come together often and talk and read and inquire and pray about the one great event which is to take place in the age to come, the one great enterprise which demands their most earnest effort, stimulates their most sacred ambition, awakens their highest hope — and that is, the establishment of righteousness and peace among all nations. They should be filled with the expectation of the coming of that day and with the desire and ambition to bear a part in labors and sacrifices which will hasten its coming. They should be educated into the feeling that they will lose the chief aim of life, the one grand object best worth living for, if they do not take an honorable part in the great, world-wide movement, which is led on by divine providence and which will be completed in the full coming of the kingdom of heaven on earth. The Sabbath day preaching from the pulpit through all the year, the conversation of the Christian household, the tone of exhortation and prayer in the meetings of the week, should impress young people with the conviction that Christians, above all things else, believe in the kingdom of God, and that they never will be satisfied with the order of things about them till God's will is done on earth by men in every condition of life as it is done by the perfect and the blessed in heaven.

In all churches and Christian homes there should be continual teaching and practice of the divine service of self-denial, the godlike excellence of giving and toiling and suffering as Christ did, for the good of the poor, the helpless, and the unworthy. Early let the child be taught to deny himself common pleasures and indulgences for the higher pleasure of giving for the relief of the needy and for the coming of the day when all people shall live as one brotherhood in Christ and all want shall be supplied. Let the child be made to understand that the demand for such service comes from his greatest and best Friend and that it is for the greatest and best cause, and that therefore it is one which he cannot honorably or rightfully deny. If he does deny it, the tone and the standard of his daily living will be let down as far as from heaven to earth; the range of his thought and aspirations will be contracted from infinity to one brief, aimless, and unsatisfactory life.

All Christian parents should talk, in the presence of their children, and with them, about Christian life and duty, Christian hope and reward, with such a tone and manner of freedom and reality that the children, without knowing it, will be educated into the missionary spirit, trained up to the desire and the expectation of the coming of the kingdom of God. The reality and the demands of that kingdom should be presented with such clearness, truthfulness, and sincerity that there shall be no such thing as exaggeration, no overwrought representation, nothing different in manner from the everyday talk of the household. The child knows very well in what tone and spirit the parents talk about the house and home and family, work and study and amusement, business and society, and the events of the day. Let him hear his parents talk, with the same air of sincerity and honesty, about the things that concern the kingdom of God. Then he will grow up to mature years in full faith that the success and joy of his life must be measured by the amount of service which he renders in carrying forward God's cause on the earth. Thus the young will be trained for the service of Christ as wisely, definitely, successfully, as the farmer is trained for the cultivation of the ground, the merchant for the transaction of business, the physician for the practice of the healing art. This most enlarged and liberal education should so completely override all other influences and instructions as to bring all the varied departments of business and occupation into its service. And all this, just because the call of Christ is first in authority and urgency, first in promise and honor, and his work is the greatest that man can undertake on earth.

I do not suppose that any intelligent and sincere Christian would think of disputing the correctness of the statements which I make. All admit that the command of Christ to publish the gospel unto all the nations is binding on all his followers and that they should give it precedence of all secular plans and engagements whatsoever. All admit that the nations need the gospel more than they need anything else, and that when it is received and obeyed universally such a period of peace and prosperity will come as has never been known on the earth. All admit that the highest glory, joy, and success of life are to be sought in the service of Christ in extending his kingdom on the earth. Nobody expects to rejoice in heaven that he escaped the great trials and sacrifices of Christian duty on earth. No one expects to go about among the hosts of the redeemed in the blessed land, telling how much money he made and kept for his own gratification, what an easy time he secured by letting the heavy burdens rest on other shoulders and the hard work be done by other hands. No one thinks it will make heaven brighter to him that he finds no one there to say, "But for your help, I should not have been here." Nobody thinks that he can be blessed and at home in the company of those who came out of great tribulation if he has to remember that the great work of establishing the kingdom of heaven on earth had no help from gifts or words or labor of his.

What we all need is to look at these great facts concerning personal duty and final salvation in their true light. When we see, as we can beyond all doubt or question, that the real joy and honor of life must come from the service of Christ, then, as rational, right-minded persons, we should choose that service with all our heart. Knowing, as we all do, that nothing will give us satisfaction in the review of the past from the borders of the other world, save that which we have done to advance the kingdom of God in our lifetime, we should set ourselves to begin our true and highest work with all our heart and strength.

Let the Church put itself before the world in the character of one united host of earnest, energetic, self-denying men, bent upon one great enterprise and making everything yield to that; let it be seen beyond all question that Christians of every name are one in the purpose and effort to bring all nations to the adoption of the one faith of the gospel, the one life of trust and obedience and love to God in all things; let the talents, riches, arts, resources now subject to the control of Christians be looked upon by them as consecrated to the demands of God's work in the world, and let children be trained up in families and churches to the early and full belief that the success and joy of life to them must be found in the service of Christ, and then the dawn of the great day of deliverance from darkness will be seen by the nations, and they will welcome its coming as the great day of the Lord God Almighty. The long, dark reign of sin and superstition, of waste and war, of poverty and misery, will give place to the reign of righteousness and peace. It will then just begin to be seen for what high dominion over the earth and all the powers therein man was created, and what still more glorious dominion and destiny await him in the endless future.

In this age of growing knowledge and startling invention and tireless activity we take it for granted that young people must have special education for success in any of the arts, trades, or professions of active life. The artist, the merchant, the manufacturer, the farmer, as well as the statesman, the lawyer, and the physician, must be taught early that his line of work is large enough to call forth all his powers and resources, and that he will be successful and satisfied with his pursuit only so far as he makes it great and honorable before the world. He never will do his best in his profession unless he feels that it is worthy of his efforts and abilities when put to the highest strain.

Now in the divine commission to disciple all nations, we have an enterprise the grandest, the most sacred, the most far-reaching and glorious that can ever inspire the efforts or employ the resources of man. The means to be employed are tried and efficient, the measures to be adopted are wise and honorable, the ends to be sought are the highest and best. The work to be done is varied and complex: it runs into all the relations of life and all the theories of faith and duty; it spreads over the whole range of human thought and culture and inquiry; it demands disciplined powers and accurate observation and patient study and personal consecration; it supplies fit and noble employment for all diversities of talent and temper and taste; it accepts and uses the least and the greatest gifts; it justifies and rewards the most costly sacrifices; it calls forth the grandest efforts; it inspires the highest hopes; it looks forward to the most triumphant and glorious conclusion.

Such is the work given the Church to do in the divine commission to disciple all nations. To take it up with assured faith and to carry it on with becoming energy, the Christian people in the home land must make it a study and an education for life. It must come to be a fundamental article in all creeds, and a first and last endeavor in all work, to fill the earth most speedily with the knowledge of God, to open for all wanderers the way of life and salvation by Jesus Christ. To this end, young men and women in Christian families and churches must be taught early to believe in the greatness and the divine authority of the missionary enterprise. They must be made to see and to feel that no movement in human society, in all the ages, is for a moment to be compared in importance with that of establishing the kingdom of righteousness and peace among all nations. They must be trained up into the full and declared purpose to answer the call of Christ, in whatever form of service they can render, for the advancement of his kingdom among men. They should be made to feel that the highest talent and the most aspiring ambition can find the most honorable and satisfying employment under the Prince and Captain of salvation. It should not be a question where they shall go or what kind of work they shall do, but how they can render the most effective service in the world-wide campaign of discipling the nations. If they are fitted for the farm or the shop, the countinghouse or the market, the professor's chair or the preacher's pulpit, for the home or the foreign field, they should hold themselves ready, and they should count it the glory and joy and success of life to fill the post to which the Master calls.

This is to be made a matter of early and continuous education in the family, in the church, and in the intercourse of Christian people with each other. Let it be understood that the Church is a divine institution, organized and maintained for the especial purpose of establishing the kingdom of God on earth, just as truly as a bank or a railroad or a manufacturing corporation is organized for the transaction of its chosen line of business. The secular corporation fails of the object of its existence when it secures no income. So the Church loses sight of its divine commission when it is making no advance in securing the conquest of the world for Christ. All this should be assumed as a matter of course, in the daily conversation of the Christian family, in the aims and motives of Christians in the transaction of business, in the modes of living and the customs of Christian society, in the course of reading and study kept up for the improvement of the mind and the enlargement of the area of thought for old and young. The training of the family and the quiet life of home, the outlook of the future, and all plans for coming days, should be in harmony with the one predominant purpose, to do the utmost to fill the world with the knowledge of the truth as it is in Jesus. The rising hopes and the young ambition of children should be stimulated and drawn out in that direction by the divine flame of Christian love burning with its holy fire upon the altar of the heart.

The whole order of service, preaching, and benevolent work in the Church should keep before the world the one great, divine idea that the Church is a brotherhood of the children of God, and that it has no higher or better aim than to do God's will on earth as it is done by the blessed in heaven. The Church has indeed no right or reason for its existence but to follow the example of the Master himself, whose most glorious mission on earth was to go about among men doing good. The young members of the flock are to be trained up into the feeling and the faith that the greatest and the most godlike man — the man whose work will last longest and be most honored and blessed when he is gone — is the man who gives himself most heartily and self-denyingly to the establishment of the kingdom of righteousness and peace on earth. The man who does that will be lifted above the narrow jealousies and petty ambitions of the world; he will have peace and good hope all the way, and when he is gone his name will be held in blessed and everlasting remembrance.

All this is to be set forth and taught in the Christian home and the church and the Sunday-school, not as a constrained or overwrought or fanatical life, but as the true life for man — the free, joyous, perfect life which best employs, disciplines, and develops all the faculties of man, best answers all the wants of man, brings forth the most complete, strong, symmetrical manhood. The Church is to be regarded as a family, a school, a college for the education of the young into such a life. The Church is to take all suitable and available measures for training up its members, old and young, to the feeling and the faith that the one thing best worth living for is the one thing set forth as first and best in the life and teaching of Jesus. Seek first the kingdom of God; seek first the personal righteousness, purity, excellence, which are qualifications for membership in God's kingdom; seek first in all earthly plans and purposes the best means of establishing God's kingdom of truth and love among men, — in that way only can the highest honor, joy, success of life be found. In that way only can our young people be trained up to have an honorable part in bringing forward that one divine event, the universal reign of right and truth and love on earth, towards which all changes and revolutions are made, by divine providence, to lead on.

Young people, when they come into the Church on profession of their faith in Christ, sometimes think they are making a great sacrifice: they are cutting themselves off from courses of life which it would be pleasant and profitable to pursue, if it were permitted. They are apt to think that, in coming into the Church and taking on themselves the responsibilities of the Christian profession, they are giving up some measure of the freedom for which their young hearts long : they are losing the enjoyment which the world offers to all who accept its principles and pursue its pleasures. They must be made to see that all such impressions are mistakes and delusions. The true life for them — the noble, free, joyous, satisfying life for them and for all, old and young — is the life of obedience to God, the life of doing good, the life of release from the narrow constraints of selfishness, and of devotion to the highest interests of mankind.

Everything which is given or done or suffered for Christ lifts up the soul; enlarges the whole area of being, action, hope; makes life better worth living, death more welcome as a happy entrance upon a still higher, happier, more glorious career of endless progress in light and truth and love. There is no greater, nobler view of life and duty than that which the gospel sets before us all. The one great idea best fitted to keep before the young to enlarge their faculties, build up their hopes, and exalt their aspirations, give them grand, ennobling views of human nature and destiny, is the idea of God present everywhere, blessing all creatures, upholding all things. As they grow up to mature years and form their plans for life, they should take it for granted that the whole world belongs to God, and everything will go right on this earth when men acknowledge God's ownership of all faculties and all possessions, and they consent to use them all as he directs. Inspire the minds of the young with the great ambition to do the most in filling the world with the truth of God, teaching and persuading all men to live lives of obedience to the eternal laws of truth, justice, and love. Make them feel that they have a personal interest in every race and nation, and in bringing all people to accept the true and divine life of faith in Christ, obedience to him, participation in his holy and beneficent work of enlightening and redeeming all mankind.

Under such instructions, given day by day kindly and faithfully in all Christian homes, preached and proclaimed every Sabbath day from every Christian pulpit, confirmed and sanctified in all meetings for Christian conference and prayer, the Church will become a mighty army, whose march is from victory to victory; the rising generation will grow up into a grander, more complete and godlike manhood than has ever yet been seen in any age of the past or in any quarter of the globe. Young people will be most effectually guarded against the frivolities of worldly pleasure and the excesses of sensual dissipation by setting before them a career which will employ all their noblest faculties, satisfy their loftiest aspirations, and give them joy and honor in every conflict. In no other way can the eager, ambitious, impulsive youth of America find fit and healthful employment for their overwrought sensibilities, a field of action worthy of their most cultivated powers, and a safeguard against every temptation to lead a selfish and sensual life.

XXVI.

COÖPERATION IN THE FIELD.

TO give the great missionary enterprise a new start forward, there must needs be earnest, hearty, intelligent coöperation and good understanding among all laborers in the foreign field. Every individual and every denomination should be left free to entertain their own preferences and adopt their own best methods of work. But there should be an adjournment, or rather an utter and positive abandonment, of all contention and controversy about ceremonial, ecclesiastical, or unessential doctrinal differences, and all should unite in the full, universal acceptance of the one supreme and essential doctrine of the cross. The first and the last and the most essential thing which the heathen need to know and believe is the way of salvation as set forth in the gospel: individual, personal rescue from the power and the guilt of sin through faith in Christ. So long as that one great fact is put first and foremost in all teaching, missionaries of every denomination can afford to work together harmoniously, side by side, in the same field, and each rejoice in the other's prosperity as truly as in his own.

There must always be diversities of taste, preference, and opinion in religious worship, usage, and teaching, as there must be diversities of temperament, adaptation, and ability. Some minds will be speculative, prone to dwell upon conjectures, theories, possibilities of doctrine and of ultimate destiny. Some minds will be straightforward, positive, practical, looking only at the straight and narrow path on which the light of divine revelation shines with clear and unquestionable distinctness. They will only walk in the way which can be traced with certainty, leaving the infinite immensity of dim conjecture and vague hypothesis, above and beyond, all unexplored. Some, by education and usage and personal taste, may have strong preferences for particular modes of worship and ordinances and ecclesiastical order. Some may have little respect for tradition and ancient usage. They may be full of the idea that they themselves are living in the best and oldest time of the world, and they may be expected to have more wisdom and experience than all the ancients. They may therefore desire to have the utmost freedom and spontaneity in all matters of church work and worship. Some may wish to give especial prominence and importance to forms and ordinances which others do not deem essential. Some may make much of a particular order in the Christian ministry or of special rules for the organization of churches and the transaction of ecclesiastical business. Others may be quite willing to have churches grow up into such forms and usages as are suited to the circumstances of peoples and countries. They will be ready to recognize any one as an authorized minister of the gospel if he preaches the truth as it is in Jesus and gives himself to the work in sincerity and love.

Let all these diversities of taste and usage and preference be allowed among Christian laborers in heathen lands. But let all bearing the Christian name and going forth into the great world field with a divine commission to disciple the nations put the one supreme doctrine of the cross so prominently before everything else in their teachings that all diversities of form and of faith, of usage and of tradition, of theory and of speculation, shall be lost sight of in comparison with that. The heathen should be made to see that Christians of all denominations are practically one, because they are working for the same end, they are ready to rejoice in the same success by whomsoever it is gained, they are perfectly agreed in regarding one thing more important than all others, and that one thing is personal salvation through faith in Jesus Christ.

All missionaries in the field should be courteous and honorable, generous and magnanimous in their intercourse with each other and in their mode of carrying on their work in the same field. They should acknowledge openly before all the heathen that they are all working for one end and in the service of the same Master, and that diversities of operation are entirely consistent with harmony of spirit and purpose. The heathen should never see or hear that different denominations of Christians, living and laboring in their countries, are disposed to ignore or slight or take advantage of each other in prosecuting the one common enterprise of establishing the kingdom of God in all the earth. Missionaries are not sent to India or China or Japan to make Episcopalians or Methodists or Presbyterians or Congregationalists, but to make disciples of Christ. That is the commission which they hold from one common Lord and Master. If they forget the commission and labor to set up a denomination, they are not fit persons for the field. They are making divisions in the host of the Lord, when it should present one united and unbroken front to the common foe.

All missionary boards, committees, and secretaries at home should plainly charge their agents that they are not sent out to promote the growth of denominational connections, but to advance the kingdom of Christ by securing the salvation of men. All teachers in theological seminaries who are preparing young men for the missionary work should labor to inspire them with the one desire and purpose to preach the gospel in its simplicity, as the power of God unto salvation, leaving all conjectures and speculations aside as forming no part of the original and divine commission. The fact that the heathen need the pure, ennobling, redeeming truth of the gospel more than they need anything else is clear and unquestionable. And they need it in its purest and plainest form, free from all the inventions and amendments of men. While that is so, it is the first duty of the missionary to preach the preaching that has been bidden him in faith and love, and leave the result with God.

I say all this, and yet I admit again, as I have done before, that there may be great diversity of opinion and of practice in heathen lands, both in regard to the actual condition of the heathen mind in respect to religion, and also in regard to the best means and methods of bringing them to accept the gospel. In China, for example, some missionaries think they find much that is good and true in Confucianism. Sometimes they talk as if they thought it needed little modification to make it harmonize with Christianity. Some talk as if they thought it had done much to prepare the way for the gospel. Other missionaries say that Confucianism is intensely atheistic, and that it takes away all sense of responsibility to God, all faith in the reality of a future life and of the spiritual and immortal nature of man. They therefore regard it as the most difficult of all the oppositions which the gospel has to overcome in China. Now, of these two classes, one makes frequent and complimentary allusions to the precepts of Confucius in the hope of disarming prejudice and preparing the mind to receive the clearer and better precepts of Christ. The other class make the least possible reference to Confucius, lest the heathen should be led to think that Christianity is only another religion of the same general character with their own, and that, while it may be good and true for western people, the Chinese will do best to stick to their own. Now, the missionaries who have such different judgments about the essential character of the religion of China can work together harmoniously, provided they agree in exalting the cross of Christ to its due place in all their teachings. Let them only vie with each other in the endeavor to show the need of redemption and the fullness with which it is provided in the gospel of Christ. Let the heathen see that, however diverse may be the mode in which the missionaries speak of Confucius, they are perfectly agreed in exalting Christ as the only and the all-sufficient Saviour. Let them see that the one thing about which Christians are all agreed is immeasurably more important than all their differences. Then there will be no loss of power for the propagation of Christianity through the collisions and controversies of Christians among themselves. There will be one fervent and united work in the field and one joy in the harvest.

There is great diversity of opinion among missionaries in China as to the degree of life and permanency which may still be observed in the old order of things in religion and in the state. Some feel sure that the power of the old pagan system has been waning for some hundreds of years: its temples and pagodas and monasteries are all of the past. They do not see it doing any great work of building or enlarging at the present day, and they see no sign that the power which built and endowed in the past will ever undertake such great establishments again. There are twelve hundred walled cities and a hundred thousand temples and religious establishments in the empire, but no one of them has been built within the present generation. The traveler, in passing through the country to-day, does not see anywhere signs of the existence of a power sufficient to build the walls that surround the one city of Peking alone. The courts in the great temples of Confucius are apt to be overgrown with weeds and bushes and wild grass. That may not always be a sign of neglect and decay in China, but to a traveler from western nations it does not seem like life and activity.

Others say that the old pagan Buddhism and Taoism are just as strong and deeply rooted in the hearts of the people as they ever were. They are not more willing to give it up now than they were two hundred years ago. They are not building and endowing great temples and monasteries as they once were, simply because a change of sovereigns has taken place and there has been a long minority in the occupancy of the throne. This apparent decadence will soon give place to high activity and great displays of power. Then again some say that the Chinese are not a religious people at all: that their incense burning and sacrifices of paper, furniture, money, servants, provisions, are only offerings to appease the spirits of the departed and keep them from injuring the living. The superstition about spirits is the most powerful sentiment now controlling the Chinese mind and that superstition existed long before Buddhism or Confucianism appeared in the country, and it still exists, independent of any philosophy or religion which the people have learned from their sages.

The Chinese hear the missionary preach about the true and the only God, and they say, "Yes, that is all right; that is what we all believe, always have believed." They say so because they have not understood what has been said, or because they do not care enough about it to try to understand, or they have put their own interpretation upon the missionary's words and given them a meaning the opposite of what he intended. Their doctrine of spirits remains untouched by anything the preacher says about God. So long as they are left to practice geomancy and astrology and demonolatry, they will not make much effort to see the difference between Buddhism and Christianity. In fact, there is very little Buddhism, pure and simple, in all China, very little regard for the temples of Buddha except as convenient places for gambling, drawing lots, telling fortunes, and propitiating spirits.

I lodged two weeks in the temple of Everlasting Rest, on the slopes of the Western Hills, overlooking the walls of Peking. Close by the door of my room was the holy house of Buddha, and there was the sacred image of the ever-sleeping god in due style and form. The incense was burning before it night and day. But in the same holy place there were boxes and barrels, old lumber and broken crockery, boards and tables on which the servants and missionaries were ironing, and tubs in which they were washing clothes. The head priest did not object to their making such use of his holy house. He did not care, the people did not care, nobody cared. But if a wall had been built up a foot higher than the walls of the temple, or a telegraph wire had been stretched across the court inside of the buildings, every Chinaman would have said that the change would give offense to the spirits of the earth and the air, and the priests and people would have been trembling with fear or burning with indignation.

Amid such contradictions and perplexities our missionaries must live and grope their way into the deep darkness of the native mind. It is not to be expected that men of equal intelligence, sincerity, and faith will all agree as to the best mode of bringing the truth of the gospel into contact with the hearts and consciences of such people. All we can ask of our brethren in the field is that each shall act upon his own free unbiased judgment of what is best, and all shall judge each other in kindness and charity. There are some who think that education is to be the grand regenerator of such blinded minds and darkened hearts. They say, Teach the heathen science, the laws of nature, the arts and inventions, the history and literature of the most cultivated and Christian nations, and then they will renounce their heathenism of course, and will be ready to embrace Christianity. They would bring together young men in large numbers in schools, put them under the personal influence of Christian teachers every day, teach them philosophy, literature, history, science, but for a while say little to them, except in a general way, about the one thing which Christ puts first before all seekers for the highest good of life. They think the time has not yet come for calling the heathen, one by one, into the open profession of faith in Christ. They are first to be converted in a general way by nations to the acknowledgment of Christianity as the one true and divine religion. The governments must first be persuaded to renounce heathenism. The people will follow their rulers, and so they will all eventually turn to Christ. Such is the theory of some in the field who are faithful in work and ardent in hope.

Some missionaries are inclined to traverse large sections of country, preaching the gospel as they go, and so bearing witness unto Jesus to many thousands for once, and then leaving them to think on what they have heard. They say that is the way that Jesus himself preached and that is the most apostolic method of bearing the divine commission unto the nations. They tell of the great multitudes to whom they have spoken, as the Master spoke to the people on the mountain or by the sea. They do not wait to see how effectual their preaching has been. They think they have done their duty by bearing witness unto the truth in such language as they can command, and then passing on to preach to other cities and villages. The people gather to hear them; they look as if they were listening and understanding. When the missionary has gone, they look at each other and express their wonder at what the stranger could be talking about. Some guess one thing, some another, but none get a correct idea of what the missionary meant to say. In a few days it is to them as if they had never seen the face or heard the voice of the stranger who came and went like the cloud of the morning and left no trace behind.

Some who go to heathen lands to preach the gospel give especial attention to the classics and sacred books of the East. They think they find much wisdom, profound lessons of truth and duty in the Confucian and Buddhistic records and traditions. Unconsciously they put Christian interpretations upon words and symbols to which the original writers and speakers gave no such meaning. So, very naturally, they find that some forms of heathenism make a near approach to Christianity, and in fact may be used as a preparation for the gospel. So they are led to think that a due combination of the best sayings and usages of heathenism with the pure precepts of Christianity will be found best fitted to raise up the eastern nations to a truer and a better life. They gladly avail themselves of opportunities to teach in heathen schools with the understanding that, in the great matter of the Christian truth which the missionary goes to teach, a seal shall be put upon their lips. They can go before their classes day by day to give instruction with a distinct agreement that they will say nothing about the beginning of all wisdom, the fear of the Lord. They hope that by making such compromises for a time, by-and-by the heathen will permit them to speak on the one great truth of the gospel message. Sometimes they even go so far as to establish schools of their own, and call them Christian schools too, and yet they carefully avoid all effort to bring their pupils, one by one, to accept and obey the special truth of divine revelation. They do so in the hope that instruction in science will prepare the way for the acceptance of the spiritual truths of the gospel.

So various are the opinions and the practice of intelligent, honest, conscientious men who go to China and India and Japan to make known the unsearchable riches of Christ to the heathen nations. Far apart as they seem to be in principle and in methods of work, they still ought to make the impression upon the disciples of Confucius and of Buddha that they are a united host and that they are all laboring for one great end — the establishment of the kingdom of Christ in all the earth. And that they can do, if always in the presence of the heathen and in their private consultations they speak of each other as brethren, they rejoice in each other's success, they put first and foremost, in all their personal influence and in all their declarations of principles, the doctrine of salvation by Jesus Christ alone.

The scholarly men, who think they find much truth in the sacred books of the East; the educationalists, who have great confidence in the power of science to scatter the darkness of superstition and prepare the way for Christianity; the medical practitioner, who has to deal with the lowest and most revolting exhibitions of vice and imbecility; the evangelist, who loves to pass through vast and populous regions, preaching as he goes, and leaving the divine word as a witness unto the people, who only partly understand its meaning; the steady, conservative, hard-working organizer of schools, colleges, hospitals ; the loud-voiced herald, who puts on the dress of the natives and goes out into the streets and cries with an exceeding great and startling cry to the people to warn them of their danger and to show them the way of safety, — must all come together, look each other in the face with kindness, confidence, and sympathy, and they must say frankly and sincerely, "We are all servants of the same Master; we are all seeking the same end ; we shall all rejoice in the success which follows effort by whomsoever put forth. Let us help each other by mutual counsel, treat each other with mutual respect and honor, commend each other to the confidence of the heathen, so that they shall see us to be all one in feeling and in faith, all one in the supreme desire to do the utmost for the instruction, the improvement, and the salvation of the people to whom we come."

Let different bands of missionaries say as much as that to each other; let them make good the words in all their intercourse with each other and with the heathen ; let them agree wholly with each other, and always confess before the heathen that the one purpose for which they have left home and country is to make all nations disciples of Jesus Christ, — then the great missionary enterprise would advance with such power and rapidity as never before. The thrones of darkness would be shaken by the strong, united assault of the armies of light.

XXVII.

RECRUITING ON THE FIELD.

THE missionary force in the foreign field needs strengthening with men and money at every point, to hold ground already gained and to move on to greater conquests. The call is constantly coming for reinforcements from the home land. But it is one of the most encouraging signs of success that efficient and faithful recruits are constantly coming in from the foreign field itself. Not only preachers, catechists, colporters, Bible readers, but the private members of the mission churches enter into the beneficent, world-embracing spirit of the new faith which they have received. It is a new and a blessed life to them to be delivered from all the restrictions of caste and race and color, and to be introduced into a divine brotherhood which is large and free enough to take in the whole family of man. So, many of them feel that it is their first duty and highest privilege to prevail on their fellow-countrymen to join that sacred society and to share the great hope which it brings to enslaved nations. Converts from among the heathen are taught in the very outset of their Christian profession that they are enrolled in the Church as volunteers in one great, consecrated army, whose campaign will be complete only with the conquest of the world.

They have all grown up under the impression that there

are many true religions in the world, and that every people may be expected to have its own, and that there must be something dishonorable and dangerous in renouncing the faith of their fathers and accepting one brought to them from a distant land. Under kind and faithful instruction they come slowly to see that there is but one true religion, which draws all men alike to the love and service of the one almighty, all-loving Father, and that in becoming Christians they are only taking the place and leading the life which is fit and becoming to all men, of every race and age and country. They are to walk worthy of their high and holy vocation that others may see the beauty and feel the power of the life they are leading. They are to bear open, honorable, and effectual testimony unto Jesus as the Saviour of all mankind, the living manifestation of the infinite love of God to man. In many cases they incur great self-denial, they are subjected to bitter persecution, they suffer the loss of friends and home and property, to be faithful to their new Master. Thus their daily testimony to the purity and the sincerity of their faith speaks louder than words in proclaiming the excellence of the truth which they have believed.

In whatever caste or calling the gospel finds the new converts, they learn to look on themselves as enrolled in the service of Christ as truly as if they had been specially ordained to the work of preaching the word of life to their benighted countrymen. Having broken loose from the most sacred traditions of their fathers and the most honored customs of social life in the community where they live, their position is trying and severe, and they must needs exercise courage and patience and faith to hold it well. But for that very reason they grow more rapidly in strength of character and in the ability to command respect and to bring others to join with them in their new faith and profession. They can preach Jesus and show the excellence of the new life upon which they have entered, in the shop, the house, the street, the market, and the field, in such a particular and personal manner as no missionary from a foreign land can preach. They can go to a thousand places which the missionary can never reach, and they can speak with millions who can never be drawn to the chapel or the church, never can be induced to stop and listen for a few moments to the preaching in the streets or under the shade of the palm and banyan by the riverside.

The heathen convert can reason, persuade, invite, entreat his fellow-countrymen in private conversation more effectively than the foreigner can do in formal and public address. In many cases what would seem to us the very weakness of his reasoning is the secret of his power with his own people, because it is according to their modes of thinking and it uses arguments and illustrations which mean little to us but are all powerful with them. He can go into his neighbors' houses or get them to come to his; he can talk of Christ and tell the gospel story as he sits with them on the earth floor and uses the same language and modes of speech they have been accustomed to use from youth up. He can talk with them as he works in the field or walks on the public road or sits in the bazar or rows in the boat. In each and every case he can commend the Jesus religion to his countrymen; he can help them to understand that it comes from the one everlasting Father and that it answers the deepest wants of the soul. He can read the gospel to his neighbors, or, if he cannot read, he can recite passages which he has committed to memory, as illiterate men can easily do all over the East. He can talk familiarly with his friends about the meaning and the spirit and power of the new religion from the West. Every new convert, in his own village and neighborhood, can make himself known as a believer in the Jesus religion and a man all in earnest to persuade others to believe the same truth and live by its instructions.

This mode of disseminating gospel truth and gathering in converts from among the heathen has grown rapidly into use of late in all parts of the great world field and it has been attended with remarkable success. By such means the heathen are taught to do their own preaching better than others can do it for them and at far less expense. In one province of China there are now fifty churches all gathered and maintained by native converts who had received no ordination as ministers and who asked no compensation for their labor, save the satisfaction of doing good. In that way the influence of one missionary is multiplied fifty or a hundred fold, and the process need only be carried on wisely and perseveringly and soon the gospel story will be told in every village of the great empire of three hundred millions of people, and they will gladly receive the testimony of truth and salvation.

In another province of China there was a young man who was a confirmed and notorious gambler. His father, in full exercise of the peculiar authority which is given to the parent in that country, had used threats and force and persuasion and ridicule to reclaim his son, but all in vain. By chance one day the young man saw what he thought was a story-teller speaking to a little company of listeners in the open street. He drew near to listen, and it was the story of the gospel that he heard from the lips of one who had learned it at the mission and who loved to tell it to all who would hear. The next Sunday he found his way into a mission chapel and there heard the truth set forth more fully. He gave up gambling at once, renounced heathenism, went home to tell his friends and neighbors. At the time when I heard the story that man had labored so effectually in preaching his new faith that his village had one of the strongest and most active churches in all China. They had no help from outside, except an occasional visit from a missionary. They paid all of their own expenses and kept up six mission stations in neighboring villages.

So everywhere, all over the great mission field of the world, the new convert, baptized and received to membership in the Christian church, is learning the best way of making known the simplest truths of the gospel to his fellow-countrymen. He stands so nearly upon their level and he has so recently broken loose from the superstitions with which they are still bound that he is the best man to waken their attention, enlist their sympathy, and help them lay hold on the new hope set before them. Fast as he learns what to believe and how to live as a Christian, the whole instruction becomes to him a discipline and a preparation for the work of bringing his friends and neighbors to join him in the Christian faith and life. Special portions of Scripture are selected for him to study and to find out how he can bring their practical meaning into contact with the minds of the gross and ignorant and debased, so as to lift them out of their degradation into the glorious light and liberty of the children of God.

When the missionary receives a new convert to the church he feels that he has gotten a man from the Lord to help him in the one great and supreme purpose for which he came on his mission to the heathen. He rejoices over the conversion of that one man, not simply or mostly because he is saved, but because he may be the means of saving many others. The missionary sets his mind at once upon the study to find out the very kind of work the new man can do best. He sets the fresh recruit to that work as directly as the contractor or the overseer sets a newly hired operative to his task and never thinks of counting him among his laborers until he is at his work. The missionary finds that the best way to guard the young convert from falling back to heathenism. The best of all bonds to bind the members of the mission church to each other and to the Master is the welcome task of bringing others to accept the truth as it is in Jesus. The heathen convert is made to understand in the very outset of his profession of Christian faith that the church which he enters is an ever-advancing and conquering army, and he joins the ranks as a volunteer that he may enter into its conflicts and share its triumph. The bare fact that he enters the church is to be understood as a declaration on his part that he will do his best to win his countrymen by every fit and honorable means to Christ.

We can never send men and women enough from Christian lands to do all the teaching and the preaching required to proclaim the gospel in all the dark places of the earth. The converted heathen must go after their brethren, every one bringing one, and in that way the whole land of the East will be filled with laborers for Christ and messengers of the great salvation. The whole dark world of heathenism will be penetrated through and through by rays from the Sun of Righteousness when every one who hears the message passes it on to others and illustrates its meaning by a life of obedience to its demands. The millions who sit in darkness and in the region of the shadow of death will awake to the discovery of the great fact that before them is set an open door out of their prison. They have only to rise up, pass through the door out into the boundless realm of the kingdom of God, and they are in a new world of light and liberty, the chains and the prison and the bondage are all behind, before them are freedom and gladness forevermore.

Just now this is the one aim most earnestly sought by all missionaries in the field : how to set the new convert at work immediately and earnestly in seeking the conversion of his neighbors, his acquaintances in the very walks of life where the message of divine truth finds him. This method of working is to be adopted, not simply as a policy, but as a principle, a prime element of doctrine and of faith. The members of every new church are banded together, not simply for their own personal safety, but as a strong, living brotherhood, organized and maintained for the special purpose of bringing all the heathen world under the dominion of Christ as Saviour and King. Nothing will do more to enlarge their hearts and lift up their hopes than the assurance that they have a commission from the divine Master to make disciples of all nations, and that Christians all round the earth are joined with them in the fulfillment of the Great Commission. They will be firm in their faith and happy in their new hopes, just so far as they are trying to bring others to Jesus.

Within the last fifty years hundreds of thousands of recruits have been gathered into the Church from the great missionary field of the world. They have been taught in the divine Word, trained for Christian work, tested by persecution, and they are to-day the living confirmation of the power and the authority of the commission to disciple all nations. To gain so much there has been a great expenditure of time and toil, of men and money, of exploration and experiment. Great resources of information have been accumulated, the results of vast and varied experience have been recorded. Explorers have gone out into the darkest places of heathenism and preparatory work has been thoroughly done in all parts of the field. Churches have been gathered, schools established, hospitals have been founded, printing presses set up, Scriptures have been translated, catechisms and text-books have been composed, fields have been marked out for visitation and occupancy. All this makes a history such as could not be written of any other fifty years since the world began.

The work of preparation has been done, vast resources

have been gathered, a great host of recruits has been enlisted from the field. Now is the time for one united, tremendus onset by all the forces in the field upon the powers of darkness. There should be a movement along the whole line, a sudden, swift, resistless advance of the hosts of the living God, in one desperate assault upon the strongholds of error and superstition in every land. The great heathen world must be made to feel that an extraordinary and an overmastering impulse has been given to all the Christian forces, and that they are determined, firmly and unitedly, not to make any further delay in strengthening entrenchments and looking out for commanding situations, but to move on with one universal and resistless charge. The impression is already made upon the heathen of all countries that Christianity is a religion for all nations and that it is destined to overspread and possess the world. In many cases they are looking out for a great and strong advance, and they wonder why the Christian forces so long delay their conquest. Let the most intelligent heathen see a strong, swift, united movement among the Christian forces in the field, let them understand that such a movement is inspired and sustained by Christians of every name throughout the world, and they will at once say that the day of confusion to their gods and contempt for their idols has come.

It will not do to rest content with reaping upon ground already gained, cultivating more thoroughly fields already won over from the enemy. The bare presence of Christian converts among the surrounding heathen will not convince the ignorant and the superstitious of the excellence of Christianity, of the superiority of its doctrines and of the life to which it leads, and thus cause them to receive it to their hearts and their homes. We must never lose sight of the aggressive character of our missionary work through a conservative and commendable desire to keep well ground already gained.

We must never forget that the divine commission commands the conquest of the whole world, the discipling of all the nations. And sometimes the best way to build up new converts and make them strong in the faith is to throw them upon their own resources. All missionaries were once driven out of Madagascar and the untrained converts were left to themselves for thirty years. They were subjected to sore and long-continued persecution, even unto death. But when the missionaries came back they found the number of Christians greater and their faith stronger than when they left. In passing through the great missionary fields of the East the Christian traveler is often saddened to find that the force in the field is only sufficient to hold the ground already gained and there are none to spare for advance. And one is often ready to raise the cry to move on and leave the new converts to keep the ground that has been held for many a year. If the vanguard is always on the march, the rear will always be on the watch. If the cry comes down from the front that new victories are gained at every step of advance, the main body will gather resources and send forward supplies. Come out from behind entrenchments and take the open field, and the display of confidence and courage will be the first step to victory.

There must needs be homes and schools and settled habitations for many. Preachers must be trained, text-books must be prepared, hospitals sustained. Nevertheless the mission force as a whole should make the impression of a conquering army, ever on the march, everywhere present with videttes and outposts always in the face of heathenism and ever advancing from victory to victory. Rather than settle down to home work and suffer themselves to be counted as one of many castes and religions, they should make the impression on the heathen that they have come to take possession of the whole land and that no nook or corner can be exempt from the invasion of the hosts of light. They should put their Christian faith, with all its high and exclusive claims, in the forefront of all their movements, medical and educational, as well as those which are distinctively evangelical. When they are charged with making proselytes and subjecting education to religion, they should not hesitate to say that that is just what they come for, and that it is the first and the sole command in their divine commission to make all nations disciples of Jesus Christ.

The missionary force in the field needs strengthening at every point, but with all its gathered recruits from among the heathen it is already strong. It need only put on strength, the strength of the Lord of hosts, and no form of heathen superstition can stand before it. Every missionary himself alone is a host, because he bears a divine commission and the power of the Almighty goes with him to his work. Unflinching courage and unconquerable energy are becoming in him because he is enlisted in a cause which can never fail. There should be a common understanding among all laborers in the field that the whole united host shall move onward with the most intense and fervid activity.

And such will be the result just as soon as missionaries in the field are sure that the Church at home has made an open, honest, entire consecration of all its resources to the fulfillment of Christ's command to disciple all nations. Let missionaries be assured that any amount of money, any needed number of men are ready to be forthcoming to sustain them in their great undertaking, and then they will relax their cautious and conservative policy, they will come out of their entrenchments and cover the whole land with the growing army of native preachers and catechists, whose best and most effective preaching is to tell the simple story of the gospel. Let missionaries know that we at home are one with them in consecration to the Master's work, and then they will enter wider fields with no fear that conquests already made will be lost when they move onward. They will give out the watchword for an advance along the whole line and their triumphant march will encompass the whole earth. When that day comes one song shall employ all nations, and the redeemed world, with millions of tongues and in all languages, shall proclaim Christ's reign on earth begun.

XXVIII.

FAITH IN SUCCESS.

TO give order and completeness to our plans, energy and perseverance to our efforts, for the conversion of the world to Christ, we must believe that the work will actually be accomplished. We must not only respect the divine authority to the command to go and preach the gospel to all the nations: we must rely upon the divine promise that the Word shall accomplish the end for which it is sent forth, the nations will heed the preaching and be saved. All Christians should be sustained by full, firm, high expectation that the kingdom of Christ is to embrace the whole world. All powers, arts, possessions, talents, inventions, are to be consecrated to him, and they are all to be used, happily and effectively, in promoting the reign of righteousness and peace. Even the implements and engines of war, which ingenious men are constantly carrying forward towards a state of complete and terrible perfection, shall in the end defeat the very purpose for which they are devised. When they have been carried so far that two armies cannot meet in conflict without inflicting immediate and utter destruction upon each other, war will become impossible. Nation will no longer rise against nation, when the weakest and the strongest are equalized in the field by the possession of the means of annihilating each other in a moment. In that day the great heroisms of the world will find a more useful and exalted employment than the slaughter of hundreds of thousands of men. The productive arts and the high-wrought sciences, which increase man's control over the power and resources of nature, will all contribute to the common good and swell the abundance of peace. The whole round earth, with all its productions, will become a garden of God for the support of the whole human family and for the multiplication of riches and beauty and blessing in every human home. The wastes and the desolations of many generations will give place to culture everywhere, and the earth, no longer impoverished by ignorance and neglect, will yield her increase in such abundance as never before.

All Christians must look forward with confident expectation to the coming of such a day, in order to labor and give and pray with becoming earnestness for the propagation of the gospel among all nations. We must believe that the truth which we carry to the utmost nations is the chosen instrumentality of the almighty God for the accomplishment of all that he desires to have done in filling the world with the abundance of blessing and peace. We must allow no doubts of the skeptic, no theories of the philosopher, no failures or hindrances in Christian work, to shake our faith in the one supreme fact of the future, that the knowledge of the Lord is to fill the earth and all nations are to become righteous. We are not apt to work on with energy in the face of difficulties and delays unless we are animated by the unfailing hope of success in the end. We shall put very little faith into the prayer, Thy kingdom come, unless we believe that the kingdom is really coming and that the will of our Father is to be done on earth as it is done by the holy and the blessed in heaven.

The command of Christ is indeed a sufficient reason for engaging in any work, even the hardest and the longest. But he commands the preaching of his gospel unto all the nations because the nations are in desperate need of the message. He came himself to our world upon his mission of mercy because men were lost and they needed nothing so much as a Saviour. He commands us to go to the uttermost parts of the earth on the same errand and for the same reason. The greatest and the most awful argument for pressing foreign missions with all possible urgency is the fact that the heathen are in that condition which Christ describes by the one word, *lost*. He commands us to make disciples, educated, consecrated Christians of the lowest and basest of mankind, because the thing needs to be done and it can be done and it will be done. We all have the opportunity to bear an honorable and efficient part in the great work. But if we decline the privilege, if we shun the duty, it will be accepted by others and we shall lose the greatest opportunity ever given to man. The Master would not have us waste our time, our efforts, our resources upon impracticable schemes for the attainment of results which he knows will never come to pass. He takes no pleasure in visionary schemes or useless enterprises. We are to preach his gospel to all the nations because the nations can be saved and he means that they shall be saved.

We are to labor and pray and give, not simply in the hope of gathering out from among the heathen nations here and there one, and leave the rest to perish under greater condemnation, because they heard the gospel and they rejected its testimony to the love of God in giving his Son for their salvation. Christ came into the world, not to condemn any, but that all through faith in him might be saved. He commands us to put his word into all the languages of men and carry it unto the ends of the earth that all men may see its light and rejoice in the brightness of its coming. It is not to select a special few and make disciples of them to the abandonment of the millions of the great heathen world that missionaries go to the ends of the earth in obedience to the command of Christ. They go to make converts, and they judge the fitness and efficiency of their labor by the number of conversions gained. They keep uppermost in mind the command of the Master, not simply to bear witness to the truth and then pass on, but to make disciples, train up a new generation of enlightened and sanctified men, to build the old wastes, to repair the desolations of many generations.

All the arts, riches, inventions, which have so greatly multiplied under the inspiring and uplifting influence of Christianity wherever it has been received, shall become the possession of the kingdom of God. They shall go on increasing a hundredfold in the future. They shall enlarge the resources and beautify the habitations of God's children in the glorious coming age, when all the heathen and the uttermost parts of the earth shall be given unto Christ for a possession. All Christians should speak and pray and give with the expectation that God's own promise will be fulfilled and that the darkness of heathenism will give place to the gospel light all over the earth.

Men like to attach themselves to enterprises which are sure to succeed. When they are called upon to risk money and time and labor and reputation upon any great undertaking, they have a right to ask what is the prospect that it will be carried through, and how far it will command the help of the mighty and the wealth of the rich and the praise of the eloquent and the approbation of the wise and the sympathy of the good. If they are sure of all that in the end, they can afford to wait for the vindication of their character and a return for their investment for many years. The financier who has succeeded in some one great undertaking, involving the expenditure of millions, finds it easy to enlist the subscriptions of the poor and the rich alike in another scheme of greater magnitude and more uncertainty.

But the one greatest and mightiest work ever undertaken in all time is the one which is most certain to succeed. It is sustained by infinite riches and power, it is guided by infinite wisdom, it is prompted by infinite love, and it can no more fail of its full accomplishment than the sun can forget to rise or the ordinances of the heavens and the earth can be changed. God himself has given his word of immutable promise that his message of salvation shall accomplish the end whereunto it is sent forth into all the earth, and all the nations shall turn unto the Lord.

When we urge men to give their time and money and labor for that one greatest enterprise of all the ages, we must do our best to fill them with the assurance of complete and glorious success. There may be wars and commotions among the nations; there may be conflicts of opinion and trials of faith; there may be changes in the customs of society and diversities in the modes of presenting the truth itself; there may be different branches of the one household of faith in Christ, and all members of the same branch may not have the same precise form of sound words in which to express their deepest convictions, — still God's word of promise shall stand, and all diversities of opinion and of practice shall blend in devotion to the same Lord and to the coming of the same reign of righteousness and peace among all nations.

In all our appeals to the people in the home land to be earnest and liberal in support of foreign missions, this one great fact of the future should ever be kept prominent and clear. The work is to be done, the heathen are to be converted, the religion of Christ is to pervade the whole earth, the knowledge, the culture, the riches, the prosperity, the peace which Christianity brings, are to become the inheritance of all nations. The education and the science, the arts and the inventions, the machines and the engines, the conquest of difficulties and the command of the forces of nature, which have thus far been attained by the most Christian nations, are but the beginnings of the riches and power and improvement which the gospel will carry with its progress among the most degraded races of men. For that great and mighty revolution in human society we ask rich men to give and strong men to work and learned and eloquent men to speak and write, and all men to pray, when we plead the cause of foreign missions, when we beseech and implore Christians in America to give their best strength and effort and faith to the fulfillment of Christ's command to disciple all the nations. The divine commission is not to speak words of truth which are only imperfectly understood and then pass on to other tribes and peoples. The messengers are to follow up the witness with labor and teaching and personal contact with heathen races until they learn the way of life and become actual disciples of Christ. When that is done all over the earth, the commission will be fulfilled, and all will say, not that the coming of Christ is near at hand, but that he has already come and filled the earth with his glory.

We must believe in the success, in the final triumph of the missionary enterprise, as surely as we believe in the power and the promise of almighty God, as surely as we believe in the constancy of God's covenant of the day and of the night. He has given his greatest and best gift for the accomplishment of the work which he commands his people to take up and carry on to the end. His love to the world, — the whole world, — his desire for the salvation of all men, are so great that he has given and done his best for the attainment of the one great end which he has most at heart with respect to men. Let the Christians of America be assured that this work of converting the nations is certain to be done, whether they do or give anything or not. But the privilege of bearing an honorable part in the greatest work of all the ages is offered them. The one cause which is certain to triumph, and which by its means will fill the earth with peace and gladness, is the cause which comes before the churches in every appeal for foreign missions.

Any man who lives in this land, calling himself a Christian and yet not interested in this greatest commission of the divine Master, needs to be taught anew what are the first elements of the doctrine of Christ. The only light which shines upon the pathway of the future for the nations, the only hope we have that they will ever learn war no more and that the wastes of wickedness will give place to abundance and peace, comes from the assurance that the truths of the gospel shall find utterance in all languages and shall be received with faith and obedience in all hearts. The great and divine work of converting the nations shall go on until it shall be seen before earth and heaven that the almighty Giver is justified for the vast expenditure of means and mercies which he has made to bring this world back to him. Bearing a part in this work ourselves, let us always speak and give and labor and pray with the tone and spirit of men who are engaged in no uncertain or doubtful enterprise. Let the Church, the whole united body of believers in all the world, silence all objections, answer all skepticisms, overcome all obstacles, by the constancy, the calm assurance of their faith in the success of their commission and the full coming of the kingdom of Christ in all the earth.